75 yrs
INDIA Vs PAKISTAN

Ravindra Padalkar

*This book is dedicated to
all my relatives
and
friends*

DISCLAIMER

This Book is based on the various references available on websites, mostly on Wikipedia which is available to everyone. This author has utilized his time to collect the data available on Wikipedia which is based on various references. The author of this book shall not be responsible for any content, information, and correctness of such information in the book. The Author shall not be prosecuted for any such content, information, pictures, references, etc. The author has not expressed his opinion in this book.

The book is all about the collection of various references, dates, incidents, pictures, stories, news, and data etc available on websites, books, and other sources only.

The reader shall not read this book unless agreed upon above.

– **Author**

CONTENTS

INTRODUCTION

India and Pakistan became independent at the same time and have now completed 75 years of independence. It will be interesting to see how both the countries progressed in the last 75 years.

First let us have a review of our History.

Entry of Mughals

The first battle with Md Ghori was fought by the Rajputs is the Battle of Tarain in 1191. In this war, Prithviraj of the Chauhan Dynasty defeated the Mohammed of Ghori, at Tarain near Thaneswar.

The Second Battle of Tarain was fought in 1192 between the Ghurid forces of Muhammad Ghori and the Rajput Confederacy of Prithviraj Chauhan. It took place near Tarain, which is 110 kilometres, north of Delhi. The battle ended in a decisive victory for the invading Ghurids and their successful penetration in north Indian plain.

The battle is regarded as a watershed event in Medieval India history as it led to the destruction of Rajput powers for a while and laid the foundation of Muslim rule in North India, which led to the establishment of Delhi Sultanate.

India was ruled by Muslims for centuries from 1192 to 1707 till the death of Auangzeb.

Although Delhi was ruled by Mughal descendants after Aurangzeb, but Marathas became powerful by then. When Mughal rule became powerless in 18th century, Nadir shah (who was Shia) plundered Delhi in 1739, massacred 20,000 people, carried away the diamond Koh-i-noor and Mayur throne.

Entry of British

The Battle of Plassey was a decisive victory of the British East India Company, under the leadership of Robert Clive, over the Nawab of Bengal and his French allies on 23 June 1757. The victory was made possible by the defection of Mir Jafar, Nawab Siraj-ud-Daulah's commander in chief. The battle helped the British East India Company take control of Bengal in 1772. Over the next hundred years, they continued to expand their control over vast territories in rest of the Indian subcontinent, including Burma.

The battle took place at Palashi (Anglicised version: Plassey) on the banks of the Hooghly River, about 150 kilometres north of Calcutta (now Kolkata) and south of Murshidabad in West Bengal, then capital of Bengal Subah. The belligerents were the British East India Company, and the Nawab Siraj-ud-Daulah, the last independent Nawab of Bengal. He succeeded Alivardi Khan (his maternal grandfather). Siraj-ud-Daulah had become the Nawab of Bengal the year before, and he had ordered the English to stop the extension of their fortification. Robert Clive bribed Mir Jafar, the commander-in-chief of the Nawab's army, and also promised to make him Nawab of Bengal. Clive defeated Siraj-ud-Daulah at Plassey in 1757 and captured Calcutta.

The battle was preceded by an attack on British-controlled Calcutta by Nawab Siraj-ud-Daulah and the Black Hole massacre. The British sent reinforcements under Colonel Robert Clive and Admiral Charles Watson from Madras to Bengal and recaptured Calcutta. Clive then seized the initiative to capture the French fort of Chandannagar. Tensions and suspicions between Siraj-ud-daulah and the British culminated in the Battle of Plassey. The battle was waged during the Seven Years' War (1756–1763), and, in a mirror of their European rivalry, the French East India Company (La Compagnie des Indes Orientales) sent a small contingent to fight against the British. Siraj-ud-Daulah had a vastly numerically superior force and made his stand at Plassey. The British, worried about being outnumbered, formed a conspiracy with Siraj-ud-Daulah's demoted army chief Mir Jafar, along with others such as Yar Lutuf Khan, Jagat Seths (Mahtab Chand and Swarup Chand), Umichand and Rai Durlabh. Mir Jafar, Rai Durlabh and Yar Lutuf Khan thus assembled their troops near the battlefield but made no move to actually join the battle. Siraj-ud-Daulah's army with about 50,000 soldiers (including defectors), 40 cannons and 10 war elephants was defeated by 3,000 soldiers of Col. Robert Clive, owing to the flight of Siraj-ud-Daulah from the battlefield and the inactivity of the conspirators. The battle ended in approximately 11 hours.

This is judged to be one of the pivotal battles in the control of Indian subcontinent by the colonial powers. The British now had a great deal of influence over the Nawab, Mir Jafar, and as a result, they were able to get important concessions for earlier losses and trade income. The British further used this revenue to increase their military might and push the other European colonial powers such as the Dutch and the French out of South Asia, thus expanding the British Empire.

Slowly, Muslims started worrying about their safety in India.

When Mahatma Gandhi started Freedom Struggle, Muslims were with the Struggle from 1919 to 1922.

But Muslims could not continue with Mahatma Gandhi, due to two major differences.

1.   Ahimsa as advised by Mahatma Gandhi and

2.   Muslims were in minority in Govt Jobs compared to Hindus.

This anxiety greatly increased over the years and in the beginning of 20th century, they found that Mahatma Gandhi's Freedom Movement is not going to give them any superiority in India (where they ruled for centuries). They started dreaming of a separate land for themselves.

India got independence after a hard struggle.

India was divided based on the religion.

Pakistan for the Muslims and India for Hindus.

Pakistan got East Pakistan as well as West Pakistan.

The areas where Muslims were in majority were given to Pakistan.

There were some so called Princely States which wanted to go Pakistan but could not do so.

The long rule of Mughals with cruelty towards the Hindus (as they called Kafirs) and rule of Britishers with apathy towards the Hindus (as they called Niggers) ended.

The Mughals killed thousands of Hindus and the Britishers killed millions of Hindus. Refer what Churchill did to Indians in 1943 Bengal famine. He said it was necessary to supply rice to the army fighting on front than to give it to these people who are fit to die.

Division of India was done based on the religion.

Muhammad Ali Jinnah said on the independence day of Pakistan that the citizens of Pakistan are free to follow their Religion without any fear.

1

(1947-1950)

<u>**INDIA**</u> - Nehru first PM of free India - National Flag of India – Refugees - Pak attacks Jammu Kashmir area - Chittaranjan Locomotive Works – Press Trust of India - Postal Department - Federation of Film Societies of India - Rs 55 Crore to Pak - Mahatma Gandhi assassinated - Annexation of Hyderabad - Industrial Finance Corporation of India - Atomic Energy Commission of India - Hindustan Aeronautics Limited - Indian Telephone Industries Limited - Indian Police Service - Films Division of India - India at the 1948 Summer Olympics - History and date of formation of Indian states since 1947 - Nationalization of RBI - Indian Rupee devalued - Atomic Minerals Directorate for Exploration and Research - Indian Council of Medical Research

<u>**PAKISTAN**</u> - Governor General – Presidents – Prime Ministers - Accession of Kalat, Balochistan - Indo-Pakistani War of 1947 - Abul A'la Maududi

INDIA

Jawaharlal Nehru became first Prime Minister of free India

It is sad, unfortunate, and scandalous that the very first election that would decide the leader of free India was manipulated. It wasn't only the election but the future of India that was rigged.

Jawaharlal Nehru appointed as Prime Minister.

As India's freedom struggle was approaching its culmination, Mahatma Gandhi made his intentions clear that Indian National Congress (INC) should be dissolved. He felt the objective of the INC was to liberate India from British rule; once that goal was accomplished, the organization had no existential purpose. Gandhi proposed that all leaders who desired public service via electoral politics should form their own political party and contest elections. This actually would have been democracy in the real sense.

It is interesting to consider the possible outcomes of such an idea.

Perhaps Nehru would have been rejected by the people, which probably would have been the end of his political journey of the dynasty. Perhaps Sardar Patel would have been India's first Prime Minister. Perhaps a newer relatively unknown face would have emerged as the nation's leader following a fractured mandate.

However, Nehru and others within the party understood that the INC had brand recognition such that they could ride the wave of goodwill earned by the party during the freedom struggle. Challengers could be implicitly or explicitly branded as a traitor for challenging the founding fathers of free India. Hence, Gandhi's advice was conveniently ignored and the INC prevailed.

However, Gandhi's advice was assiduously followed in another matter. In 1946, an internal election was held to decide the President for the INC would eventually become the first Prime Minister of independent India. Among the candidates were Jawaharlal Nehru, Acharya Kripalani, and Sardar Patel.

The INC working committee and the various state committees had to send in nominations for their preferred candidates. From the very beginning, Gandhi openly favoured Nehru. Gandhi had explained his rationale behind backing Nehru 'Jawaharlal cannot be replaced today whilst the charge is being taken from the British. He, a Harrow boy, a Cambridge graduate, and a barrister, is wanted to carry on the negotiations with the Englishmen.'

Gandhi also felt that Nehru was better known abroad and could help India play a role in international affairs. Even Maulana Azad endorsed Nehru three days before the last date of nomination. He wrote in his autobiography, published posthumously in 1959: "After weighing the pros and cons I came to the conclusion that the election of Sardar Patel would not be desirable in the existing circumstances. Taking all facts into consideration it seemed to me that Jawaharlal should be the new President...."

The results showed that the members of INC had a drastically different opinion. Sardar Patel who was known to be a great executive, organizer, and leader, won 12 out of 15 state committees, the other state committees abstained from the process. Nehru did not receive any nominations. This was a unanimous choice for Patel while Nehru was resoundingly rejected. Sardar Patel was on his way to becoming India's first Prime Minister.

When Gandhi conveyed the results to Nehru, instead of humbly accepting the popular mandate, Nehru's reaction was that of total silence. Gandhi realized that while that Patel would agree to work as Nehru's deputy, the reverse would most certainly not happen. Thus Gandhi intervened and asked Patel to withdraw his nomination.

Gandhi unwittingly introduced the anti-democratic culture of the 'party high commands' overruling state units for inter-party matters. In deference to Gandhi, Kripalani nominated Nehru and withdrew from the contest. Patel who regarded Gandhi as his mentor then willingly stepped aside in favour of Nehru. Such a supreme sacrifice is unthinkable in contemporary times.

There were two major reasons why Patel accepted Gandhi's request. Firstly, unlike Nehru, he never had coveted positions or posts, for him satisfaction was solely derived in his service to the nation. Secondly, Patel also knew that Nehru was not one to take rejection well. He had an inkling that Nehru would probably reject playing deputy to Patel and in fact become a fierce opponent of Patel and an impediment as he governed the nation.

He knew Nehru had his myriad supporters who would also join his faction of opposing Patel. Patel understood that this division between him and Nehru would further divide a nation that was already plagued with various problems and was about to undergo an almost cataclysmic partition.

National Flag of India

The version of the flag closest to the current one came into existence in 1923. It was designed by Pingali Venkayya and had saffron, white and green stripes with the spinning wheel placed in the white section. It was hoisted on April 13, 1923, in Nagpur during an event commemorating the Jallianwallah Bagh Massacre. It was named the Swaraj Flag and became the symbol of India's demand for Self-rule led by the Indian National Congress.

The resolution to adopt the tricolor as the National Flag of India was passed in 1931. On July 22, 1947, the Constituent Assembly of India adopted the Swaraj Flag as the National Flag of Sovereign India with the Ashok Chakra replacing the spinning wheel.

Refugees

Millions of people suddenly found themselves miles from their supposed new homeland. The sudden separation also resulted in communal violence across the Indian sub-continent with massacres reported on both sides.

At least 14 million people were displaced and as many as one million were killed in the violence.

The Partition of India in 1947 was the change of political borders and the division of other assets that accompanied the dissolution of the British Raj in the Indian subcontinent and the creation of two independent dominions in South Asia: India and Pakistan. The Dominion of India is today the Republic of India, and the Dominion of Pakistan—which at the time comprised two regions lying on either side of India—is now the Islamic Republic of Pakistan and the People's Republic of Bangladesh. The partition was outlined in the Indian Independence Act 1947. The change of political borders notably included the division of two provinces of British India, Bengal and Punjab. The majority Muslim districts in these provinces were awarded to Pakistan and the majority non-Muslim to India. The other assets that were divided included the British Indian Army, the Royal Indian Navy, the Royal Indian Air Force, the Indian Civil Service, the railways, and the central treasury. Provisions for self-governing independent Pakistan and India legally came into existence at midnight on 14 and 15 August 1947 respectively.

The partition caused large-scale loss of life and an unprecedented migration between the two dominions. Among refugees who survived, it solidified the belief that safety lay among co-religionists. In the instance of Pakistan, it made palpable a hitherto only-imagined refuge for the Muslims of British India. The migrations took place hastily and with little warning. It is thought that between 14 million and 18 million people moved, and perhaps more. Excess mortality during the period of the partition is usually estimated to have been around one million. The violent nature of the partition created an atmosphere of hostility and suspicion between India and Pakistan that affects their relationship to this day.

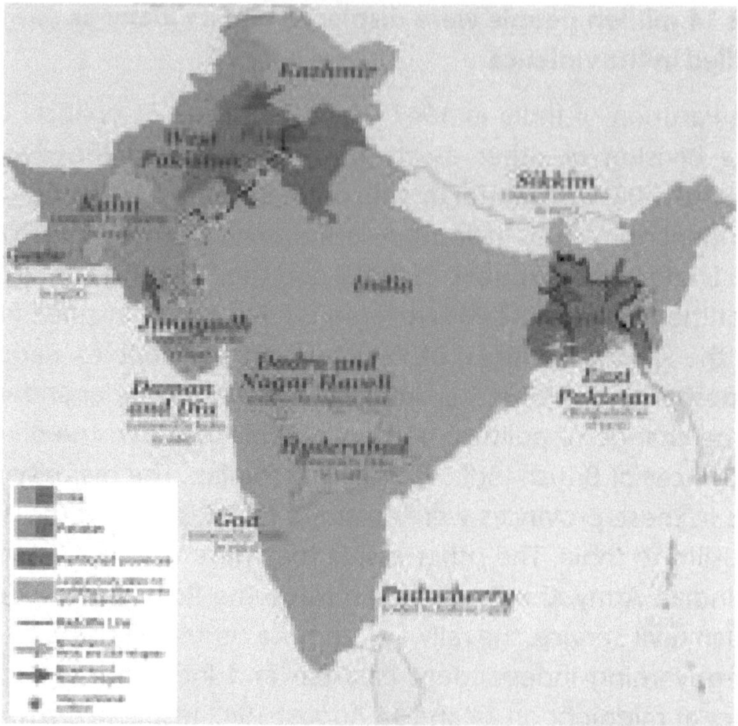

The partition of India: green regions were all part of Pakistan by 1948, and orange ones part of India. The darker-shaded regions represent the Punjab and Bengal provinces partitioned by the Radcliffe Line. The grey areas represent some of the key princely states that were eventually integrated into India or Pakistan.

Mountbatten administered the independence oath to Jinnah on the 14th, before leaving for India where the oath was scheduled on the midnight of the 15th. On 14 August 1947, the new Dominion of Pakistan came into being, with Muhammad Ali Jinnah sworn in as its first Governor-General in Karachi. The following day, 15 August 1947, India, now Dominion of India, became an independent country, with official ceremonies taking place in New Delhi, Jawaharlal Nehru assuming the office of prime minister. Mountbatten remained in New Delhi for 10 months, serving as the first governor-general of an independent India until June 1948. Gandhi remained in Bengal to work with the new refugees from the partitioned subcontinent.

After oath taking ceremony, Nehru addressed to the Nation. "Long years ago, we made a tryst with destiny. Now the time has come when we shall redeem our pledge - not wholly or in full measure - but very substantially. At the stroke of the midnight hour, when the world sleeps, India will awake to life and freedom."

Massive population exchanges occurred between the two newly formed states in the months immediately following the partition. There was no conception that population transfers would be necessary because of the partitioning. Religious minorities were expected to stay put in the states they found themselves residing. An exception was made for Punjab, where the transfer of populations was organized because of the communal violence affecting the province; this did not apply to other provinces.

"The population of undivided India in 1947 was approx 390 million. After partition, there were 330 million people in India, 30 million in West Pakistan, and 30 million people in East Pakistan (now Bangladesh)." Once the boundaries were established, about 14.5 million people crossed the borders to what they hoped was the relative safety of religious majority. The 1951 Census of Pakistan identified the number of displaced persons in Pakistan at 7,226,600, presumably all Muslims who had entered Pakistan from India; the 1951 Census of India counted 7,295,870 displaced persons, apparently all Hindus and Sikhs who had moved to India from Pakistan immediately after the partition. The overall total is therefore around 14.5 million, although since both censuses were held about 4 years after the partition, these numbers include net population increase following the mass migration.

Pak attacks Jammu Kashmir area

27 October 1947: The Spectacular Rescue of Kashmir

By Brig Amar Cheema

Celebrated as the Infantry Day by the Indian Army, 27th October, 1947, was truly spectacular in the annals of Indian History – Not only did the Post-Independence Indian Army come into its own, but it was also the finest hour for the Indian Air Force and the brave Kashmiris who collectively contributed in their own way to the 'rescue' of Kashmir. This piece covering these fateful events is an extract from the book, 'The Crimson Chinar: A Politico-Military Perspective of the Kashmir War.'

The Military Situation and Initial Indian Responses

News of the Pakistan sponsored Qabali invasion reached Delhi on 24 October via two channels. Generals Auchinleck and Lochhart were informed by the officiating C-in-C of the Pakistan Army, General Gracey, and by the evening, the second input came through Mr. R L Batra, the Deputy Prime Minister of Kashmir, who had flown to Delhi with an urgent request from the Maharaja. His mission requesting for immediate help also conveyed the willingness of the Maharaja to accede to India to save his state from the 'Marauders' as he dubbed the Qabalis, who by then had already ravaged Uri and had the same state was feared for Baramulla.

The next day the Defence Cabinet Committee (DCC), chaired by Lord Mountbatten held their first meeting. Against strong opposition from the Service Chiefs and from Lord Mountbatten himself, it was decided to help Kashmir militarily. However, what could be adduced as delaying tactics, it was decided to send Mr. Menon to Srinagar to make an 'on the spot' assessment. As a consequence, Menon and Batra flew to the valley the same afternoon.

Concurrent to these developments in Delhi, Sheikh Abdullah sent Bakshi Ghulam Mohammed and GM Sadiq to Pakistan to meet Mr. Jinnah and/or Mr. Liaquat Ali Khan. This move of Sheikh Abdullah proved abortive as Jinnah sensing victory did not deem it prudent to meet the emissaries, now that success was within his reach. This enraged the Sheikh and he flew to Delhi and met Pundit Nehru. In fact he was there when Batra reached Nehru's house on 24 October. On the same day Pundit Nehru informed Prime Minister Attlee of the developments and that India was considering military intervention. Mr Attlee responded by requesting both Nehru and Liaquat to avoid precipitating the situation which could lead to a military confrontation.

When Menon flew back the next morning, Mr. Mahajan, the Prime Minister of Kashmir, also flew in with him and he carried the letter seeking accession to India. Thus, 26 October was the date when after a stormy DCC session, the decision was taken to send Indian troops to the rescue of the state. The situation had become so acrimonious, that the Indian Ministers were constrained to state that since the British officers opposed the operation, they could step down and it was Mountbatten's intervention that saved the situation. However, after this ugly turn of events, he took upon himself to become the de facto military advisor for the impending Indian operation.

Chittaranjan Locomotive Works -

In the late 1930s, a committee consisting of M/s Humphries and Shrinivasan was created to consider the economic possibilities of establishing locomotive manufacturing facilities in India. The initial project at Chandmari, East of Kalyani in West Bengal, was found to be unsuitable due to the partition. A new survey led to the present site at Chittaranjan being established, which was approved by the railway board in 1947. A survey of the proposed area began on January 9, 1948; the rocky soil was an advantage in erecting structural foundations, and the undulating terrain solved the problem of drainage for the township. The Damodar Valley Corporation envisioned hydro-electric and thermal power stations in the area, assuring adequate power availability for the project.

The project was launched as Loco Building Works in 1950 to produce 120 average-sized steam locomotives. It also had the capacity to manufacture 50 spare boilers. Production of steam locomotives commenced on January 26, 1950. The first President of India, Rajendra Prasad, dedicated the first steam locomotive to the nation on 1 November 1950, and on the same day, the Loco Building Works was renamed as Chittaranjan Locomotive Works after Deshbandhu Chittaranjan Das. The nearby Mihijam Station was also renamed as Chittaranjan.

Press Trust of India

The Press Trust of India Ltd., commonly known as **PTI**, is the largest news agency in India. It is headquartered in New Delhi and is a nonprofit cooperative among more than 500 Indian newspapers. It has over 500 full-time employees as of 1 January 2022, including about 400 journalists. It also has nearly 400 part-time correspondents in most of the district headquarters of the country. PTI also has correspondents in major capitals and important business centres around the world. It took over the operations of the Associated Press of India from Reuters in 1948–49. It provides news coverage and information of the region in both English and Hindi.

Postal Department

India Post is a government-operated postal system in India, part of the Department of Post under the Ministry of Communications. Generally known as the Post Office, it is the most widely distributed postal system in the world. Warren Hastings had taken initiative under East India Company to start the Postal Service in the country in 1766. It was initially established under the name "Company Mail". It was later modified into a service under the Crown in 1854 by Lord Dalhousie. Dalhousie introduced uniform postage rates (universal service) and helped to pass the India Post Office Act 1854 which significantly improved upon 1837 Post Office act which had introduced regular post offices in India. It created the position Director General of Post for the whole country.

It is involved in delivering mail (post), remitting money by money orders, accepting deposits under Small Savings Schemes, providing life insurance coverage under Postal Life Insurance (PLI) and Rural Postal Life Insurance (RPLI) and providing retail services like bill collection, sale of forms, etc. The DoP also acts as an agent for the Indian government in discharging other services for citizens such as old age pension payments and Mahatma Gandhi National Rural Employment Guarantee Scheme (MGNREGS) wage disbursement. With 154,965 post offices (as on March 2017), India Post is the widest postal network in the world.

Post-independence stamps

Brown-and-pink stamp depicting a temple

India attained independence on 15 August 1947. Thereafter, the Indian Posts and Telegraph Department embarked on a broad-based policy for the issuance of stamps. On 21 November 1947 the first new stamp was issued by independent India. It depicts the Indian flag with the patriots' slogan, Jai Hind ("long live India"), at the top right-hand corner. The stamp was valued at three and one-half annas. A memorial to Mahatma Gandhi was issued 15 August 1948 on the first anniversary of independence. One year later a definitive series appeared, depicting India's broad cultural heritage (primarily Hindu, Buddhist, Muslim, Sikh and Jain temples, sculptures, monuments and fortresses). A subsequent issue commemorated the beginning of the Republic of India on 26 January 1950. Definitives included a technology-and-development theme in 1955, a series depicting a map of India in 1957 (denominated in naya paisa—decimal currency) and a 1965 series with a wide variety of images. The old inscription "India Postage" was replaced in 1962 with "भारत *INDIA*", although three stamps (issued from December 1962 to January 1963) carried the earlier inscription.

Federation of Film Societies of India

Federation of Film Societies of India (FFSI) is the umbrella body of film-screening societies in India. FFSI is currently a member of the International Federation of Film Society that has its Central Office in Paris. The international organisation is an associate member of UNESCO.

History

FFSI was established on 13 December 1959 with its Registered and Central Offices in Calcutta (now Kolkata) by the coming together of a group of officials representing six existing film societies in the country, namely Calcutta Film Society, Delhi Film Society, Madras Film Society, Patna Film Society, Bombay Film Society and Roorkee Film Society. The moving spirit behind the concept was the eminent film director-writer-music composer-screenplay writer-graphic artist-type font designer-short story writer Satyajit Ray who along with his colleagues from the Bengali language film industry came together to join hands to bring international cinema and Indian regional film efforts before a generation of young audiences who were until then provided only with commercial Indian cinema fare. The first executive committee of this federation comprised Satyajit Ray as president, three vice-presidents, namely Ms Ammu Swaminathan (Madras), Robert Hawkins (Bombay), S. Gopalan (Delhi), two joint secretaries, Ms Vijaya Mulay (Delhi) and Chidananda Dasgupta (Calcutta), Diptendu Pramanick and Abul Hasan as joint treasurers, and members R Anantharaman, K L Khandpur, Jag Mohan, A Rehman, A Roychowdhury and Ms. Rita Ray.

The creation of FFSI could be said to be the culmination of the development of a film society movement which first took seeds in Britain in the early 1920s. India received the idea as a colony of the Imperial administration when a member of the British movement reached Bombay to attempt create a similar organisation in 1937. The effort failed because England went to war and dragged its colonies along thereby diverting the native resources away from arts and culture. It sealed the fate of the Amateur Film Society opened in Bombay until the WWII came to a close. When peace returned to India, film activities were revived in all its main production centres and Satyajit Ray found himself working in the film unit of Jean Renoir on his outdoor drama The River.

In 1947 the Calcutta Film Society was formed. The idea of film societies could now germinate in other cities, and new units were formed working independently from Delhi (1956), Bombay, Madras (1957), Roorkee, Patna (1958). In 1959, Agra and Faizabad also reported the formation of their own film clubs.

Chidananda Dasgupta, working in the USIS Center in Delhi, and Satyajit Ray, already an international film celebrity, were both exposed to world cinema and being also colleagues known to each other, decided to take the next big step to bring the various film societies together under an umbrella organisation to create the Federation.

The creation of the Federation helped the film clubs to now bargain with the national government to begin exchange of feature films under bilateral cultural exchanges. Soon a new traffic of films from the socialist and European countries started. Indian audiences began to learn of the existence of new alternate cinema other than the American and British English speaking film fare. Film historians began to call for corrections of the distortions of Imperial India. A banned Charles Chaplin was now free to send his films into India; Sergei Eisenstein's Battleship Potemkin was allowed public screenings from 1955.

On an average, FFSI members have been screening about 230 films annually drawn from about 65 nations. It holds about a dozen major film festivals for its members. A major annual international commitment is to manage the 'Open Forum' section of the International Film Festival of India held in Goa, and similar activities in Kolkata, and Trivandrum International Film Festivals.

Rs 55 Crore to Pak

It was 13 Jan 1948; Mahatma Gandhi started his last fast. He had laid down two conditions for ending his fast. The first, for communal amity; all mosques and houses belonging to the Muslims in Delhi be vacated and handed over to them: The second, was to pay to Pakistan 55 crores as its share of the treasury on Partition. Both the conditions were met by 18 Jan 1948 and Gandhi broke his fast by exercising his extra-constitutional moral authority over the Provisional Government of India.

Gandhi was an apostle of 'Non-violence', however, ironically his experiment with non-violence was a grand failure where an estimated 1-2 million people of the subcontinent lost their lives in barbarous bloody communal violence and a displacement of over 14 million refugees. It was also a grand failure on the part of Britain and its Viceroy Mountbatten who left the country with blood dripping from their hands. Even the Government of India headed by Nehru was overwhelmed by the situation and was wringing its feeble hands in sheer helplessness and frustration.

The millions who came from Pakistan to India had survived murderous raids and attacks, came carrying their little bundles of clothes, utensils, bespattered, hungry, and literally were in great pain and penury. There were large-scale communal riots in Calcutta, Nao Khali, Delhi, Punjab (both East and West), Bihar, and umpteen places in both West and East Pakistan. The carnage if recounted is a gory chapter in Human History, as to how humans can forget humanity? These refugees who had taken shelter in mosques and vacant houses were pulled out brutally by their own countrymen and dumped on the streets in the biting cold of Delhi's winter; to satisfy Gandhi, who was ensconced in Birla House.

To recount the events at that point in time; Pakistan had invaded the State of J&K in Oct 1947 and India was in the midst of raging Indo-Pak War 1947/48. It was a crucial period when India had averted the loss of Srinagar and had regained Baramulla and Uri. Heavy fighting was going on in Naoshera, Rajouri, Skardu, and Tithwal. Mirpur had fallen and the Indian Garrison at Poonch was under siege. It was during this critical time in the war that Gandhi laid out his second condition to pay Pakistan Rs 55 crores. Never a country at war has funded the enemy. Yes; we paid Pakistan the money that enabled it to drag the war by a year more!

Mahatma Gandhi assassinated

Mahatma Gandhi was assassinated by Nathuram Godse on 30th Jan 1948.

At 05:05 pm on 30 January 1948, as Gandhi made his way to a prayer meeting on a raised lawn behind Birla House, a mansion in New Delhi, where he was staying, Godse stepped out of the crowd flanking his path to the dais. He fired three bullets into Gandhi's chest. Gandhi fell immediately, sending the attendant crowd into a state of shock. Herbert Reiner Jr., a 32-year-old vice-consul at the new American embassy in Delhi, was the first to rush forward and grasp Godse by the shoulders, spinning him into the arms of some military personnel, who disarmed him. Reiner then held Godse by the neck and shoulders until he was taken away by the military and police. Reiner reported later that in the moments before he apprehended him, Godse looked a little stunned at how easily he had carried out his plan. Gandhi was taken back to his room in Birla House, where he died soon thereafter.

NATHURAM GODSE'S LAST SPEECH

16th May 2021, 15:38.52 hrs.

With the permission of the Supreme Court, the speech of Hon'ble Nathuram Godse was published - Why I killed Gandhi. For 60 years it was forbidden! As you all know - on January 30, 1948, Godse shot and killed Gandhiji.

He did not escape from the scene of the shooting! He surrendered! The lawsuit was filed against 17 others, including Godse.

During the trial, a request was made to the Chief Justice so that Nathuram could speak about why he killed Gandhiji.

Permission was granted but subject to conditions! Your speech should not go outside the court as per the instructions of the government. Later, after a long lawsuit against this condition by his younger brother Gopal Godse, after about 60 years, permission was granted to keep his speech in public.

1. Nathuram thought - Gandhiji's policy of non-violence and Muslim appeasement is turning Hindus into cowards. Ganesh Shankar Vidyarthi was brutally killed by Muslims in Kanpur. And that Ganeshji was influenced by Gandhiji's style of thought -

    Gandhiji remained silent in his assassination!

2. The 1919 Jallianwala Bagh massacre was in full swing. Gandhi was asked to file a case against General Dyer, the villain who committed this heinous murder. But Gandhi had cleanly refused.

3. Gandhi sowed the seeds of communalism in India by supporting the Khilafat movement! He used to describe himself only as a benefactor of Muslims. Mopla Muslims killed 1500 Hindus in Kerala and converted 2000 Hindus! Gandhiji did not even oppose!

4. Netaji Subhash Chandra Bose won the Tripura session of the Congress with overwhelming support. But Gandhi's favourite candidate was Sita Ramayana! Subhash Chandra Bose was later forced to resign.

5. On March 23 1931, Bhagat Singh was hanged. The whole country requested Gandhi to stop the execution. Gandhi did not make this request considering Bhagat Singh's activity as inappropriate!

6. Gandhiji asked Hari Singh, the king of Kashmir, to resign - because Kashmir is a Muslim-majority state! He told Hari Singh to go to Kashi and do penance! But in the case of Nizam of Hyderabad is silent. Gandhiji's policy changed, especially with religion. Later, due to the activism of Sardar Vallabhbhai Patel, Hyderabad was kept with India.

7. At that time the killing of Hindus was going on in Pakistan. Several Hindus migrated to India to save their lives. They took refuge in a mosque in Delhi. Muslims began to oppose it. On a terrible winter night, mothers, sisters, children and the elderly were all forcibly evicted from the mosque. Gandhi remained silent!

8. Gandhi arranged to read the Qur'an and pray in the temple! Instead, he could not arrange to read the Gita in any mosque! Numerous Hindus and Brahmins protested against it - Gandhi did not bother.

9. Sardar Vallabhbhai Patel won the Lahore Congress, but Gandhi insisted on giving the post to Nehru. He was perfect in making his wish come true. Dharna, fasting, anger, stopping the conversation - with the help of these tricks he used to blackmail. He did not judge the decision either right or wrong.

10. On 14th June 1947, there was a meeting of the All India Congress Committee in Delhi. The topic of discussion was the partition of

India. This proposal was to be rejected. But strangely, Gandhi supported the proposal to divide the country. This is what he said one day - if he wants to divide the country, he has to do it on his dead body! Millions of Hindus have died, but he has remained silent! He never ordered the Muslims to maintain peace - as much as the advice is only on the Hindus!

11. Gandhi gave birth to "Muslim flattery" in the guise of secularism. When Muslims opposed making Hindi the state language - Gandhi admitted! He gave a strange solution - "Hindustani" (Hindi and Urdu Khichri)! He began calling Badsha Ram, Begum Sita to say!

12. He bowed his head in opposition to some Muslims and did not allow "Bande Mataram" to become the national anthem!

13. Gandhiji has repeatedly called Chhatrapati Shivaji, Maharana Pratap, Guru Gobind Singh misguided patriots! But there he used to call Muhammad Ali Jinnah "Qaeda Azam"! What a strange thing!

14. In 1931, the National Congress formed a committee to decide what the national flag of independent India would look like. This committee unanimously decided that there would be a flag of deep saffron cloth with a spinning wheel in the middle. But Gandhiji's insistence is to make it Teranga! All depended on his will!

15. When the proposal to rebuild the Somnath temple was put in Parliament on the initiative of Sardar Vallabhbhai Patel, he opposed it. He was not even in the cabinet! But strangely enough, he started a hunger strike on January 13 1948 - to build a mosque in Delhi at the government's expense! Why this duplicity? He may not think Hindus are Indians! Well, were you a Hindu at all?

16. It was decided by Gandhiji's mediation that - After independence, India will give ₹75,00,00,000 to Pakistan. ₹20,00,00,000 was given at the beginning. The rest was 55 crores was to give later. But on October 22, 1947, Pakistan invaded Kashmir! For this betrayal of Pakistan, the Union Cabinet decided that the rest of the money

would not be given to Pakistan. But he sat down with a stick! Started blackmail again - hunger strike again. In the end, the government was forced to pay the remaining ₹55,00,00,000 to traitorous Pakistan!

Seeing his love for Jinnah and 'blind Pakistan love', I can say that he was the father of Pakistan - not India. He speaks in support of Pakistan at every moment - no matter how unjust Pakistan's claim!

THESE ARE SOME STATEMENTS OF NATHURAM GODSE GIVEN IN COURT.

I have a lot of respect for him. But no patriot can divide the country and we cannot allow any patriot to divide the country and favour a particular community. I did not kill Gandhi - I killed him – killed him. I had no choice but to assassinate Gandhiji. He was not my enemy - but his decision brought danger to the country. When a person has no other way - then to take the right path to do the right thing.

I was disturbed by Gandhiji's support in building the Muslim League and Pakistan. Gandhiji went on a hunger strike to get Rs 55 crore for Pakistan. The plight of the Hindus who migrated to India for persecution in Pakistan stunned me. Unbroken Hindu state was not possible for Gandhiji to bow down to the Muslim League. It was unbearable for me to see my mother split into pieces for one of her sons. I became a foreigner in my own country. He was abiding by all the injustices of the Muslim League. I decided that I must kill Gandhiji to save Mother India from disintegration and misery. And that is why I killed Gandhi.

I knew I would be hanged for it and I was ready for it. And if it is a crime to protect the motherland here - then I will commit such a crime again and again - every time. And until the Indus River flows into the whole of India – do not immerse my bones. At the time of my execution, I had a saffron flag in one hand and a map of the whole of India in the other. Before I go to the gallows, I want to say the victory of Mother India.

"O Mother India - I am very sorry that I have been able to serve you only this."

Annexation of Hyderabad

Operation Polo was the code name of the Hyderabad "police action" in September 1948, by the newly independent Dominion of India against Hyderabad State. It was a military operation in which the Indian Armed Forces invaded the Nizam-ruled princely state, annexing it into the Indian Union.

At the time of Partition in 1947, the princely states of India, who in principle had self-government within their own territories, were subject to subsidiary alliances with the British, giving them control of their external relations. With the Indian Independence Act 1947, the British abandoned all such alliances, leaving the states with the option of opting for full independence. However, by 1948 almost all had acceded to either India or Pakistan. One major exception was that of the wealthiest and most powerful principality, Hyderabad, where the Nizam, Mir Osman Ali Khan, Asaf Jah VII, a Muslim ruler who presided over a largely Hindu population, chose independence and hoped to maintain this with an irregular army. The Nizam was also beset by the Telangana rebellion, which he was unable to crush.

In November 1947, Hyderabad signed a standstill agreement with the Dominion of India, continuing all previous arrangements except for the stationing of Indian troops in the state. Claiming that it feared the establishment of a Communist state in Hyderabad. Nizam's power had weakened because of the Telangana Rebellion and the rise of a radical militia known as the Razakars whom he could not put down. India invaded the state in September 1948, following a crippling economic blockade, and multiple attempts at destabilizing the state through railway disruptions, the bombing of government buildings, and raids on border villages. After the defeat of Razakars, the Nizam signed an instrument of accession, joining India.

The operation led to massive violence on communal lines, at times perpetrated by the Indian Army. The Sunderlal Committee, appointed by Indian prime minister Jawaharlal Nehru, concluded that between 30,000-40,000 people had died in total in the state, in a report which was not released until 2013. Other responsible observers estimated the number of deaths to be 200,000 or higher.

Operation Polo

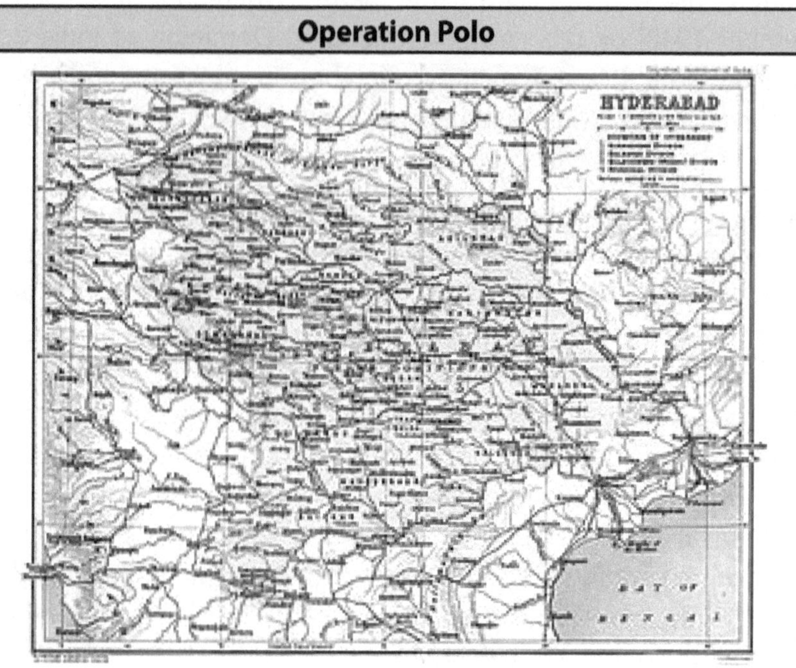

The State of Hyderabad in 1909 (excluding Berar)

Date 13-18 September 1948 (5 days)

Hyderabad State (parts of South and Western Location, India)

Indian Victory

Result – Annexation of Hyderabad to the Union of India

35,000 Indian Armed Forces Vs 22,000 Hyderabad State Forces & 2 lakh irregulars (Razakars)

Killed Indian Armed Forces 10

Hyderabad State Forces 807 killed 1647 POWs

Razakars 1373 killed, 1911 captured

Around 1 lakh civilians killed

Industrial Finance Corporation of India (IFCI)

IFCI Ltd (IFCI) was set up as a Statutory Corporation ("The Industrial Finance Corporation of India") in 1948 for providing medium and long term finance to industry. In 1993, after repeal of the Industrial Finance Corporation Act, IFCI became a Public Limited Company, registered under the Companies Act, 1956. IFCI is also registered with the Reserve Bank of India (RBI) as a Systemically Important Non-Deposit taking Non-Banking Finance Company (NBFC-ND-SI) and is also a notified Public Financial Institution under Section 2(72) of the Companies Act, 2013.

Atomic Energy Commission of India

The Atomic Energy Commission of India is the governing body of the Department of Atomic Energy (DAE), Government of India. The DAE is under the direct charge of the Prime Minister.

The Indian Atomic Energy Commission was set up on 3 August 1948 under the late Department of Scientific Research. A resolution passed by the Government of India later replaced the commission by "Atomic Energy Commission of India" on 1 March 1954 under the Department of Atomic Energy with Homi J. Bhabha as secretary and more financial and executive powers, headquartered in Mumbai, Maharashtra.

The functions of the Atomic Energy Commission are: (i) to organize research in atomic science in the country (ii) to train atomic scientists in the country (iii) to promote nuclear research in commission's own laboratories in India (iv) to undertake prospecting of atomic minerals in India and to extract such minerals for use on industrial scale.

India achieved a major success in terms of breakthrough in science and technology when the Atomic Energy Commission (AEC) detonated an underground nuclear device at Pokhran in the deserts of Rajasthan on 18 May, 1974.

It has five research centres in India viz.

- Bhabha Atomic Research Centre (BARC), Mumbai
- Indira Gandhi Centre for Atomic Research (IGCAR), Kalpakkam (Tamil Nadu)

- ♦ Raja Ramanna Centre for Advanced Technology (RRCAT), Indore
- ♦ Variable Energy Cyclotron Centre (VECC), Kolkata
- ♦ Atomic Minerals Directorate for Exploration and Research (AMD), Hyderabad.

It also gives financial assistance to autonomous national institutes doing research in the field and has various other organisations under it.

Hindustan Aeronautics Limited

Hindustan Aeronautics Limited (HAL) is an Indian public sector aerospace and defence company, headquartered in Bangalore. Established on 23 December 1940, HAL is one of the oldest and largest aerospace and defense manufacturers in the world. HAL began aircraft manufacturing as early as 1942 with licensed production of Harlow PC-5, Curtiss P-36 Hawk and Vultee A-31 Vengeance for the Indian Air Force. HAL currently has 11 dedicated Research and development (R&D) centres and 21 manufacturing divisions under 4 production units spread across India. HAL is managed by a board of directors appointed by the President of India through the Ministry of Defence, Government of India. HAL is currently involved in designing and manufacturing of fighter jets, helicopters, jet engine and marine gas turbine engine, avionics, software development, spares supply, overhauling and upgrading of Indian military aircraft.

The HAL HF-24 Marut fighter-bomber was the first indigenous fighter aircraft made in India.

History

HAL was established as Hindustan Aircraft Limited in Bangalore on 23 December 1940 by Walchand Hirachand in association with the then Kingdom of Mysore. Walchand Hirachand became chairman of the company. The company's office was opened at a bungalow called "Eventide" on Domlur Road.

The organisation and equipment for the factory at Bangalore was set up by William D. Pawley of the Intercontinental Aircraft Corporation of New York. Pawley obtained a large number of machine-tools and equipment from the United States.

The Indian Government bought a one-third stake in the company and by April 1941 by investing ₹25 lakh as it believed this to be a strategic imperative. The decision by the government was primarily motivated to boost British military hardware supplies in Asia to counter the increasing threat posed by Imperial Japan during Second World War. The Kingdom of Mysore supplied two directors, Air Marshal John Higgins was resident director. The first aircraft built was a Harlow PC-5. On 2 April 1942, the government announced that the company had been nationalised when it had bought out the stakes of Seth Walchand Hirachand and other promoters so that it could act freely. The Mysore Kingdom refused to sell its stake in the company but yielded the management control over to the British Indian Government.

In 1943 the Bangalore factory was handed over to the United States Army Air Forces but still using Hindustan Aircraft management. The factory expanded rapidly and became the centre for major overhaul and repair of American aircraft and was known as the 84th Air Depot. The first aircraft to be overhauled was a Consolidated PBY Catalina followed by every type of aircraft operated in India and Burma. When returned to Indian control two years later the factory had become one of the largest overhaul and repair organisations in the East. In the post war reorganisation the company built railway carriages as an interim activity.

After India gained independence in 1947, the management of the company was passed over to the Government of India. The total number of broad- gauge coaches manufactured by the Hindustan Aircraft Limited during the year 1954 is 158.

Hindustan Aeronautics Limited (HAL) was formed on 1 October 1964 (the Registrar of Companies has a registration date of 16 August 1963) when Hindustan Aircraft Limited joined the consortium formed in June by the IAF Aircraft Manufacturing Depot, Kanpur (at the time manufacturing HS748 under licence) and the group recently set up to manufacture MiG-21 under licence, with its new factories planned in Koraput, Nasik and Hyderabad. Though HAL was not used actively for developing newer models of fighter jets, except for the HF-24 Marut, the company has played a crucial role in modernisation of the Indian Air Force. In 1957 company started manufacturing Bristol Siddeley Orpheus jet engines under licence at new factory located in Bangalore.

Indian Telephone Industries Limited

ITI Limited, earlier known as Indian Telephone Industries Limited, is a central public sector undertaking in India. It is under the ownership of Department of Telecommunications, Ministry of Communications, Government of India. It was founded in 1948 as a departmental factory, incorporated as a public company in 1950 and today has six manufacturing facilities at Bengaluru, Naini, Mankapur, Raebareli, Palakkad and Srinagar which produce a range of switching, transmission, access and subscriber premises equipment. It is headquartered at Bengaluru. It has multi-locational electronic assembly and mechanical manufacturing facilities, countrywide marketing and customer support centers and in-house R&D for absorption of technology, indigenous development of products for in-house manufacturing. It produces GSM mobile equipments at its Mankapur and Raebareli facilities. These two facilities supply more than nine million lines per annum to both domestic as well as foreign markets. The Palakkad unit is responsible for data handling with assembly and personalization of smart cards and electronic manufacturing facilities for PCB's, HDPE Pipe, Smart Energy Meters, Micro PC under Smart City Mission etc. It also produces Information and Communication Technology (ICT) equipments such as network management systems, encryption and networking for internet connectivity, and secure communications networks and equipment for the defense. The company has 1924 employees as on August 1, 2023. On 01-10-2020, ITI Limited signed a contract with Defense to implement Rs 7796 Crore ASCON Phase-IV project.

Indian Police Service

The Indian Police Service (abbr. IPS) is a civil service under the All India Services. It replaced the Imperial Police in 1948, a year after India became independent from the British Raj.

Along with the Indian Administrative Service (IAS) and the Indian Forest Service (IFS), the IPS is one of the All India Services – its officers are employed by both the Union Government and the individual states.

The service commands and provides leadership to State police forces and Union territories' police forces, Central Armed Police Forces (BSF,

SSB, CRPF, CISF, and ITBP), the National Security Guard (NSG), National Disaster Response Force (NDRF), Intelligence Bureau (IB), Research and Analysis Wing (R&AW), Special Protection Group (SPG), National Investigative Agency (NIA) and the Central Bureau of Investigation (CBI).

Films Division of India

The Films Division of India (FDI), commonly referred as Films Division, was established in 1948 following the independence of India. It was the first state film production and distribution unit, under the Ministry of Information and Broadcasting, Government of India, with its main intent being to "produce documentaries and news magazines for publicity of Government programmes" and the cinematic record of Indian history.

FDI was divided into four wings; these are Production, Distribution, International Documentary and Short Film Festival. The Division produces documentaries/news magazines from its headquarters in Mumbai, films on defence and family welfare from New Delhi and featurettes focussing on rural India from the regional centres at Calcutta now (Kolkata) and Bangalore. In 1990, it was started at the annual Mumbai International Film Festival, for documentary, short and animation films at Mumbai. It housed a museum of cinema, the National Museum of Indian Cinema (NMIC), inaugurated on 19 January 2019.

In March 2022, it was merged with National Film Development Corporation.

India at the 1948 Summer Olympics

India competed at the 1948 Summer Olympics in Wembley Park, London, England. 79 competitors, all men, took part in 39 events in 10 sports. It was the first time that India competed as an independent nation at the Olympic Games.

The Indian field hockey team defeated the British team to win the country's first gold medal at the 1948 Summer Olympics. It was the country's first Olympic gold medal since India became independent.

History and date of formation of Indian states since 1947

Before independence, India was divided into 565 princely states. These indigenous princely states believed in independent governance, which was the biggest obstacle in building a strong India.

At this time India had three types of states (1) 'Territories of British India', (2) 'Princely states' and the colonial territories of France and Portugal.

After the Indian independence; 562 princely states had nodded to join the Indian Confederation except Hyderabad, Junagadh, Bhopal and Kashmir.

Since the Indian independence the boundaries of the Indian states keep on changing year by year.

From 565 princely states and 17 provinces before partition, to 14 states and 6 Union Territories following the Reorganisation of States in 1956 to 29 states and 7 union territories in 2014, now after the bifurcation of Jammu & Kashmir to 28 states and 9 Union Territories after it.

Bhopal

The state of Bhopal was also one of the princely states that declined the integration of princely states. The situation in Bhopal was slightly different from other states where a Muslim Nawab, Hamidullah Khan, was ruling the Hindu-dominated population. The Nawab of Bhopal was ordered a close aide of the Muslim League & thus strictly opposed the integration of princely

states. Lord Mountbatten offered the Nawab of Bhopal the Instrument of Accession. The Nawab of Bhopal refused to sign the Accession claiming the protection of Muslim rights in a Hindu-dominated state. By July 1947, he finally accepted and signed the Instrument of Accession as the people of Bhopal also realized that the Nawab was only interested in gaining power.

Junagarh

The princely state of Junagarh was situated in southwestern Gujarat. This state also showed disinterest in merging with the Indian union. It comprised a large Hindu population and was ruled by a Muslim Nawab, Muhammad Mahabat Khanji III. The king of Junagarh had initially agreed to merge with Pakistan on 15th September 1947, claiming it adjoined Pakistan by sea. Later on, two states, Mangrol and Babariawad, under the purview of Junagarh, announced their independence by acceding to the Indian union. The Nawab, in response, forcefully took control of these states by adopting military measures. The rulers of Mangrol and Babariawad pleaded for assistance from the Indian Government.

Looking at the complex situation, Sardar Patel & V.P. Menon tried to convince the Dewan of Junagarh to call for a plebiscite. After many clashes & hardships, the plebiscite was held, resulting in Junagarh acceding to India.

Nationalization of RBI

1st January, 1949

The Reserve Bank of India was nationalised with effect from 1st January, 1949 on the basis of the Reserve Bank of India (Transfer to Public Ownership) Act, 1948. All shares in the capital of the Bank were deemed transferred to the Central Government on payment of a suitable compensation.

Indian Rupee devalued

The Indian rupee has been devalued three times by the government of India in the past. Due to a shortage of funds within the government, the value of the Indian rupee was reduced in 1949. Due to the war with China and Pakistan in 1966, the Indian rupee was devalued. The Indian government once more devalued the rupee in 1991 during a financial crisis.

Devaluation of Currency in India

In macroeconomics and contemporary monetary policy, a **devaluation is the formal setting by a monetary authority of a lower exchange rate for the national currency** in relation to a foreign reference currency or currency basket in a fixed-exchange-rate system. Devaluation is the intentional reduction in the value of a nation's currency.

- The currency's value may be reduced at the government's discretion.

- **Depreciating a currency lowers the cost of exports** and can aid in reducing trade deficits.

- Devaluing a currency can be beneficial during such a time when an economy is paralyzed due to a variety of factors.

- The value of the Indian rupee was devalued on numerous occasions in the past, and these actions eventually improved both the economy and the value of the currency.

- Due to a lack of funds, the Indian government **devalued the rupee in 1949, 1966, during the war with China and Pakistan, and in 1991**, during an economic downturn.

Atomic Minerals Directorate for Exploration and Research

Atomic Minerals Directorate for Exploration and Research (AMD), with headquarters at Hyderabad and seven regional centers, is the oldest unit of the Department of Atomic Energy (India) (DAE), Government of India. The principal mandate of the organisation is to carry out geological exploration and discover mineral deposits required for nuclear power programme of India.

Central Reserve Police Force

The Central Reserve Police Force (CRPF) is a reserve gendarmerie and internal combat force in India under the authority of the Ministry of Home Affairs (MHA) of the Government of India. It is one among the Central Armed Police Forces. The CRPF's primary role lies in assisting the State/Union Territories in police operations to maintain law and order and counter-insurgency. It is composed of Central Reserve Police Force (Regular) and Central Reserve Police Force (Auxiliary).

It came into existence as the Crown Representative's Police on 27 July 1939. After Indian independence, it became the Central Reserve Police Force on the enactment of the CRPF Act on 28 December 1949. Besides law and order and counter-insurgency duties, the CRPF has played an increasingly large role in India's general elections. This is especially true for the erstwhile state of Jammu and Kashmir, Bihar, and in the North East, with the presence of unrest and often violent conflict. During the Parliamentary elections of September 1999, the CRPF played a major role in the security arrangements. Of late, CRPF contingents are also being deployed in UN missions.

With 246 battalions and various other establishments, the CRPF is considered India's largest central armed police force and has a sanctioned strength of more than 300,000 personnel as of 2019.

Indian Council of Medical Research

The Indian Council of Medical Research (ICMR), the apex body in India for the formulation, coordination and promotion of biomedical research, is one of the oldest and largest medical research bodies in the world.

The ICMR is funded by the Government of India through the Department of Health Research, Ministry of Health and Family Welfare. In 2007, the organization established the Clinical Trials Registry - India, which is India's national registry for clinical trials.

ICMR's 26 national institutes address themselves to research on specific health topics like tuberculosis, leprosy, cholera and diarrhoeal diseases, viral diseases including AIDS, malaria, kala-azar, vector control, nutrition, food & drug toxicology, reproduction, immuno-haematology, oncology, medical statistics, etc. Its 6 regional medical research centres address themselves to regional health problems, and also aim to strengthen or generate research capabilities in different geographic areas of the country.

The council's research priorities coincide with National health priorities such as control and management of communicable diseases, fertility control, maternal and child health, control of nutritional disorders, developing alternative strategies for health care delivery, containment within safety limits of environmental and occupational health problems; research on major non-communicable diseases like cancer, cardiovascular diseases, blindness, diabetes and other metabolic and haematological disorders; mental health research and drug research (including traditional remedies). These efforts are undertaken with a view to reduce the total burden of disease and to promote health and well-being of the population.

PAKISTAN

The head of state of Pakistan from independence until Pakistan became a republic in 1956 was the Pakistani monarch. The British Parliament passed Mountbatten's plan. He became the first Governor-General of independent India and Mohammed Ali Jinnah the Governor-General of Pakistan.

Pakistan was one of the realms of the Commonwealth of Nations that shared the same person as sovereign and head of state. The Pakistani monarch was represented in the dominion by the Governor-General of Pakistan, whom the monarch appointed on the advice of the Pakistani government.

The Pakistani monarch and the Federal Legislature of Pakistan constituted the Parliament of Pakistan. All executive powers of Pakistan rested with the sovereign. All laws in Pakistan were enacted only with royal assent, granted by the Governor-General on behalf of the sovereign. The Governor-General was also responsible for summoning, proroguing, and dissolving the Federal Legislature. The governor-general chose and appointed the Council of Ministers and dismissed them at his discretion. All Pakistani ministers of the Crown held office at the pleasure of the Governor-General. The Governor-General of Pakistan was also exempted from any proceedings against him in any Pakistani court.

During partition, the trains full with dead bodies of Hindus were coming from Pakistan. These were the unfortunate people who wanted to come to India by leaving all their assets in Pakistan. India was shocked to see such a scene.

"Hans ke liya hai Pakistan, lad ke lenge Hindustan". We have taken Pakistan easily (smiling). We will take Hindustan by fighting, was the popular slogan in those days.

India is an enemy country, is taught to the children in Pakistan in the schools. This poison has a long lasting effect.

List of governors-general of Pakistan

The following is a list of people who served as governor-general of Pakistan.

1. Muhammad Ali Jinnah — 14 August 1947 to 11 September 1948

2. Sir Khawaja Nazimuddin — 14 September 1948 to 17 October 1951

3. Sir Ghulam Muhammad — 17 October 1951 to 7 August 1955

4. Iskander Mirza — 7 August 1955 to 23 March 1956

The President of Pakistan is the head of state of the Islamic Republic of Pakistan.

The complete list of Presidents of Pakistan includes the persons sworn into the office as President of Pakistan following the proclamation of the Islamic Republic of Pakistan in 1956.

There have been a total of 13 Presidents. The first President was Iskander Ali Mirza who entered office on 23 March 1956. The current office holder is Arif Alvi, who took charge on 9 September 2018, following his victory in the 2018 elections.

Presidents of Pakistan

1. Iskander Mirza (Republican Party) 23 March 1956 to 27 October 1958

2. Ayub Khan (Martial Law) 27 October 1958 to 25 March 1969

3. Yahya Khan (Martial Law) 25 March 1969 to 20 December 1971

4. Zulfiqar Ali Bhutto (Pakistan Peoples Party) 20 December 1971 to 14 August 1973

5. Fazal Ilahi Chaudhry (Pakistan Peoples Party) 14 August 1973 to 16 September 1978

6. Muhammad Zia-ul-Haq (Martial Law) 16 September 1978 to 17 August 1988

7. Ghulam Ishaq Khan (Independent) 17 August 1988 to 18 July 1993

8. Wasim Sajjad (Acting) (Pakistan Muslim League (N)) 18 July 1993 to 14 November 1993

9. Farooq Leghari (Pakistan Peoples Party) 14 November 1993 to 2 December 1997

10. Wasim Sajjad (Acting) (Pakistan Muslim League (N)) 2 December 1997 to1 January 1998

11. Muhammad Rafiq Tarar (Pakistan Muslim League) 1 January 1998 to 20 June 2001

12. Pervez Musharraf (Martial Law) 20 June 2001 to 18 August 2008

13. Muhammad Mian Soomro (Acting) Pakistan Muslim League (Q) 18 Aug 2008 to 9 Sep 2008

14. Asif Ali Zardari (Pakistan Peoples Party) 9 September 2008 to 9 September 2013

15. Mamnoon Hussain (Pakistan Muslim League (N)) 9 Sep 2013 to 9 Sep 2018

16. Arif Alvi (Pakistan Tehreek-e-Insaf) 9 Sep 2018

1. <u>Muhammad Ali Jinnah</u>

   Muhammad Ali Jinnah (born Mahomedali Jinnahbhai; 25 December 1876 – 11 September 1948) was a barrister, politician and the founder of Pakistan. Jinnah served as the leader of the All-India Muslim League from 1913 until the inception of Pakistan on 14 August 1947, and then as the Dominion of Pakistan's first Governor-General until his death.

   As the first Governor-General of Pakistan, Jinnah worked to establish the new nation's government and policies, and to aid the millions of Muslim migrants who had emigrated from neighbouring India to Pakistan after the two states' independence, personally supervising the establishment of refugee camps. Jinnah died at age 71 in September 1948, just over a year after Pakistan gained independence from the United Kingdom. He left a deep and respected legacy in Pakistan. Innumerable streets, roads and localities in the world are named after Jinnah.

Several universities and public buildings in Pakistan bear Jinnah's name. He is revered in Pakistan as the Quaid-e-Azam ("Great Leader") and Baba-e-Qaum ("Father of the Nation"). His birthday is observed as a national holiday in Pakistan. According to his biographer, Stanley Wolpert, Jinnah remains Pakistan's greatest leader.

2. <u>Khawaja Nazimuddin</u>

Sir Khawaja Nazimuddin (19 July 1894 – 22 October 1964) was a Pakistani politician and statesman who served as the second governor-general of Pakistan from 1948 to 1951 and later as the second Prime Minister of Pakistan from 1951 to 1953. He was one of the leading founding fathers of Pakistan and the first Bengali to have governed Pakistan.

Nazimuddin ascended to Governor-General in 1948 after the death of Jinnah, before becoming Prime Minister in 1951 following the assassination of his predecessor, Liaquat Ali Khan. His term was marked by constant power struggles with his own successor as Governor-General, Ghulam Muhammad, as law and order deteriorated amid the rise of the Bengali language movement and protests in his native Dhaka in 1952, and religious riots in Lahore a year later. The latter crisis saw the first instance of martial law, limited to the city, and led to Ghulam Muhammad dismissing Nazimuddin on 17 April 1953.

Prime Ministers of Pakistan

Liaquat Ali Khan (1 October 1895 – 16 October 1951) was a Pakistani lawyer, politician and statesman who served as the first prime minister of Pakistan from 1947 until his assassination in 1951. He was one of the leading figures of the Pakistan Movement and is revered as Quaid-e-Millat ("Leader of the nation").

Khan's premiership oversaw the beginning of the Cold War, in which Khan's foreign policy sided with the United States-led Western Bloc over the Soviet Union-led Eastern Bloc. He promulgated the Objectives Resolution, in 1949, which stipulated Pakistan to be an Islamic democracy.

He also held cabinet portfolio as the first foreign minister, defence minister, and frontier regions minister from 1947 until his assassination in 1951. Prior to the part, Khan briefly tenured as Finance minister of British India in the Interim Government that undertook independence of Pakistan and India, led by Louis Mountbatten, the then-Viceroy of India.

In March 1951, he survived an attempted coup by left-wing political opponents and segments of the Pakistani military. While delivering a speech in the Company Bagh of Rawalpindi, Khan was shot dead by an Afghan militant Said Akbar for unknown reasons. Khan was posthumously given the title Shaheed-e-Milat ('Martyr of the Nation') and is honored as one of Pakistan's greatest prime ministers.

His government faced serious challenges including the dispute over Kashmir with India, forcing Khan to approach his counterpart the Prime Minister of India Jawaharlal Nehru. A settlement was reached to end the fighting, while Nehru also referred the issue to the United Nations. Ali Khan sent the recommendation to Jinnah to appoint Abdul Rashid as the country's first Chief Justice, and Justice Abdur Rahim as President of the Constitutional Assembly, both of them were also founding fathers of Pakistan. Some of the earliest reforms Khan took were to centralise the Muslim League, and he planned and prepared the Muslim League to become the leading authority of Pakistan.

As Prime Minister Ali Khan took initiatives to develop educational infrastructure, science and technology in the country, with the intention of carrying the vision of successful development of science and technology to aid the essential foreign policy of Pakistan.

Khan's government authorised the establishment of the Sindh University. Under his government, science infrastructure was slowly built but he continued inviting Muslim scientists and engineers from India to Pakistan, believing it essential for Pakistan's future progress.

In 1947, Khan and his Finance minister Malick Ghulam proposed the idea of Five-Year Plans, by putting the country's economic system on investment and capitalism grounds. Focusing on an initial planned economic system under the directives of private sector and consortium industries in 1948, economic planning began to take place during his time in office, but soon collapsed partly because of unsystematic and inadequate staffing. Khan's economic policies were soon heavily dependent on United States aid to the country. In spite of planning an independent economic policy, Khan's economic policies focused on the United States' aid programme.

Accession of Kalat

The princely state of Kalat in Balochistan acceded to the Dominion of Pakistan on 27 March 1948, after having declared independence earlier on 15 August 1947. It was accepted by the Governor General Muhammad Ali Jinnah on 31 March, making Kalat an integral part of Pakistan. The accession was a stormy affair. Whether it had the consensus of its subjects remains disputed and Insurgencies against the state of Pakistan continue till the present day.

27th March: The day of occupation of Balochistan by Pakistan

London [UK], March 28 (ANI): After World War II, Britain and its allies were threatened by Russia and its socialism, socialism which was becoming a ray of hope for the subjugated oppressed nations of the world, Russia's growing popularity in the region was a wake-up call for the Western powers.

In this regard, Balochistan had great geographical worth. If the Soviet Union had succeeded in setting foot here, it would have been a moment of reflection for the West.

Therefore, the UK needed a watchdog in the region, which she was getting in the form of Pakistan by breaking United India, so the UK, along with Pakistan's cunning leader Muhammad Ali Jinnah, took away the constitutional status and independence of the state of Kalat.

In March 1948, Jinnah fraudulently trapped the Jam of Lasbela Jam Ghulam Qadir, Wali of Makuran Nawab Bhai Khan and Nawab Noshirwani of Kharan, he succeeded in convincing them of his political machinations.

On other hand, Jinnah pressurised and urged Khan of Kalat to join Pakistan, even though no law of the world recognizes that any part of an independent country should be forcibly annexed without its will and intention. But Pakistan's treacherous leader Jinnah, along with Britain, put this unconstitutional move into practice.

Meanwhile, The Khan of Kalat was raising his voice against these unconstitutional moves, on the orders of Sir Douglas Gracie, the COAS of Pakistan, the Pakistani army raided the coastal areas of Balochistan towards Panjgur, which later became annexation of Kalat on March 27.

On March 27, 1948, a newborn Pakistani state attacked and forcefully annexed the sovereign Baloch state on gunpoint, since the occupation of Balochistan in 1948 Baloch people have been observing March 27 as a black day.

From the very day of forcible occupation, the Baloch resistance movement has started and it was led by Agha Abdul Karim Khan, who was then the governor of Makoran state and younger brother of Khan of Kalat (Balochistan) Mir Ahmed Yar Khan.

Historically Kalat was the capital of Balochistan, And Balochistan was called Kalat State, whereas Jhalawan, Makoran, Kharan, and Lasbela were provinces of Kalat state. Even though the Rulers (Walis) of states met with Mohammad Ali Jinnah and merge their states with Pakistan but these provinces had no legal or constitutional rights to annex with Pakistan because these provinces were under the direct control of the Kalat state and governors were appointed by Kalat the central government and the Wali's were also members of the upper chamber (Aiwan e Bala) of Kalat state.

And they had already taken the oath from the assembly for the safety and sovereignty of Balochistan.

March 27 has been observed as a black day by the Baloch nation. They protest, hoist black flags on their houses and wear black, hand bands to express the hatred against the occupation.

Pro Freedom political parties stage a protest and arrange awareness campaigns and seminars in Balochistan and worldwide to highlight Pakistani atrocities in Balochistan.

Baloch have been fighting against slavery and for the sovereignty of their homeland Balochistan since the first day of Occupation, Baloch have fought five wars against Pakistan to regain the sovereign state of Balochistan but Pakistan quelled those insurgencies with the help of

China, neighbouring countries and used the US-supplied weapons and jets against Baloch insurgents.

The new ongoing insurgency; which was started two decades ago said to be the most powerful and ideological Baloch movement.

Thousands of Balochs have been killed and thousands are forcibly abducted in military aggressions since 1948. Houses are being burned, livestock and other assets are being looted on a daily basis in military operations.

Balochs have never accepted Pakistani slavery and they have been struggling for their self-determination, however, there have been ups and downs in the Baloch national liberation struggle. (ANI)

This report is auto-generated from ANI news service.

The Partition of India came in 1947 with the sudden grant of independence. It was the intention of those who wished for a Muslim state to have a clean partition between independent and equal "Pakistan" and "India" once independence came.

Nearly one third of the Muslim population of India remained in the new India.

Inter-communal violence between Hindus, Sikhs and Muslims resulted in between 200,000 and 2 million casualties leaving 14 million people displaced.

Princely states in India were provided with an Instrument of Accession to accede to either India or Pakistan.

Indo-Pakistani War of 1947

The war, also called the First Kashmir War, started in October 1947 when Pakistan feared that the Maharaja of the princely state of Kashmir and Jammu would accede to India. Following partition, princely states were left to choose whether to join India or Pakistan or to remain independent. Jammu and Kashmir, the largest of the princely states, had a majority Muslim population and significant fraction of Hindu population, all ruled by the Hindu Maharaja Hari Singh. Tribal Islamic forces with support from the army of Pakistan attacked and occupied parts of the princely state forcing the Maharaja to sign the Instrument of Accession of the princely state to the Dominion of India to receive Indian military aid. The UN Security Council passed Resolution 47 on 22 April 1948. The fronts solidified gradually along what came to be known as the Line of Control. A formal cease-fire was declared at 23:59 on the night of 1 January 1949. India gained control of about two-thirds of the state (Kashmir Valley, Jammu and Ladakh) whereas Pakistan gained roughly a third of Kashmir (Azad Kashmir, and Gilgit-Baltistan). The Pakistan controlled areas are collectively referred to as Pakistan administered Kashmir.

Muhajirs – The Muslims who went from India to Pakistan after the partition, were called Muhajirs. They were always differentiated from the Muslims who were staying in Pakistan before the partition. This was another major problem with Pakistan as a country. This type of thinking never created t unity amongst all the people.

Unlike Pakistan, Indians accepted the refugees those came from Pakistan after the partition whole heartedly with sympathy without any prejudice.

Abul A'la Maududi

Sayyid Abul A'la al-Maududi (25 September 1903 – 22 September 1979) was an Islamic scholar, Islamist ideologue, Muslim philosopher, jurist, historian, journalist, activist, and scholar active in British India and later, following the partition, in Pakistan. Described by Wilfred Cantwell Smith as "the most systematic thinker of modern Islam", his numerous works, which "covered a range of disciplines such as Qur'anic exegesis, hadith, law, philosophy, and history", were written in Urdu, but then translated into English, Arabic, Hindi, Bengali, Tamil, Telugu, Kannada, Burmese, Malayalam and many other languages. He sought to revive Islam, and to propagate what he understood to be "true Islam". He believed that Islam was essential for politics and that it was necessary to institute sharia and preserve Islamic culture similarly as to that during the reign of the Rashidun Caliphs and abandon immorality, from what he viewed as the evils of secularism, nationalism and socialism, which he understood to be the influence of Western imperialism.

He founded the Jamaat-e-Islami, the then largest Islamic organization in Asia. At the time of the Indian independence movement, Maududi and the Jamaat-e-Islami actively worked to oppose the partition of India. After it occurred, Maududi and his followers shifted their focus to politicizing Islam and generating support for making Pakistan an Islamic state. They are thought to have helped influence General Muhammad Zia-ul-Haq to introduce the Islamization in Pakistan, and to have been greatly strengthened by him after tens of thousands of members and sympathizers were given jobs in the judiciary and civil service during his administration. He was the first recipient of the Saudi Arabian King Faisal International Award for his service to Islam in 1979. Maududi was part of establishing and running of Islamic University of Madinah, Saudi Arabia.

He was the second person in history whose absentee funeral was observed in the Kaaba, after King Ashama ibn-Abjar. Maududi is acclaimed by the Jamaat-e-Islami, Muslim Brotherhood, Islamic Circle of North America, Hamas and other organizations.

2

(1951-1970)

INDIA - Constitution of India - National Symbols of India - Election Commission of India - First Asian Games in Delhi in 1951 - Five-Year Plans of India - Indian general election - Assam earthquake - Indian Navy - Supreme Court of India - Liaquat–Nehru Pact - Indo-Nepal Treaty - Vallabhbhai Patel - Council of Scientific and Industrial Research – Helsinki Olympics - Constitution of Jammu and Kashmir - Indo-China War of 1962 – 1964 Summer Olympics, Tokyo- India's first Prime Minister dies - Indo-Pakistani War of 1965 - Tashkent Declaration - Lal Bahadur Shastri - Indira Gandhi - Indira Gandhi afraid of Sam Manekshaw - 1966 anti-cow slaughter agitation -1967 Koynanagar earthquake – 1968 Summer Olympics, Mexico - How India overcame food emergency, attained self-sufficiency – The Split in Indian National Congress – ISRO - Nationalization of Banks

PAKISTAN – Governor General – Presidents – Prime Ministers - Muttahida Qaumi Movement (MQM)

INDIA

Constitution of India

The Constitution of India is the supreme law of India. The document lays down the framework that demarcates fundamental political code, structure, procedures, powers, and duties of government institutions and sets out fundamental rights, directive principles, and the duties of citizens. It is the longest written national constitution in the world.

It imparts constitutional supremacy (not parliamentary supremacy, since it was created by a constituent assembly rather than Parliament) and was adopted by its people with a declaration in its preamble. Parliament cannot override the constitution.

B. R. Ambedkar and Constitution of India on a 2015 postage stamp of India

It was adopted by the Constituent Assembly of India on 26 November 1949 and became effective on 26 January 1950. The constitution replaced the Government of India Act 1935 as the country's fundamental governing document, and the Dominion of India became the Republic of India. To ensure constitutional autochthony, its framers repealed prior acts of the British parliament in Article 395. India celebrates its constitution on 26 January as Republic Day.

The constitution declares India a sovereign, socialist, secular, and democratic republic, assures its citizens justice, equality, and liberty, and endeavours to promote fraternity. The original 1950 constitution is preserved in a nitrogen-filled case at the Parliament House in New Delhi.

Background

In 1928, the All Parties Conference convened a committee in Lucknow to prepare the Constitution of India, which was known as the Nehru Report.

M. N. Roy is called the Pioneer of Indian Constitution, as the draft constituted by him is said to be "by far the most populist and radical of the manifestos of the 'New India'".

With the exception of scattered French and Portuguese exclaves, India was under the British rule from 1858 to 1947. From 1947 to 1950, the same legislation continued to be implemented as India was a dominion of United Kingdom for these three years, as each princely state was convinced by Sardar Patel and V. P. Menon to sign the articles of integration with India, and the British Government continued to be responsible for the external security of the country. Thus, the constitution of India repealed the Indian Independence Act 1947 and Government of India Act 1935 when it became effective on 26 January 1950. India ceased to be a dominion of the British Crown and became a sovereign, democratic republic with the constitution. Articles 5, 6, 7, 8, 9, 60, 324, 366, 367, 379, 380, 388, 391, 392, 393, and 394 of the constitution came into force on 26 November 1949, and the remaining articles became effective on 26 January 1950 which is celebrated every year in India as Republic Day.

The song Jana-gana-mana, composed originally in Bangla by Rabindranath Tagore, was adopted in its Hindi version by the Constituent Assembly as the National Anthem of India on January 24, 1950.

List of National Symbols of India

1. The National Flag - Tiranga

    The national flag of India is made of three colors. It has three stripes of equal length with saffron at the top, white in the middle, and green at the bottom. The center which is the white strip is embellished with Ashok chakra which is navy blue. Ashok chakra has 24 spokes which depict the 24 hours. The national flag of India was designed by Pingali Venkayya. The three colors of the national flag are of huge significance. The saffron stripe indicates sacrifice and courage, the white stripe in the middle represents purity, peace, and honesty, and the green stripe represents faith and chivalry.

2. National Emblem - National Emblem of India

    The national emblem of India is the lion capital of Ashoka at Sarnath. It was adopted as the national emblem of India on 26th January 1950. The motto inscribed below the national emblem is an integral part of India which says Satyamev Jayate in Devnagri script which means truth alone triumphs in English.

3. National Currency – Indian Rupee Similarly,

4. National Calendar - Saka Calendar, 5. Oath of Allegiance - National Pledge

5. National River – Ganga, 7. National Heritage Animal - Indian Elephant

6. National Animal - Royal Bengal Tiger, 7. National Bird - Indian Peacock

8. National Tree - Indian Banyan, 9. National Song - Vande Mataram

10. National Anthem - Jana Gana Mana, 11. National Aquatic Animal - Ganges River Dolphin

12. National Vegetable - Pumpkin, 13. National Fruit – Mango

14. National Flower – Lotus

Election Commission of India

The Election Commission of India (ECI) is a constitutional body. It was established by the Constitution of India to conduct and regulate elections in the country. Article 324 of the Constitution provides that the power of superintendence, direction, and control of elections to parliament, state legislatures, the office of the President of India, and the office of vice-president of India shall be vested in the election commission. Thus, the Election Commission is an all-India body in the sense that it is common to both the Central government and the state governments.

The body administers elections to the Lok Sabha, Rajya Sabha, State Legislative Assemblies, State Legislative Councils and the offices of the President and Vice President of the country. The Election Commission operates under the authority of Constitution per Article 324, and subsequently enacted Representation of the People Act. The commission has the powers under the Constitution, to act in an appropriate manner when the enacted laws make insufficient provisions to deal with a given situation in the conduct of an election. It is a permanent constitutional body.

First Asian Games were held in Delhi between March 4-11 in 1951

The Asian Games was first held in 1951 in New Delhi. They were held from March 4 to March 11, 1951. 491 athletes from 11 Asian National Olympic Committees participated in 57 events. 57 events from eight sports and disciplines. Japan won the most number of medals with 60 to their tally, out of which 24 were gold. India had 15 golds and 51 overall medals, they won the most number of bronzes with 20.

Five-Year Plans of India

First Plan (1951-1956)

The first Indian prime minister, Jawaharlal Nehru, presented the First Five-Year Plan to the Parliament of India and needed urgent attention. The First Five-year Plan was launched in 1951 which mainly focused in the development of the primary sector. The First Five-Year Plan was based on the Harrod–Domar model with few modifications.

This five years plan's president was Jawaharlal Nehru and Gulzarilal Nanda was the vice-president. The motto of first five years plan was ' Development of agriculture' and the aim was to solve different problems that formed due to the partition of the nation, second world war. Rebuilding the country after independence was the vision of this plan. Another main target was to lay down the foundation for industry, agriculture development in the country and to provide affordable healthcare, education in low price to people.

The total planned budget of ₹2,069 crore (₹2,378 crore later) was allocated to seven broad areas: irrigation and energy (27.2%), agriculture and community development (17.4%), transport and communications (24%), industry (8.6%), social services (16.6%), rehabilitation of landless farmers (4.1%), and for other sectors and services (2.5%). The most important feature of this phase was active role of state in all economic sectors. Such a role was justified at that time because immediately after independence, India was facing basic problems—deficiency of capital and low capacity to save.

1951–52 Indian general election

General elections were held in India between 25 October 1951 and 21 February 1952. India attained independence on 15 August 1947 and set up an Election Commission two years later. In March 1950, Sukumar Sen was appointed as the first Chief Election Commissioner. A month later, the Indian Parliament passed the Representation of the People Act which provided the conduct for election for the Houses of Parliament and the Houses of Legislature for each state. It was conducted under the provisions of the Indian Constitution, which was adopted on 26 November 1949. Elections to most of the state legislatures took place simultaneously.

A total of 1,949 candidates competed for 489 seats in the Lok Sabha. More than 173 million people out of an overall population of about 360 million were eligible to vote, making it the largest election conducted at the time. Voter turnout was 45.7%.

The Indian National Congress (INC) won a landslide victory, winning 364 of the 489 seats and 45% of the total votes polled. This was over four times as many votes as the second-largest party. Jawaharlal Nehru became the first democratically elected Prime Minister of the country.

After the adoption of the constitution on 26 November 1949, the Constituent Assembly continued to act as the interim parliament. The interim cabinet was headed by Jawaharlal Nehru and consisted of 15 members from diverse communities and parties. Various members of this cabinet resigned from their posts and formed their own parties to contest the elections.

A total of 173,212,343 voters were registered (excluding Jammu and Kashmir) out of a population of 361,088,090 according to the 1951 Census of India. All Indian citizens over the age of 21 were eligible to vote.

1950 Assam–Tibet earthquake

The 1950 Assam–Tibet earthquake, also known as the Assam earthquake, occurred on 15 August and had a moment magnitude of 8.7. The epicentre was located in the Mishmi Hills. It is the strongest earthquake ever recorded on land and is tied with the 2012 Indian Ocean Earthquakes as the strongest Strike-slip earthquake to date.

Occurring on a Tuesday evening at 7:39 pm Indian Standard Time, the earthquake was destructive in both Assam (India) and Tibet (China), and approximately 4,800 people were killed. The earthquake is notable as being the largest recorded quake caused by continental collision rather than subduction, and is also notable for the loud noises produced by the quake and reported throughout the region.

The earthquake occurred in the rugged mountainous areas between the Himalayas and the Hengduan Mountains. The earthquake was located just south of the McMahon Line between India and Tibet, and had devastating effects in both regions. This great earthquake has a calculated magnitude of 8.7 and is regarded as one of the most important since the introduction of seismological observing stations.

It was the sixth largest earthquake of the 20th century. It is also the largest known earthquake to have not been caused by an oceanic subduction. Instead, this quake was caused by two continental plates colliding.

Aftershocks were numerous; many of them were of magnitude 6 and over and well enough recorded at distant stations for reasonably good epicentre location. From such data the Indian Seismological Service established an enormous geographical spread of this activity, from about 90 deg to 97 deg east longitude, with the epicentre of the great earthquake near the eastern margin.

Indian Navy

Founded on 26th January 1950, The Indian Navy (IN) is the maritime branch of the Indian Armed Forces. The President of India is the Supreme Commander of the Indian Navy. The Chief of Naval Staff, a four-star admiral, commands the navy. As a blue-water navy, it operates significantly in the Persian Gulf Region, the Horn of Africa, the Strait of Malacca, and routinely conducts anti-piracy operations and partners with other navies in the region. It also conducts routine two to three month-long deployments in the South and East China seas as well as the western Mediterranean Sea simultaneously.

The primary objective of the navy is to safeguard the nation's maritime borders, and in conjunction with other Armed Forces of the union, act to deter or defeat any threats or aggression against the territory, people or maritime interests of India, both in war and peace. Through joint exercises, goodwill visits and humanitarian missions, including disaster relief, the Indian Navy promotes bilateral relations between nations.

As of June 2019, Indian Navy has 67,252 active and 75,000 reserve personnel in service and has a fleet of 150 ships and submarines, and 300 aircraft. As of September 2022, the operational fleet consists of 2 active aircraft carriers and 1 amphibious transport dock, 8 landing ship tanks, 11 destroyers, 13 frigates, 2 ballistic missile submarines, 16 conventionally-powered attack submarines, 18 corvettes, one mine countermeasure vessel, 4 fleet tankers and numerous other auxiliary vessels, small patrol boats and sophisticated ships. It is considered as a multi-regional power projection blue-water navy.

Supreme Court of India

In 1861, the Indian High Courts Act 1861 was enacted to create high courts for various provinces and abolish Supreme Courts at Calcutta, Madras and Bombay and also the sadar adalats in presidency towns in their respective regions. These new high courts had the distinction of being the highest courts for all cases till the creation of the Federal Court of India under the Government of India Act 1935. The Federal Court had the jurisdiction to solve disputes between provinces and federal states and hear appeals against judgement of the high courts. The first CJI of India was H. J. Kania.

The Supreme Court of India came into existence on 28 January 1950. It replaced both the Federal Court of India and the Judicial Committee of the Privy Council, which were then at the apex of the Indian court system. The first proceedings and inauguration, however, took place on

28 January 1950 at 9:45 am, when the judges took their seats; which is thus regarded as the official date of establishment.

The Supreme Court of India is the supreme judicial authority and the highest court of the Republic of India. It is the final court of appeal for all civil and criminal cases in India. It also has the power of judicial review. The Supreme Court, which consists of the Chief Justice of India and a maximum of fellow 33 judges, has extensive powers in the form of original, appellate and advisory jurisdictions.

As the apex constitutional court, it takes up appeals primarily against verdicts of the High Courts of various states and tribunals. As an advisory court, it hears matters which are referred by the President of India. Under judicial review, the court invalidates both normal laws as well as constitutional amendments that violate the Basic structure doctrine. It is required to safeguard the fundamental rights of citizens and settles legal disputes among the central government and various state governments.

Its decisions are binding on other Indian courts as well as the union and state governments. As per the Article 142 of the Constitution, the court is conferred with the inherent jurisdiction to pass any order deemed necessary in the interest of complete justice which becomes binding on the President to enforce. The Supreme Court replaced the Judicial Committee of the Privy Council as the highest court of appeal since 28 January 1950, two days after India was declared a republic.

With the Indian Constitution granting it far-reaching authority to initiate actions, exercise appellate authority over all other courts in the country with the power to review constitutional amendments, India's Supreme Court is regarded as one of the most powerful supreme courts in the world.

Liaquat-Nehru Pact

The Liaquat–Nehru Pact (or the Delhi Pact) was a bilateral treaty between India and Pakistan in which refugees were allowed to return to dispose of their property, abducted women and looted property were to be returned, forced conversions were unrecognized, and minority rights were confirmed.

The treaty was signed in New Delhi by the Prime Minister of India Jawahar Lal Nehru and the Prime Minister of Pakistan Liaquat Ali Khan on April 8, 1950. The treaty was the outcome of six days of talks sought to guarantee the rights of minorities in both countries after the Partition of India and to avert another war between them.

This pact also introduced visa system for refugees and free passage of refugees across border was restricted.

Minority commissions were set up in both countries. More than one million refugees migrated from East Pakistan (now Bangladesh) to West Bengal in India.

Indo-Nepal Treaty

The 1950 India-Nepal Treaty of Peace and Friendship (official name: Treaty of Peace and Friendship Between the Government of India and Government of Nepal) is a bilateral treaty signed by the Kingdom of Nepal and the Republic of India to establish a close strategic relationship between the two South Asian neighbours. The treaty was signed at Kathmandu on 31 July 1950 by the last Rana Prime Minister of Nepal Mohan Shumsher Jang Bahadur Rana and Indian ambassador to Nepal, Chadreshwar Narayan Singh and came into force the same day as per Article 9 of the Treaty. Rana rule in Nepal ended just 3 months after the treaty was signed. The treaty allows free movement of people and goods between the two nations and a close relationship and collaboration on matters of defence and foreign policy.

Vallabhbhai Patel

Vallabhbhai Jhaverbhai Patel (31 October 1875 – 15 December 1950), commonly known as Sardar Vallabhai Patel, was an Indian independence nationalist and barrister who served as the first Deputy Prime Minister and Home Minister of India from 1947 to 1950. He was a senior leader of the Indian National Congress, who played a significant role in the country's struggle for independence and its political integration. In India and elsewhere, he was often called Sardar, meaning "Chief" in Hindi, Urdu, Bengali and Persian. He acted as the Home Minister during the political integration of India and the Indo-Pakistani War of 1947.

Death

Patel's health declined rapidly through the summer of 1949. He later began coughing blood, whereupon Maniben began limiting his meetings and working hours and arranged for a personalised medical staff to begin attending to Patel. The Chief Minister of West Bengal and doctor Bidhan Roy heard Patel make jokes about his impending end, and in a private meeting Patel frankly admitted to his ministerial colleague N. V. Gadgil that he was not going to live much longer. Patel's health worsened after 2 November, when he began losing consciousness frequently and was confined to his bed. He was flown to Bombay on 12 December on advice from Dr Roy, to recuperate as his condition was deemed critical. Nehru, Rajagopalachari, Rajendra Prasad, and Menon all came to see him off at the airport in Delhi. Patel was extremely weak and had to be carried onto the aircraft in a chair. In Bombay, large crowds gathered at Santacruz Airport to greet him. To spare him from this stress, the aircraft landed at Juhu Aerodrome, where Chief Minister B. G. Kher and Morarji Desai were present to receive him with a car belonging to the Governor of Bombay that took Vallabhbhai to Birla House.

After suffering a massive heart attack (his second), Patel died on 15 December 1950 at Birla House in Bombay. In an unprecedented and unrepeated gesture, on the day after his death more than 1,500 officers of India's civil and police services congregated to mourn at Patel's residence in Delhi and pledged "complete loyalty and unremitting zeal" in India's service. Numerous governments and world leaders sent messages of condolence upon Patel's death, including Trygve Lie, the Secretary-General of the United Nations, President Sukarno of Indonesia, Prime Minister Liaquat Ali Khan of Pakistan and Prime Minister Clement Attlee of the United Kingdom.

In homage to Patel, Prime Minister Jawaharlal Nehru declared a week of national mourning. Patel's cremation was planned at Girgaum Chowpatty, but this was changed to Sonapur (now Marine Lines) when his daughter conveyed that it was his wish to be cremated like a common man in the same place as his wife and brother were earlier cremated. His cremation in Sonapur in Bombay was attended by a crowd of one million including Prime Minister Jawaharlal Nehru, Rajagopalachari and President Rajendra Prasad.

Council of Scientific and Industrial Research

The Council of Scientific and Industrial Research abbreviated as CSIR, was established by the Government of India in September 1942 as an autonomous body that has emerged as the largest research and development organisation in India. CSIR is also among the world's largest publicly funded R&D organisation which is pioneering sustained contribution to S&T human resource development in the country.

As of 2013, it runs 37 laboratories/institutes, 39 outreach centres, 3 Innovation Centres and 5 units throughout the nation, with a collective staff of over 14,000, including a total of 4,600 scientists and 8,000 technical and support personnel. Although it is mainly funded by the Ministry of Science and Technology, it operates as an autonomous body through the Societies Registration Act, 1860.

The research and development activities of CSIR include aerospace engineering, structural engineering, ocean sciences, life sciences and healthcare including diagnostics, metallurgy, chemicals, mining, food, petroleum, leather, and environmental science.

India at the 1952 Summer Olympics

India competed at the 1952 Summer Olympics in Helsinki, Finland. 64 competitors, 60 men and 4 women, took part in 42 events in 11 sports. This marked the second time India had competed as an independent republic.

India won 2 medals.

1 Gold in Men's Field Hockey &

1 Bronze in Wrestling by Khashaba Jadhav

Gold

- Kunwar Digvijai Singh (c), Leslie Claudius, Keshav Dutt, Chinadorai Deshmutu, Randhir Singh Gentle, Grahanandan Singh, Ranganandhan Francis, Jaswant Singh Rajput, Balbir Singh Sr., Dharam Singh, Govind Perumal, Raghbir Lal, Udham Singh, and Muniswamy Rajgopal — Field hockey, Men's Team Competition.

Bronze

♦ Khashaba Jadhav — Wrestling, Men's Freestyle Bantamweight

1 naya paisa (Indian coin)

The Indian One Naya paisa was a unit of currency equaling 1/100 (one-hundredth) of the Indian rupee. The symbol for paisa is p. In 1955, India adopted metric system for coinage and amended the "Indian Coinage Act". Subsequently, one paisa coins were introduced on 1 April 1957. From 1957 to 1964, one paisa coin was called "Naya Paisa" and on 1 June 1964, the term "Naya" was dropped and the denomination was simply called "One paisa". Naya paisa coin has been demonetized and is no longer a Legal tender.

History

Prior to 1957, Indian rupee was not decimalised and the rupee from 1835 to 1957 AD was further divided into 16 annas. Each anna was further divided into four Indian paisas and each paisa into three Indian pies till 1947 when the pie was demonetized. In 1955, India amended the "Indian Coinage Act" to adopt the metric system for coinage. Paisa coins were introduced in 1957, but from 1957 to 1964 the coin was called "Naya Paisa". On 1 June 1964, the term "Naya" was dropped and the denomination was simply called "One paisa". Naya paisa coins were issued as a part of "The Decimal Series".

Constitution of Jammu and Kashmir

The Constitution of Jammu and Kashmir was the legal Constitution which established the framework for the state government of the Indian state of Jammu and Kashmir. The constitution was adopted on 17 November 1956, and came into effect on 26 January 1957. It was rendered infructuous on 5 August 2019 by an order signed by the President of India and ceased to be applicable on that date. It also included Ladakh.

The Constitution of India granted special status to Jammu and Kashmir among Indian states, and it was the only state in India to have a separate constitution. Article 370 of the Constitution of India stated that Parliament of India and the Union government jurisdiction extends over limited matters with respect to State of Jammu and Kashmir, and in all other matters not specifically vested in Federal government, actions have to be supported by state legislature. Also, unlike other states, residual powers were vested with the state government. Because of these constitutional provisions, the State of Jammu and Kashmir enjoyed a special but temporary autonomous status as mentioned in Part XXI of the Constitution of India. Among notable and visible differences with other states, till 1965, the head of state in Jammu and Kashmir was called Sadr-i-Riyasat (Head of State) whereas in other state, the title was Governor, and the head of government was called Prime Minister in place of Chief Minister in other states.

On 5 August 2019, the President of India issued a presidential order, namely, The Constitution (Application to Jammu and Kashmir) Order, 2019 (C.O. 272) under Article 370 making all the provisions of Constitution of India applicable to the State of Jammu and Kashmir and this has rendered the Constitution of Jammu and Kashmir infructuous from that date. Now the Constitution of India is applicable to Jammu and Kashmir, like all other states and union territories of India.

India at the 1956 Summer Olympics

India competed at the 1956 Summer Olympics in Melbourne, Australia. 59 competitors, 58 men and 1 woman, took part in 32 events in 8 sports.

India won 1 Gold medal in Men's Field Hockey.

India at the 1960 Summer Olympics

India competed at the 1960 Summer Olympics in Rome, Italy. 45 competitors, all men, took part in 20 events in 6 sports. India won its only medal (Silver Medal) in men's Field Hockey. Milkha Singh misses bronze medal by finishing 4th in Men's 400m in athletics.

Panshet Dam

Panshet Dam, also called Tanajisagar Dam, is a dam on the Ambi river, a tributary of the Mutha River, about 50 km (31 mi) southwest of the city of Pune in western India.The dam was constructed in late 1950s for irrigation and, along with three other dams nearby, Varasgaon, Temghar and Khadakwasla, it supplies drinking water to Pune.

History

Panshet Dam burst in its first year of storing water on 12 July 1961, when the dam wall burst, because of the total absence of reinforced cement concrete (RCC) strengthening in the conduit through the earthen dam. Plain unreinforced concrete blocks were used instead due to a shortage of steel. causing massive flooding in Pune. An estimated 1,000 people died from the resulting flood.

Location

It is about 50 km (31 mi) from Pune and about 180 km (110 mi) from Mumbai.

Specifications

The height of the dam above its lowest foundation is 63.56 m (208.5 ft) while the length is 1,039 m (3,409 ft). The volume content is 4.190 km3 (1.005 cu mi) and gross storage capacity is 303,000 m3 (10,700,000 cu ft).

Purpose

- Irrigation
- Water supply

Indo-China War of 1962

The Sino-Indian War also known as the Indo-China War of 1962, was a military conflict between China and India that took place from October to November 1962. It was a military escalation of the Sino-Indian border dispute. Fighting occurred along India's border with China, in India's North-East Frontier Agency East of Bhutan, and in Aksai Chin West of Nepal.

There had been a series of violent border skirmishes between the two countries after the 1959 Tibetan uprising, when India granted asylum to the Dalai Lama. Chinese military action grew increasingly aggressive after India rejected proposed Chinese diplomatic settlements throughout 1960–1962, with China resuming previously banned "forward patrols" in Ladakh after 30 April 1962. Amidst the

Cuban Missile Crisis, China abandoned all attempts towards a peaceful resolution on 20 October 1962, invading disputed territory along the 3,225-kilometre (2,004 mi) border in Ladakh and across the McMahon Line in the northeastern frontier. Chinese troops pushed Indian forces back in both theatres, capturing all of their claimed territory in the Western theatre and the Tawang Tract in the Eastern theatre. The conflict ended when China unilaterally declared a ceasefire on 20 November 1962, and simultaneously announced its withdrawal to its pre-war position, the effective China–India border (also known as the "Line of Actual Control").

Much of the fighting comprised mountain warfare, entailing large-scale combat at altitudes of over 4,000 metres (13,000 feet). Notably, the war took place entirely on land, without the use of naval or air assets by either side.

As the Sino-Soviet split deepened, the Soviet Union made a major effort to support India, especially with the sale of advanced MiG fighter-aircraft. Simultaneously, the United States and the United Kingdom refused to sell advanced weaponry to India, further compelling it to turn to the Soviets for military aid.

Govt of India was taken by surprise by China invasion.

With Panchsheel Agreement, Indian ministers were saying that not no army is required as there is no danger of any external attack. The requirement of arms and ammunitions was a totally neglected category. Soldiers did not have adequate provision of suitable dress including shoes to fight in the chilling cold weather of the Himalayas. Insufficient arms & ammunitions aggravated the problems further. In all such adverse situation, our soldiers fought bravely to the surprise of China.

So finally China declared cease fire.

The 1954 Sino-Indian Agreement, also called the Panchsheel Agreement, officially the Agreement on Trade and Intercourse between Tibet Region of China and India, was signed by China and India in Peking on 29 April 1954. The preamble of the agreement stated the Panchsheel, or the five principles of peaceful coexistence, that China proposed and India favored. The agreement reflected the adjustment of the previously existing trade relations between Tibet and India to the changed context of India's decolonization and China's assertion of suzerainty over Tibet.

The agreement expired on 6 June 1962, as per the original term limit, in the midst of the Sino-Indian border tensions. It was not renewed. By October of that year, war broke out between the two sides.

India at the 1964 Summer Olympics

India competed at the 1964 Summer Olympics in Tokyo, Japan. 53 competitors, 52 men and 1 woman, took part in 42 events in 8 sports.

India won 1 Gold Medal in Men's Field Hockey.

India's first Prime Minister Jawaharlal Nehru dies after a five-month illness

Nehru's health began declining steadily in 1962. In the spring of 1962, he was affected with a viral infection over which he spent most of April in bed. In the next year, through 1963, he spent months recuperating in Kashmir. Some writers attribute this dramatic decline to his surprise and chagrin over the Sino-Indian War, which he perceived as a betrayal of trust. Upon his return from Dehradun on 26 May 1964, he was feeling quite comfortable and went to bed at about 23:30 as usual. He had a restful night until about 06:30. Soon after he returned from the bathroom, Nehru complained of pain in the back. He spoke to the doctors who attended to him for a brief while, and almost immediately he collapsed. He remained unconscious until he died at 13:44. His death was announced in the Lok Sabha at 14:00 local time on 27 May 1964; the cause of death was believed to be a heart attack. Draped in the Indian national Tri-colour flag, the body of Jawaharlal Nehru was placed for public viewing. "Raghupati Raghava Rajaram" was chanted as the body was placed on the platform. On 28 May, Nehru was cremated in accordance with Hindu rites at the Shantivan on the banks of the Yamuna, witnessed by 1.5 million mourners who had flocked into the streets of Delhi and the cremation grounds.

Indo-Pakistani War of 1965

After watching Indo-China war, Pak thought that they can get some advantage by waging war against India.

The Indo-Pakistani War of 1965, also known as the Second India–Pakistan War or the Second Kashmir War was an armed conflict between Pakistan and India that took place from April 1965 to September 1965. The conflict began following Pakistan's Operation Gibraltar, which was designed to infiltrate forces into Jammu and Kashmir to precipitate an insurgency against Indian rule. The seventeen-week war caused thousands of casualties on both sides and witnessed the largest engagement of armored vehicles and the largest tank battle since World War II. Hostilities between the two countries ended after a ceasefire was declared through UNSC Resolution 211 following a diplomatic intervention by the Soviet Union and the United States, and the subsequent issuance of the Tashkent Declaration. Much of the war was fought by the countries' land forces in Kashmir and along the border between India and Pakistan. This war saw the largest amassing of troops in Kashmir since the Partition of India in 1947, a number that was overshadowed only during the 2001–2002 military standoff between India and Pakistan. Most of the battles were fought by opposing infantry and armored units, with substantial backing from air forces, and naval operations.

Tashkent Declaration

Tashkent Declaration was signed between India and Pakistan on 10 January 1966 to resolve the Indo-Pakistani War of 1965. Peace was achieved on 23 September through interventions by the Soviet Union and the United States, both of which pushed the two warring countries towards a ceasefire in an attempt to avoid any escalation that could draw in other powers.

Background

The meeting was hosted by the Soviet Union in the city of Tashkent, Uzbekistan, from 4 to 10 January 1966 in an attempt to create a more permanent settlement between the warring sides.

The Soviets, represented by Soviet politician Aleksei Kosygin, moderated between Indian Prime Minister Lal Bahadur Shastri and Pakistani President Muhammad Ayub Khan.

Declaration

A declaration was released that was hoped to be a framework for lasting peace by stating that the Indian military and the Pakistani military would pull back to their pre-conflict positions, their pre-August lines, no later than 25 February 1966; neither nation would interfere in each other's internal affairs; economic and diplomatic relations would be restored; there would be an orderly transfer of prisoners of war, and both leaders would work towards improving bilateral relations.

Aftermath

The treaty was heavily criticized in both countries, as Indians and Pakistanis were expecting more concessions to their respective sides than what had been agreed upon. In accordance with the Tashkent Declaration, talks were held at the ministerial level on 1 and 2 March 1966. Despite the fact that these talks were unproductive, the diplomatic exchange continued throughout the spring and summer, though stark differences of opinion on the Kashmir conflict culminated in the lack of a resolution from bilateral discussions.

In India, the agreement was criticized because it did not contain a no-war pact or any renunciation of guerrilla warfare across Kashmir. After the Tashkent Declaration was signed, Indian Prime Minister Lal Bahadur Shastri died under mysterious circumstances in Tashkent; his sudden death led to the rise of conspiracy theories claiming that he was poisoned. Journalist, conspiracy theorist, and holocaust denier Gregory Douglas claimed he conducted a series of interviews with American intelligence officer Robert Crowley in 1993. According to Douglas, Crowley claimed that the Central Intelligence Agency assassinated Shastri as well as Indian nuclear scientist Homi J. Bhabha (who died on Air India Flight 101) in order to thwart the development of India's nuclear weapons programme. The Indian government has refused to declassify a report on his death under the claim that it would harm India's foreign relations, cause disruption in the country, and breach parliamentary privileges.

In Pakistan, the agreement caused widespread distress; social upset was exacerbated after Pakistani President Muhammad Ayub Khan went into seclusion in the ceasefire's aftermath, as demonstrations and riots erupted across the country. However, Khan later addressed the nation on 14 January 1966 and explained the rationale behind the agreement. Although he was eventually able to quell the unrest, the Tashkent Declaration greatly damaged Khan's image, and was one of the factors that ultimately led to his downfall in 1969.

Lal Bahadur Shastri

Lal Bahadur Shastri (2 October 1904 – 11 January 1966) was an Indian politician and statesman who served as the second prime minister of India from 1964 to 1966. He previously served as the sixth Home Minister of India from 1961 to 1963.

Jawaharlal Nehru died in office on 27 May 1964. Then Congress Party President K. Kamaraj was instrumental in making Shastri Prime Minister on 9 June. Shastri, though mild-mannered and soft-spoken, was a Nehruvian socialist and thus held appeal to those wishing to prevent the ascent of conservative right-winger Morarji Desai.

In his first broadcast as prime minister, on 11 June 1964, Shastri stated:

There comes a time in the life of every nation when it stands at the cross-roads of history and must choose which way to go. But for us, there need be no difficulty or hesitation, no looking to right or left. Our way is straight and clear—the building up of a socialist democracy at home with freedom and prosperity for all, and the maintenance of world peace and friendship with all nations.

Shastri died in Tashkent, Uzbekistan (then Soviet Union) on 11 January 1966, one day after signing a peace treaty to end the 1965 Indo-Pakistan War. *Many among Shastri's supporters and close relatives, refused at the time, and have refused since, to believe the circumstances of his death and allege foul play. Conspiracy theories appeared within hours of his death and have thereafter persisted.* He was eulogized as a national hero and the Vijay Ghat memorial established in his memory. Upon his death, Gulzarilal Nanda once again assumed the role of acting Prime Minister until the Congress Party elected Indira Gandhi over Morarji Desai to officially succeed Shastri.

Indira Gandhi

Indira Gandhi (19 November 1917 – 31 October 1984) was an Indian politician and stateswoman who served as the third Prime Minister of India from 1966 to 1977 and again from 1980 until her assassination in 1984. She was India's first and, to date, only female Prime Minister, and a central figure in Indian politics as the leader of the Indian National Congress. Gandhi was the daughter of Jawaharlal Nehru, the first prime minister of India, and the mother of Rajiv Gandhi, who succeeded her in office as the country's sixth prime minister. Furthermore, Gandhi's cumulative tenure of 15 years and 350 days makes her the second-longest-serving Indian prime minister after her father.

Indira Gandhi afraid of Sam Manekshaw

"When are you taking over," Indira asked Manekshaw

Three years before the 1971 Bangladesh war which made him a national hero, Field Marshal Sam Manekshaw was suspected of planning a coup to topple the Indira Gandhi-led government and the apprehension had been conveyed to him by none other than the then Prime Minister herself.

Manekshaw, however, allayed these fears triggered by insinuations by some of Gandhi's Cabinet colleagues. The country's only Field Marshal, who died last month, had disclosed this in an address at an IGNOU convocation, which was perhaps one of his last speeches.

"Mrs Gandhi called me to her office. She was very worried. 'Everybody says you are taking over. When are you taking over', she asked," Manekshaw said in the speech. The Army Chief asked the Prime Minister as to why she was thinking so. Gandhi replied that her ministers were saying so.

"You can't," Manekshaw quoted Gandhi as saying.

"I said you are right Prime Minister. My daughter when she comes from convent sings the nursery rhyme, 'You mind your business, I mind mine. You kiss your own sweetheart, I kiss mine'. I do not interfere with politics and politicians,"

Manikshaw told Gandhi during the meeting. "You have appointed them. You sack them" -- was the Army Chief's contention aimed at allaying Gandhi`s fears.

He also requested Gandhi not to let the people and the country start thinking that he was going to do the same thing in India what Gen Yahya Khan did in Pakistan.

However, he asked for more freedom as the Chief of Army Staff.

1966 anti-cow slaughter agitation

7 November 1966, a group of Hindu protestors, led by ascetics, Naga sadhus and backed by Rashtriya Swayamsevak Sangh and Bharatiya Jana Sangh (aka Jan Sangh), approached the Indian Parliament to protest to criminalize cow slaughter. The incident resulted in a riot which ended with a death toll of 7 people and hundreds were injured. The total damage was estimated at about 1 billion rupees by city officials; numerous vehicles were destroyed, along with numerous shops.

The episode was the culmination of a long-term movement by the Hindu Right to protect the cow, a traditional symbol of reverence in Hindu society. A meeting in late 1965 involving lobbying groups, Naga sadhus and many religious dharma acharyas and influential Hindu religious orders initiated a year-long program of demonstrations and picketing, culminating in the planned march to the Parliament. Jan Sangh was a participant in the march. The march attracted hundreds of thousands of people for that peaceful march outside the parliament.

The "protection of the cow" policy has commanded huge political significance in the subcontinent in precolonial spans; the Mughal emperor Akbar had banned the killing of cows, and cow slaughter was treated as a capital offense in many Hindu and Sikh-ruled states.

Overall, the agitation propelled the Hindu Right into the foreground of national politics for the first time; simultaneously, Gandhi's successful negotiation helped establish her image as a resolute leader who later had the tenacity to lead a weakened Congress after the 1969 split. The episode also played a significant role in Gandhi's choosing to shift away from the staunch secular ideals displayed by her father, embracing the Hindu way of life and enabling communal politics.

How India overcame food emergency, attained self-sufficiency

Subramani Ra Mancombu writes in The Hindu Business Line

From facing a food shortage in 1964 to becoming a foodgrain-surplus nation, we've come a long way, thanks to the Green Revolution

"Sacrifice one meal at least a week!". This was Prime Minister Lal Bahadur Shastri's plea to Indians in 1965 when India was at war with Pakistan. It was one of the various struggles the country had to undergo in meeting food demand for its burgeoning population. It is another story that today we grow surplus foodgrains.

According to late C Subramaniam, the architect of India's Green Revolution, a US team of experts visiting India had predicted in 1964 an "intractable agricultural problem that would lead to the death of millions in the 1970s". It was to be proved wrong later. The food emergencies that India faced after Independence extended till the Green Revolution was launched in 1967. An expert termed agricultural production as a "statistical uncertainty".

India signed a long-term Public Law (PL) 480 agreement to get food aid under Government agricultural trade development assistance, with the US in 1954. The agreement was signed a few more times before the US ended it in the late 1960s as Lal Bahadur Shastri and then Indira Gandhi were not willing to make policy changes, especially to allow privatisation of the industrial sector, in return for food aid.

Advent of agricultural science

C Subramaniam, who became the Food and Agriculture Minister in Shastri's Cabinet, wrote in "Green Revolution" that he favoured the introduction of science and technology in farming. He also called agricultural scientists for a "frank and free discussion" on the status of agricultural science. "I had to listen to a tale of woe," he wrote.

Subramaniam came up with two-point formula. One, to provide price incentives to farmers and two, to go in for science and technology application. The price incentives proposal was opposed by Finance Minister TT Krishnamachari and the Planning Commission. The argument was price incentives would result in high subsidies and new technology would lead to fertiliser imports. But he won Shastri's confidence and got a panel to make recommendations favouring his formula.

When Indira Gandhi became the prime minister, she not only backed Subramaniam fully but made him a member of the Planning Commission that helped redraft the Fourth Plan with higher financial allocation for agriculture. The Indian Agriculture Research Institute (IARI) was set up giving priority to agricultural research among other reforms he carried out.

The minister then took up the issue with agricultural scientists among whom the younger lot was optimistic that Indian farmers would adopt new technologies and new varieties. The Government decided to go ahead but opponents pointed out that a huge amount of foreign exchange would be spent on importing fertilisers.

Subramaniam argued that it would be more important to be self-sufficient in food production than to import foodgrains. India needed a huge quantity of fertilisers, estimated to cost $250 million then. It needed foreign financial aid and India managed to get it from then US President Lydon B Johnson. The rest is history.

In the 1968 rabi harvest, India produced 16.5 mt of wheat, over 30 per cent more than the highest before that. In two years' time, wheat production was double the average output during 1960-65. The Green Revolution had got going.

1967 Koynanagar earthquake

The 1967 Koynanagar earthquake occurred near Koynanagar town in Maharashtra, India on 11 December local time. The magnitude 6.6 shock hit with a maximum Mercalli intensity of VIII (Severe). It occurred near the site of Koyna dam, raising questions about induced seismicity, and claimed at least 177 lives and injured over 2,200.

Damage

More than 80% of the houses were damaged in Koyana Nagar Township, but it did not cause any major damage to the dam except some cracks which were quickly repaired. There have been several earthquakes of smaller magnitude there since 1967. The earthquake caused a 10–15 cm (3.9–5.9 in) fissure in the ground which spread over a length of 25 kilometers (16 mi). Some geologists believe that the earthquake was due to reservoir-triggered seismic activity, but senior project officials have repeatedly denied this conclusion.

India at the 1968 Summer Olympics

India competed at the 1968 Summer Olympics in Mexico City, Mexico. 25 competitors, all men, took part in 11 events in 5 sports.

India won 1 Bronze medal in Men's Field Hockey.

ISRO

The Indian Space Research Organisation is the national space agency of India. It operates as the primary research and development arm of the Department of Space (DoS), which is directly overseen by the Prime Minister of India, while the Chairman of ISRO also acts as the executive of DoS. ISRO is primarily responsible for performing tasks related to space-based operations, space exploration, international space cooperation and the development of related technologies. ISRO is one of the six government space agencies in the world that possesses full launch capabilities, can deploy cryogenic engines, can launch extraterrestrial missions and operate a large fleet of artificial satellites. ISRO is one of the four government space agencies to have soft landing (uncrewed) capabilities.

ISRO was previously know as the Indian National Committee for Space Research (INCOSPAR), set up under Jawaharlal Nehru in 1962 recognising the need for space research. INCOSPAR grew and became ISRO in 1969, within the Department of Atomic Energy (DAE). In 1972, the government of India set up a Space Commission and the DoS, bringing ISRO under it. The establishment of ISRO thus institutionalised space research activities in India. It has since been managed by DoS, which also governs various other institutions in India in the domain of astronomy and space technology.

The Split in Indian National Congress

The Indian National Congress (Organisation) also known as Congress (O) or Syndicate/Old Congress was a political party in India formed when the Congress party split following the expulsion of Indira Gandhi.

On 12 November 1969, the Prime Minister of India, Indira Gandhi was expelled from the Congress party for violating the party discipline. The party finally split with Indira Gandhi setting up a rival organization Indian National Congress (Requisitionists), which came to be known as Congress (R) or Indicate/New Congress. In the All India Congress Committee, 446 of its 705 members walked over to Indira's side. K Kamaraj and later Morarji Desai were the leaders of the INC(O).

INC(O) led governments in Bihar under Bhola Paswan Shastri, Karnataka under Veerendra Patil, and in Gujarat under Hitendra K Desai. It was also a part of the Janata Morcha that ruled Gujarat under Babubhai J. Patel from 1975–1976 during the emergency era.

The split can in some ways be seen as a left-wing/right-wing division. Indira wanted to use a populist agenda in order to mobilize popular support for the party. The regional party elites, who formed the INC(O), stood for a more right-wing agenda, and distrusted Soviet help.

Nationalisation of Banks

Despite the provisions, control and regulations of the Reserve Bank of India, banks in India except the State Bank of India (SBI), remain owned and operated by private persons. By the 1960s, the Indian banking industry had become an important tool to facilitate the development of the Indian economy. At the same time, it had emerged as a large employer, and a debate had ensued about the nationalization of the banking industry. Indira Gandhi, the then Prime Minister of India, expressed the intention of the Government of India in the annual conference of the All India Congress Meeting in a paper entitled Stray thoughts on Bank Nationalization.

Thereafter, the Government of India issued the Banking Companies (Acquisition and Transfer of Undertakings) Ordinance, 1969 and nationalized the 14 largest commercial banks with effect from the midnight of 19 July 1969. These banks contained 85 percent of bank deposits in the country. Within two weeks of the issue of the ordinance, the Parliament passed the Banking Companies (Acquisition and Transfer of Undertaking) Bill, and it received presidential approval on 9 August 1969.

The following 14 banks were nationalized in 1969:

- Allahabad Bank (now Indian Bank)
- Bank of Baroda
- Bank of India
- Bank of Maharashtra
- Central Bank of India
- Canara Bank
- Dena Bank (now Bank of Baroda)
- Indian Bank
- Indian Overseas Bank
- Punjab National Bank
- Syndicate Bank (now Canara Bank)
- UCO Bank
- Union Bank of India
- United Bank of India (now Punjab National Bank)

PAKISTAN

It was believed that Pakistan was ruled by 3 "A"s. Allah, Army & America.

Governor General of Pakistan

1. Malik Ghulam Muhammad

Sir Malik Ghulam Muhammad (20 April 1895 – 29 August 1956) was a Pakistani politician and economist who served as the third governor-general of Pakistan from 1951 to 1955.

Educated at the Aligarh Muslim University (AMU), he joined the Indian Civil Service as a chartered accountant at the Indian Railway Accounts Service before being promoted to join the Ministry of Finance under Liaquat Ali Khan in 1946. After the Independence of Pakistan in 1947, he joined the Liaquat administration as the country's first Finance Minister where he helped draft the first five-year plans to alleviate the national economy. He co-founded Mahindra & Mohammed in 1945 (later Mahindra & Mahindra in 1948) with Jagdish Chandra Mahindra and Kailash Chandra Mahindra.

Following the assassination of prime minister Liaquat Ali Khan in 1951, Malik was invited to be the Governor-General by Sir Khawaja Nazimuddin who himself took over the government as Prime Minister. Nationwide violence in the aftermath of the language movement in East Bengal and religious riots in Lahore made him dismiss the Nazimuddin administration using the reserve powers to restore stability. In 1955, he was forced to resign from the post of Governor-General due to worsening of his health conditions by then-Interior Minister Iskandar Ali Mirza, who himself took control of the office. After resignation, he fought a brief but unsuccessful battle with his illness, that ultimately resulted in his death in 1956.

His personal image is viewed negatively by Pakistan's historians, criticized for giving rise to political intrigue, undermining the civilian control of the military by authorizing martial law in Pakistan, and devaluing nascent democratic norms by sacking the Constituent Assembly of Pakistan during Prime Minister Bogra's tenure.

2. <u>Iskandar Ali Mirza</u>

Iskandar Ali Mirza (13 November 1899 – 13 November 1969) was a Bengali-Pakistani politician, statesman and military general who served as the Dominion of Pakistan's fourth governor-general of Pakistan from 1955 to 1956, and then as the Islamic Republic of Pakistan's first president of Pakistan from 1956 to 1958.

Playing a crucial role in the ousting of Governor-General Sir Malik Ghulam, Mirza assumed his position in 1955 and was elected as the first President of Pakistan when the first set of Constitution was promulgated in 1956. His presidency, however, was marked with political instability which saw his unconstitutional interferences in the civilian administration that led to the dismissal of four prime ministers in a mere two years. Facing challenges in getting the political endorsements and reelection for the presidency, Mirza surprisingly suspended the writ of the Constitution by imposing martial law against his own party's administration governed by Prime Minister Feroze Khan on 8 October 1958, enforcing it through his army commander General Ayub Khan who dismissed him when the situation between them escalated, also in 1958. Mirza lived in the United Kingdom for the remainder of his life and was buried in Iran in 1969.

Presidency (1956–58)

On 12 September 1956, he established and became vice-president of the Republican Party that was in direct conflict with the Muslim League, mainly due to disagreements on the idea of republicanism and conservatism. Unable to keep the substantial pressure on Mirza's Republic Party eventually led the Muslim League's successful demand for the resignation of Prime Minister Muhammad Ali on 12 September 1956.

Upon these developments, President Mirza invited the Awami League to form the central government that appointed Huseyn Suhrawardy as the Prime Minister, who made an alliance with the Republican Party, to take over charge of the government.

Despite Mirza and Suhrawardy both being Bengalis and hailing from West Bengal, the two leaders had very different views of running the central government and both leaders were in brief conflict, causing harm to the unity of the nation. Prime Minister Suhrawardy found it extremely difficult to govern effectively due to the issue of One Unit, alleviating the national economy, and President Mirza's constant unconstitutional interference in the Suhrawardy administration.

President Mirza demanded the resignation of Prime Minister Suhrawardy and turned down his request to seek a motion of confidence at the National Assembly. Threatened by President Mirza's dismissal, Prime Minister Suhrawardy tendered his resignation on 17 October 1957 and was succeeded by I. I. Chundrigar but he too was forced to resign in a mere two months.

President Mirza had widely lacked the parliamentary spirit, distrusting the civilians to ensure the integrity and sovereignty of the country. His unconstitutional interference in the civil administration made the elected prime ministers effectively unable to function, as he had dismissed four elected prime ministers in a matter of two years. On his last nomination, he appointed Feroz Khan as the seventh Prime Minister of the country, who had been supported by the Awami League and the Muslim League.

3. <u>Muhammad Ayub Khan (Martial Law)</u>

Muhammad Ayub Khan (14 May 1907 – 19 April 1974) was a Pakistani military officer and politician who served as the second president of Pakistan from 1958 to 1969. He previously served as the third Commander-in-Chief of the Pakistan Army from 1951 to 1958.

As president, Khan appointed Muhammad Musa to replace him as commander-in-chief. He aligned Pakistan with the United States, and allowed American access to air bases inside Pakistan, most notably the airbase outside of Peshawar, from which spy missions over the Soviet Union were launched. Relations with neighboring China were strengthened but his alignment with the US worsened relations with the Soviet Union in 1962. He launched Operation Gibraltar against India in 1965, leading to an all-out war. It resulted in a stalemate and peace was restored via the Tashkent Declaration. Domestically, Ayub subscribed to the laissez-faire policy of Western-aligned nations at the time. Khan privatized state-owned industries, and liberalized the economy generally. Large inflows of foreign aid and investment led to the fastest-growing economy in South Asia. His tenure was also distinguished by the completion of hydroelectric stations, dams, and reservoirs. Under Ayub, Pakistan's space program was established, and the country launched its first uncrewed space-mission by 1962. However, the failure of land reforms and a weak taxation system meant that most of this growth landed in the hands of the elite. In 1965, Khan entered the presidential race as the Convention Muslim League's candidate to counter the opposition candidate Fatima Jinnah. Ayub won the elections and was re-elected for a second term. In 1967, disapproval of price hikes of food prompted demonstrations across the country led by Zulfikar Ali Bhutto. Following protests in East Pakistan, Ayub resigned in March 1969 and appointed Yahya Khan. Later, fighting a brief illness, he died in 1974.

Khan remains the country's longest-serving president and second-longest serving head of state. His legacy remains mixed; his era is often dubbed the "Decade of Development". Khan is credited with economic prosperity and industrialisation. He is denounced by critics for beginning the first of the intelligence agencies' incursions into national politics, for concentrating wealth in a corrupt few hands, and for geographically discriminatory policies that later led to the Bangladesh Liberation War.

Presidency (1958–1969)

1958 military coup

Under threat of being dismissed, Prime Minister H.S. Suhrawardy resigned and Prime Minister I.I. Chundiragar took over the post but in a mere two months he too tendered his resignation after losing a vote of no confidence in the National Assembly. The Constituent Assembly then elected Sir Feroz Noon for the post of the prime minister; Noon had much wider support from the western Republican Party, the eastern Awami League, and the Krishak Sramik.

This new alliance threatened President Iskander Mirza because Suhrawardy and Feroz began campaigning to become prime minister and president in the upcoming general elections. Also, the conservative

Pakistan Muslim League, led by its President A.Q. Khan, was threatening to engage in civil disobedience. These events were against President Mirza hence he was willing to dissolve even Pakistan's One Unit for his advantage.

On 7 October 1958, President Mirza abrogated the Constitution after sending a letter to Prime Minister Feroz announcing the coup d'état. Most of the country's politicians only became aware of the coup the next morning; only U.S. Ambassador to Pakistan James Langley was kept fully informed of political developments in the country. President Mirza appointed General Ayub chief martial law administrator (CMLA), who then declared martial law.

The regime came to power with the intent of instituting widespread reform. Like Mirza, Ayub advocated for greater centralization of power, and his ruling style was more American than British. He "vowed to give people access to speedier justice, curb the crippling birth rate, and take appropriate steps, including land reforms and technological innovation, to develop agriculture so that the country could feed itself".

Ayub finally "restored civil administration", although he maintained the Presidency and relied on an intricate web of spy agencies to maintain supremacy over the bureaucracy, including calling upon civilian intelligence agencies.

In 1960, a referendum, that functioned as the Electoral College, was held that asked the general public: "Do you have confidence in Muhammad Ayub Khan?". The voter turnout was recorded at 95.6% and such confirmation was used as impetus to formalise the new system – a presidential system. Ayub Khan was elected president for the next five years and decided to pay his first state visit to the United States with his wife and also daughter Begum Naseem Aurangzeb in July 1961. Highlights of his visit included a state dinner at Mount Vernon, a visit to the Islamic Center of Washington, and a ticker tape parade in New York City.

Constitutional and legal reforms

A constitutional commission was set-up under the Supreme Court to implement the work on the Constitution that was led by Chief Justice

Muhammad Shahabuddin and Supreme Court justices. The commission reported in 1961 with its recommendations but President Ayub remained unsatisfied; he eventually altered the constitution so that it was entirely different from the one recommended by the Shahabuddin Commission. The Constitution reflected his personal views of politicians and the restriction of using religions in politics. His presidency restored the writ of government through the promulgated constitution and restored political freedom by lifting the martial law enforced since 1958.

The new Constitution respected Islam, but did not declare Islam as the state religion and was viewed as a liberal constitution. It also provided for election of the president by 80,000 (later raised to 120,000) Basic Democrats who could theoretically make their own choice but who were essentially under his control. He justified this as analogous to the American Electoral College and cited Thomas Jefferson as his inspiration. The Ayub administration "guided" the print newspapers through his takeover of key opposition papers and, while Ayub Khan permitted a National Assembly, it had only limited powers.

On 2 March 1961, he passed and signed the "Muslim Family Laws" bill through the ordinance under which unmitigated polygamy was abolished. Consent of the current wife was made mandatory for a second marriage, and brakes were placed on the practice of instant divorce under Islamic tradition, where men could divorce women by saying:"I divorce you" three times.

Industrialization and rural development through constructing modern national freeways are considered his greatest achievements and his era is remembered for successful industrialization in the impoverished country. Strong emphasis on capitalism and foreign direct investment (FDI) in the industry is often regarded as the "Great Decade" in the history of the country (both economical and political history). The "Decade of Development" was celebrated, which highlighted the development plans executed during the years of Ayub's rule, the private consortium companies and industries, and is credited with creating an environment where the private sector was encouraged to establish medium and small-scale industries in Pakistan. This opened up avenues for new job opportunities and thus the economic graph of the country started rising.

He oversaw the development and completion of mega projects such as hydroelectric dams, power stations, and barrages all over the country. During 1960–66, the annual GDP growth was recorded at 6.8%.

Several hydroelectric projects were completed, including the Mangla Dam (one of the world's largest dams), several small dams and water reservoirs in West Pakistan, and one dam in East Pakistan, the Kaptai Dam. President Ayub authorized planning of nuclear power plants, overriding the concerns of his own finance minister, Muhammad Shoaib, about their cost. Initially, two nuclear power plants were to be established in the country: one in Karachi and the other in Dhaka. Dr. Abdus Salam. supported by the President, personally approved the project in Karachi while the project in East Pakistan never materialized.

Defence spending

During the Ayub era, the navy was able to introduce submarines and slowly modified itself by acquiring warships. However, Ayub drastically reduced funding of the military in the 1950s and de-prioritized nuclear weapons in the 1960s. The military relied on donations from the United States for major weapons procurements. Major funding was made available for military acquisitions and procurement towards conventional weaponry for conventional defence. In the 1960s, the Pakistani military acquired American produced conventional weapons such as Jeep CJs, M48 Patton and M24 Chaffee tanks, M16 rifles, F-86 fighter airplanes, and the submarine PNS Ghazi; all through the US Foreign Military Sales program. In 1961, President Ayub started the nation's full fledged space program in cooperation with the air force, and created the Suparco civilian space agency that launched sounding rockets throughout the 1960s.

Ayub directed Pakistan's nuclear technology efforts towards electrical power generation, disregarding recommendations to use it for military purposes. He reportedly spent Rs. 721 million on civilian nuclear power plants and related education of engineers and scientists.

Ayub Khan filled more and more civil administrative positions with army officers, increasing the military's influence over the bureaucracy. He expanded the size of the army by more than half from the early 1960s to

1969, and maintained a high level of military spending as a percentage of GDP during that period, peaking in the immediate aftermath of the Indo-Pakistani War of 1965.

Foreign policy

The main feature of Ayub Khan's foreign policy was prioritized relations with the United States and Europe. Foreign relations with the Soviet Union were downplayed. He enjoyed support from President Dwight Eisenhower in the 1950s and, working with Prime Minister Ali Khan, forged a military alliance with the United States against regional communism. His obsession towards modernization of the armed forces in the shortest time possible saw relations with the United States as the only way to achieve his organizational and personal objectives as he argued against civilian supremacy that would affect American interests in the region as a result of an election.

The Central Intelligence Agency leased Peshawar Air Station in the 1950s and spying into the Soviet Union from the air station grew immensely, with Ayub's full knowledge, during his presidency. When these activities were exposed in 1960 after a U-2 flying out of the air station was shot down and its pilot captured by the USSR, President Ayub was in the United Kingdom on a state visit. When the local CIA station chief briefed President Ayub on the incident, Ayub shrugged his shoulders and said that he had expected this would happen at some point.

The resulting Soviet ire severely compromised the national security of Pakistan. Ayub Khan had to publicly offer his apologies to the Soviet Union after USSR Secretary General Nikita Khrushchev made a threat to bomb Peshawar.

President Ayub directed his Foreign Office to reduce tensions with the Soviet Union by facilitating state visits by Soviet Premier Kosygin and Soviet Foreign Minister Gromyko and agreeing to downplay relations with the United States.

In 1963, Ayub signed the historic Sino-Pakistan Frontier Agreement with China despite US opposition.

During 1961–65, Ayub lost much of his support from President John Kennedy and President Lyndon Johnson as they sought closer relations with India. President Johnson placed an embargo on both nations during the war in 1965. Relations with the Soviet Union were eventually normalized when the Soviets facilitated a peace treaty between Pakistan and India in 1965, and reached a trade treaty with Pakistan the following year. In 1966–67, Ayub wrestled with the United States' attempt to dictate Pakistan's foreign policy, while he strengthened relations with the Soviet Union and China. Despite initiatives to normalize relations with the Soviet Union, Ayub Khan remained inclined towards the United States and the western world, receiving President Johnson in Karachi in 1967.

In 1961–62, Ayub paid a state visit to the United Kingdom. He attracted much attention from the British public when his involvement in the Christine Keeler affair was revealed.

In 1959, Ayub Khan's interest in building defence forces had already diminished when he made an offer of joint defense with India during the Sino-Indo clashes in October 1959 in Ladakh, in a move seen as a result of American pressure and a lack of understanding of foreign affairs. Upon hearing this proposal, India's Prime Minister Nehru reportedly countered, "Defence Minister Ayub: Joint Defence on what?" India remained uninterested in such proposals and Prime Minister Nehru decided to push his country's role in the Non-Aligned Movement. In 1960, President Ayub, together with Prime Minister Nehru, signed the Indus Waters Treaty brokered by the World Bank. In 1962, after India was defeated by China, Ayub Khan disguised a few thousand soldiers as guerillas and sent them to Indian Kashmir to incite the people to rebel. In 1964, the Pakistan Army engaged with the Indian Army in several skirmishes, and clandestine operations began.

The war with India in 1965 was a turning point in his presidency, and it ended in a settlement reached by Ayub Khan at Tashkent, called the Tashkent Declaration, which was facilitated by the Soviet Union. The settlement was perceived negatively by many Pakistanis and led Foreign Minister Zulfiqar Ali Bhutto to resign his post and take up opposition to Ayub Khan. According to Morrice James, "For them (Pakistanis) Ayub had betrayed the nation and had inexcusably lost face before the Indians."

Ayub Khan's main sponsor, the United States, did not welcome the move and the Johnson administration placed an economic embargo that caused Pakistan to lose US$500 million in aid and grants that had been received through consortium. Ayub Khan could not politically survive in the aftermath of the 1965 war with India and fell from the presidency after surrendering presidential power to Army Commander General Yahya in 1969.

Slowly Pakistan moved to Martial Law Administration which was to become a rule in future.

Prime Ministers

Khawaja Nazimuddin

Sir Khawaja Nazimuddin (19 July 1894 – 22 October 1964) KCIE was a Pakistani politician and statesman who served as the second governor-general of Pakistan from 1948 to 1951 and later as the second prime minister of Pakistan from 1951 to 1953. He was one of the leading founding fathers of Pakistan and the first Bengali to have governed Pakistan.

Altaf Hussain (Pakistani politician)

Altaf Hussain (born 17 September 1953 in Karachi) is a British Pakistani politician who is known as the founder of the Muttahida Qaumi Movement. He holds United Kingdom citizenship and has been living in exile in the UK since the start of Operation Clean-up. Since 2015, he has been a fugitive from the Anti Terrorism Court of Pakistan on the charges of murder, targeted killing, treason, inciting violence and hate speech. He went on trial in the UK in January 2022 for promoting terrorism and unrest through hate speech in Pakistan, and was acquitted the next month. He had fled the country in 1992 after a crackdown against his party was launched.

Altaf Hussain was born on 17 September 1953 to Nazir Hussain and Khurseed Begum in Karachi. Before the independence of Pakistan, Hussain's parents resided at their ancestral home in Nai ki Mandi, Agra, U.P., British India. His father was an officer with the Indian Railways. His paternal grandfather Mohammad Ramazan was the Grand Mufti of Agra and his maternal grandfather Pir Haji Hafiz Rahim Bakhsh Qadri was a religious scholar. Hussain's siblings include four sisters and six brothers.

Following the partition of India in 1947, a wide-scale migration of Muslims ensued, mostly from the various states in the Dominion of India to the newly established Dominion of Pakistan. Hussain's parents were initially reluctant to leave everything behind in Agra to resettle in Pakistan but were later forced by Hussain's elder brother to reconsider. Upon emigrating to Pakistan, the family settled in Karachi. They were provided with government housing in Abyssinia Lines reserved for Muhajirs (people and families migrating from the Dominion of India).

Hussain's elder brother Nasir Hussain was later employed by the government and given a small dwelling on Jehangir Road. The family subsequently left their government allotted residence and moved in with Nasir. The family later moved again in the 1970s to a small house in Azizabad, which later became the headquarters of Hussain's political party, the Muttahida Qaumi Movement (MQM; formerly the Muhajir Qaumi Movement).

Education and non-political career

Hussain received his early education from the Government Comprehensive School in Azizabad. He later enrolled in the Government Boys Secondary School to complete his matriculation in 1969. For the first year of his intermediate education in pre-medical sciences, he attended the National College Karachi. He later moved to City College Karachi for his second year.

In 1974, Hussain graduated from the Islamia Science College with a Bachelor of Science. In 1979, he graduated from the University of Karachi with a Bachelor of Pharmacy. After graduating, Hussain began his career as a trainee at the Seventh-day Adventist Hospital in Karachi while simultaneously working for a multinational pharmaceutical company.

Short-lived military service

In 1970, General Yahya Khan introduced the National Service Cadet Scheme (NSCS), making it compulsory for higher secondary scholars to enlist with the army. According to the MQM, Altaf Hussain enlisted with the Pakistan

Army through the NSCS and was assigned to the 57th Baloch Regiment as soldier number 2642671. Upon completion of his training his regiment was assigned from Hyderabad to Karachi, from where it was sent to East Pakistan via ships.

Political career

After the Pakistan Civil War came to an end in 1971, Hussain returned to West Pakistan to wilfully join with the regular army. In the MQM's version of events, the selection officer rejected him because his parents were Muhajirs from India, even when he insisted he was born in Pakistan. This is quoted as one of the many instances that formulated Hussain's future political aspirations. The political struggle of the All Pakistan Muhajir Students Organisation (APMSO) shifted to include the issue of stranded Pakistanis in Bangladesh, and on 14 August 1979, Hussain participated in a demonstration at the Mazar-e-Quaid for the safe return of stranded Pakistanis, also called Biharis. Following the demonstration, he was arrested and sentenced on 2 October 1979 to nine months imprisonment and flogging with five strokes. Hussain was later released on 28 April 1980 after he had served his sentence.

The urban centres of Karachi and Hyderabad had increasingly become ethnically diverse and riots along ethnic lines were commonplace. In May 1985, a Pathan minivan driver struck and killed a Muhajir schoolgirl, inciting the first Pathan-Muhajir ethnic riot. Later, following an unsuccessful raid on an Afghan heroin processing and distribution centre in Sohrab Goth by security forces, the Afghans attacked Muhajir residents of Aligarh Colony, which instigated the bloody riots of December 1986. These riots saw the popularity of the MQM and its leader Altaf Hussain rise and the party's ideology was greatly influenced as a result.

Before October 1986, the urban city of Hyderabad was largely dominated by the Sindhi nationalist party Jeay Sindh Qaumi Mahaz (JSQM) founded by G. M. Syed, giving rise to the nationalist slogan Sindhudesh. The only Muhajir political movement countering the JSQM was led by Syed Mubarak Ali Shah, Nawab Zahid Ali Khan and Nawab Muzaffar Hussain. After their deaths, the Urdu-speaking people of Hyderabad were without a charismatic Muhajir leader.

On 31 October 1986, Hussain gave his first public address in Hyderabad at the site of the historic Pacco Qillo, where he was greeted by a crowd. After his address, his message was well received by the Urdu-speaking people of Hyderabad, and he was able to fill the void left by the deaths of the Muhajir leaders. Hussain and a few of his companions were arrested by security personnel after his address, implicating him in several alleged criminal cases. His arrest enraged his supporters, who launched public movements for his release. The charges against him and his companions were later dropped and they were released from Karachi Central Prison on 24 February 1987.

In 1987 the government began widespread arrests of MQM workers all over Sindh. Hussain surrendered to law enforcement on 30 August 1987 on the condition that the arrests of his party's workers be stopped immediately. During Hussain's imprisonment, the MQM placed highly in the local elections of 1987, and there was pressure to release him. He was released on 7 January 1988.

In early 1987, Hussain issued the MQM's Charter of Purpose, which formed the basis for the party's ideology. The charter was paramount in addressing many of the "long-standing grievances" of Sindhi nationalists, and a cooperative arrangement was worked out between the MQM and various Sindhi nationalist parties in early 1988. Apart from the points stipulated in the party's original resolution, Hussain also introduced the idea of Muhajir being a fifth subnationality of Pakistan alongside the Punjabis, Pathans, Balochis, and Sindhis.

Hussain said that while he was admitted to Abbasi Shaheed Hospital in 1988, Late Hameed Gul, Inter-Services Intelligence (ISI) chief at the time, sent him a briefcase full of money via Brigadier Imtiaz Ahmed. He said the intention was to bribe him into joining the military establishment-led Islami Jamhoori Ittehad coalition which was against the Pakistan People's Party (PPP), but he rejected the offer. Later both Ahmed and Gul confirmed the statement.

The 1988 general election indicated that the voting patterns in Sindh were based on ethnic lines, as the PPP and the MQM won almost all of the province's seats in the National Assembly. The PPP had derived its support from the Sindhi population in the province, and the MQM from the Muhajirs. In less than four years since its founding, the MQM had emerged as the third-largest political party in Pakistan.

The PPP had been successful in Sindh but didn't fare well in the other provinces and had to resort to forming a coalition government. Hussain and his party offered their support, but insisted on a formal agreement between the PPP and the MQM. This 59-point MQM-PPP accord, known as the Karachi Declaration, was signed on 2 December 1988. It reiterated many of the points defined in the earlier MQM charter. However, when Benazir Bhutto came into power, she was unwilling or unable to commit to her part of the bargain. Her reluctance in this matter was largely interpreted by Muhajirs as pro-Sindhi and anti-Muhajir. When the declaration was not implemented violence erupted between the APMSO and the PSF, the student wings of the MQM and the PPP, respectively.

After Bhutto's disavowal, Hussain approached Nawaz Sharif, leader of the IJI, which was an opposition coalition opposed to the Bhutto government. As a result of their meeting, a formal agreement between the MQM and the IJI came to pass. However, when Sharif later came into power, he did not honour those commitments either. Hussain became increasingly harsh and hostile in his opinions regarding the governing parties and would often accuse them of political hypocrisy. Due to the perception that striving for justice in a constitutional capacity was futile, ethnic militancy thrived. The gulf between Muhajirs and Sindhis widened, leading to several cases of ethnic cleansing in Hyderabad. Hussain favours peace between India and Pakistan and is a vocal advocate of bridging gaps between the two neighbouring rivals.

Pakistan at the 1956 Summer Olympics

Pakistan competed at the 1956 Summer Olympics in Melbourne, Australia. 55 competitors, all men, took part in 43 events in 8 sports. They won their first medal at this level, winning the silver in the men's field hockey competition.

Pakistan at the 1960 Summer Olympics

Pakistan competed at the 1960 Summer Olympics in Rome, Italy. 44 competitors, all men, took part in 35 events in 7 sports. Here, they won their first Olympic Games gold medal by defeating India in the final of the men's hockey competition. The country also landed their first individual Olympic Games medal, a bronze, through welterweight wrestler Mohammad Bashir in the freestyle contests. Making this Pakistan's most successful Olympics to date.

Pakistan at the 1964 Summer Olympics

Pakistan competed at the 1964 Summer Olympics in Tokyo, Japan. 41 competitors, all men, took part in 29 events in 7 sports. This time round, they won a silver medal in the men's field hockey team competition.

Pakistan at the 1968 Summer Olympics

Pakistan competed at the 1968 Summer Olympics in Mexico City, Mexico. **The only medal won was a gold medal in men's field hockey.** The contingent included only 20 sports persons — 18 hockey players and two wrestlers. Pakistan took part in only two disciplines at the Olympiad.

3

(1971-1980)

INDIA - Privy Purse in India - Bangladesh Liberation War - The Man Inside Sam Manekshaw -Indo-Pakistani War of 1971 - Simla agreement - Smiling Buddha – 1972 Olympics at Munich, W. Germany - The Emergency (India) - 1977 Indian general election - Janata Party - 1980 Olympics in Moscow, USSR

PAKISTAN - Yahya Khan - Zulfikar Ali Bhutto - Fazal Ilahi Chaudhry - Muhammad Zia-ul-Haq - Muhammad Junejo - Benazir Bhutto - 1972 Summer Olympics - 1976 Summer Olympics

INDIA

Privy Purse in India

In India, a privy purse was a payment made to the ruling families of erstwhile princely states as part of their agreements to first integrate with India in 1947 after the independence of India, and later to merge their states in 1949, thereby ending their ruling rights.

The privy purses continued to be paid to the royal families until the 26th Amendment in 1971, by which all their privileges and allowances from the central government ceased to exist, which was implemented after a two-year legal battle.

In some individual cases, privy purses were continued for life for individuals who had held ruling powers before 1947; for instance, HH Maharani Sethu Lakshmi Bayi's allowance was reinstated after a prolonged legal battle, and lasted until she died in 1985.

Bangladesh Liberation War

The Bangladesh Liberation War also known as the Bangladesh War of Independence, or simply the Liberation War in Bangladesh was a revolution and armed conflict sparked by the rise of the Bengali nationalist and self-determination movement in East Pakistan, which resulted in the independence of Bangladesh. The war began when the Pakistani military junta based in West Pakistan—under the orders of Yahya Khan—launched Operation Searchlight against the people of East Pakistan on the night of 25 March 1971, initiating the Bangladesh genocide.

In response to the violence, members of the Mukti Bahini—a guerrilla resistance movement formed by Bengali military, paramilitary and civilians—launched a mass guerrilla war against the Pakistani military, liberating numerous towns and cities in the war's initial months. At first, the Pakistan Army regained momentum during the monsoon, but Bengali guerrillas counterattacked by carrying out widespread sabotage, including through Operation Jackpot against the Pakistan Navy, while the nascent Bangladesh Air Force flew sorties against Pakistani military bases. India joined the war on 3 December 1971, after which Pakistan launched preemptive air strikes on northern India. The subsequent Indo-Pakistani War involved fighting on two fronts; with air supremacy achieved in the eastern theatre, and the rapid advance of the Allied Forces of Mukti Bahini and the Indian military, Pakistan surrendered in Dhaka on 16 December 1971, in what remains to date the largest surrender of armed personnel since the Second World War.

The Man Inside Sam Manekshaw

Abhishek @Come on India Jun 29, 2021, 08:33 IST

He was also famous for his witty wit and sense of humour. A story is with Yahya Khan. Yahya and he was posted in Delhi in 1947 and his red coloured motorcycle was loved by Yahya. After partition, when Yahya decided to go to Pakistan, he took that motorcycle with him and promised Sam Manekshaw that he would send 1,000 rupees of that motorcycle after reaching Pakistan. But after reaching there, he forgot his promise.

Years later, at the time of the 1971 war, both were the Chiefs of Army Staff of their respective countries. After winning the war, Sam jokingly said, "I waited for 24 years for that check which never came, finally he paid the loan taken in 1947 by giving half of his country."

In a career spanning more than four decades in the Army, he held several important positions. He was also instrumental in the accession of Kashmir to India in 1948. He was given the command of the 4th Corps after the defeat in 1962 from China. And now talk about his achievement which is one of the most important events not only in his life but in independent India.

On 16 December we celebrate Victory Day to commemorate the victory over Pakistan in the 1971 war, Sam Manekshaw is the architect of this victory, when a large number of refugees from Bangladesh started coming to India, Indira Gandhi called him and asked him to attack in East Pakistan, refusing which Manekshaw said that the army was not ready for war and asked for time to prepare for war. In this way, he persuaded Mrs Gandhi not to attack immediately and made a comprehensive strategy for the war.

It was the result of his strategy and efficient leadership that despite being more in numbers, Pakistan had to surrender and India took 93000 of its soldiers as prisoners of war.

Once in a conversation, when asked about his biggest achievement, he said that he did not punish any soldier from the post of second lieutenant to field marshal. And he called it the biggest achievement of his career. This answer defines his personality.

When Outlook magazine conducted a survey with IBN Seven about the greatest Indian post-independence in 2013, Sam Manekshaw was ranked 15th, though he will remain in the top 5 on my list of greatest Indian. The Government of India has already honoured him with the country's second-highest civilian award, Padma Vibhushan, but he is one of the few who deserve Bharat Ratna more than anyone. And Bharat Ratna will be the true tribute to this great Indian.

Indo-Pakistani War of 1971

The Indo-Pakistani War of 1971 or the Third India–Pakistan War was an armed conflict between India and Pakistan that occurred during the Bangladesh Liberation War in East Pakistan from 3 December 1971 to 16 December 1971.

The official de-jure war began with Pakistan airforce-affiliated Operation Chengiz Khan, which consisted of preemptive aerial strikes on 11 Indian air stations resulting in minor damages and the suspension of counter-air operations for a mere few hours. The strikes led to India declaring war on Pakistan, marking its entry into the war for East Pakistan's independence, on the side of Bengali nationalist forces. India's entry expanded the existing conflict, with Indian and Pakistani forces engaging on both the eastern and western fronts.

Thirteen days into the war, India had achieved total superiority in East Pakistan, while it also had sufficient superiority in West Pakistan, which later resulted in the Eastern defence of Pakistan signing a joint instrument of surrender, the second-largest in recorded history after the German surrender in World War II on 16 December 1971 in Dhaka. This marked the official end of the conflict and the formation of East Pakistan as the new nation of Bangladesh. Approximately 93,000 Pakistani servicemen were taken prisoner by the Indian Army, including 79,676 to 81,000 uniformed personnel of the Pakistan Armed Forces along with some Bengali soldiers who had remained loyal to Pakistan. The remaining 10,324 to 12,500 prisoners were civilians, either family members of the military personnel or collaborators (Razakars).

It is estimated that members of the Pakistani military and supporting pro-Pakistani Islamist militias killed between 300,000 and 3,000,000 civilians in Bangladesh. As a result of the conflict, a further eight to ten million people fled the country to seek refuge in India.

During the 1971 Bangladesh war for independence, members of the Pakistani military and supporting pro-Pakistani Islamist militias called the Razakars raped between 200,000 and 400,000 Bangladeshi women and girls in a systematic campaign of genocidal rape.

In the Pakistani general elections held on 7 December 1970, the Awami League won 167 out of 169 seats belonging to East Pakistan in the

National Assembly of Pakistan, as well as a landslide in the East Pakistan Provincial Assembly. The Awami League emerged as the single largest party in the federal parliament of Pakistan. With 167 seats, it was past the halfway mark of 150 seats in the 300 member National Assembly and had the right to form a government of its own. Sheikh Mujib was widely considered to be the Prime Minister-elect, including by President Yahya Khan.

Here Pakistan made a historic blunder. People in East Pakistan were there brothers. Had they allowed Sheikh Mujibur Rahman to become Prime Minister, the problem would have been solved easily and could not have escalated. But West Pakistan wanted Punjabi dominance and did not want to hand over power to their brothers of East Pakistan. Otherwise East & West Pakistan together would have been powerful by now. They should have believed in peaceful co-existence.

Simla agreement

The Simla Agreement, also spelled Shimla Agreement, was a peace treaty signed between India and Pakistan on 2 July 1972 in Shimla, the capital city of the Indian state of Himachal Pradesh. It followed the Indo-Pakistani War of 1971, which began after India intervened in East Pakistan as an ally of Bengali rebels who were fighting against Pakistani state forces in the Bangladesh Liberation War. The Indian intervention proved decisive in the war and led to East Pakistan's breakaway from its union with West Pakistan and the emergence of the independent state of Bangladesh.

The treaty's official purpose was stated to serve as a way for both countries to "put an end to the conflict and confrontation that have hitherto marred their relations" and to conceive the steps to be taken for further normalization of India–Pakistan relations while also laying down the principles that should govern their future interactions.

Details of the Simla agreement

The treaty was signed in Simla (also spelt "Shimla") in India by Zulfiqar Ali Bhutto, the President of Pakistan, and Indira Gandhi, the Prime Minister of India. The agreement also paved the way for diplomatic recognition of

Bangladesh by Pakistan. Technically, the document was signed at 0040 hours in the night of 3 July; despite this official documents are dated 2 July 1972. Some of the major outcomes of the Simla Agreement are:

- Both countries will "settle their differences by peaceful means through bilateral negotiations". India has, many a times, maintained that Kashmir dispute is a bilateral issue and must be settled through bilateral negotiations as per Simla Agreement, 1972 and thus, had denied any third party intervention even that of United Nations.

- The agreement converted the cease-fire line of 17 December 1971 into the Line of Control (LOC) between India and Pakistan and it was agreed that "neither side shall seek to alter it unilaterally, irrespective of mutual differences and legal interpretations". Many Indian bureaucrats have later argued that a tacit agreement, to convert this LOC into international border, was reached during a one-on-one meeting between the two heads of government. However, Pakistani bureaucrats have denied any such thing. This identification of a new "cease-fire line" by both the states has been argued by India as making United Nations Military Observer Group in India and Pakistan insignificant. As according to India, the purpose of UNMOGIP was to monitor the cease-fire line as identified in Karachi agreement of 1949 which no longer exists. However, Pakistan have a different take on this issue and both countries still host the UN mission.

The agreement has not prevented the relationship between the two countries from deteriorating to the point of armed conflict, most recently in the Kargil War of 1999. In Operation Meghdoot of 1984 India seized all of the inhospitable Siachen Glacier region where the frontier had been clearly not defined in the agreement (possibly as the area was thought too barren to be controversial); this was considered as a violation of the Simla Agreement by Pakistan. Most of the subsequent deaths in the Siachen Conflict have been from natural disasters, e.g. avalanches in 2010, 2012, and 2016.

India at the 1972 Summer Olympics

India competed at the 1972 Summer Olympics in Munich, West Germany. 41 competitors, 40 men and no woman, took part in 27 events in 7 sports.

India won 1 Bronze medal in Men's Field Hockey.

Pakistan won 1 Silver Medal and West Germany 1 Gold Medal in Men's Field Hockey.

The field hockey tournament at the 1972 Summer Olympics was the 12th edition of the field hockey event at the Summer Olympics. Final matchwas played between West Germany and Pakistan.

The West German victory was the first title by a European nation since 1920, but this was marred by the behavior of Pakistani players, fans, and officials: during the last ten minutes of the gold-medal match, the umpires had to stop play twice so that Pakistani fans who had invaded the pitch could be removed, while Pakistani players and officials repeatedly remonstrated with the umpires throughout that time.

At the final whistle, Pakistani fans and officials invaded the pitch and assaulted West German police and stadium security before storming the tournament officials' table and pouring a bucket of water over International Hockey Federation president Rene Frank, while the players stormed their locker room before proceeding to destroy it.

At the medal ceremony, the Pakistani players refused to wear their silver medals or face the West German flag as it was raised, and turned their backs as the West German national anthem was played.

The eleven Pakistani players were banned for life from their national team, but after a high-level apology, the ban was reduced to two years, and eight of them played at the 1976 Olympics.

Smiling Buddha

Operation Smiling Buddha (MEA designation: Pokhran-I) was the assigned code name of India's first successful nuclear bomb test on 18 May 1974. The bomb was detonated on the army base Pokhran Test Range (PTR), in Rajasthan, by the Indian Army under the supervision of several key Indian generals.

Pokhran-I was also the first confirmed nuclear weapons test by a nation outside the five permanent members of the United Nations Security Council. Officially, the Indian Ministry of External Affairs (MEA) characterised this test as a "peaceful nuclear explosion". Indira Gandhi, then the Prime Minister of India, saw a massive rise in popularity following this test. After this, a series of nuclear tests were carried out in 1998 under the name Pokhran-II.

The court verdict that prompted Indira Gandhi to declare Emergency

Hindustan Times | By Satya Prakash, New Delhi

The June 12, 1975 verdict of the Allahabad High Court convicting then Prime Minister Indira Gandhi of electoral malpractices and debarring her from holding any elected post falls in this category.

Seldom does a court verdict change the course of history of a country.

The June 12, 1975 verdict of the Allahabad High Court convicting then Prime Minister Indira Gandhi of electoral malpractices and debarring her from holding any elected post falls in this category. The verdict delivered by Justice Jagmohanlal Sinha, it is widely believed, led to imposition of Emergency in India on June 25, 1975.

Indira Gandhi had won the 1971 Lok Sabha election from Rae Bareli Lok Sabha seat in Uttar Pradesh convincingly defeating socialist leader Raj Narain, who later challenged her election alleging electoral malpractices and violation of the Representation of the People Act, 1951. It was alleged that her election agent Yashpal Kapoor was a government servant and that she used government officials for personal election related work.

While convicting Indira Gandhi of electoral malpractices, Justice Sinha disqualified her from Parliament and imposed a six-year ban on her holding any elected post.

"The respondent no. I (Indira Gandhi) was thus guilty of a corrupt practice under section 123(7) of the Act....accordingly stands disqualified for a period of six years from the date of this order...," Justice Sinha pronounced to a stunned Indira Gandhi who was present in person in the court. But on an appeal filed by Indira Gandhi, Justice VR Krishna Iyer – a vacation judge of the Supreme Court - on June 24, 1975 granted a conditional stay on Justice Sinha's verdict allowing her to continue as Prime Minister. However, she was debarred from taking part in parliamentary proceedings and draw salary as an MP.

Interestingly, the very next day she imposed the Emergency suspending all fundamental rights, putting opposition leaders in jails and imposing censorship on the media.

While the Emergency was in force, the Supreme Court later overturned her conviction on November 7, 1975.

The Emergency (India)

The Emergency in India was a 21-month period from 1975 to 1977 when Prime Minister Indira Gandhi had a state of emergency declared across the country.

Officially issued by President Fakhruddin Ali Ahmed under Article 352 of the Constitution because of prevailing "internal disturbance", the Emergency was in effect from 25 June 1975 and ended on 21 March 1977. The order bestowed upon the prime minister the authority to rule by decree, allowing elections to be cancelled and civil liberties to be suspended. For much of the Emergency, most of Gandhi's political opponents were imprisoned and the press was censored. Several other human rights violations were reported from the time, including a mass campaign for vasectomy spearheaded by her son Sanjay Gandhi. The Emergency is one of the most controversial periods of Indian history since its independence. The final decision to impose an emergency was proposed by Indira Gandhi, agreed upon by the President of India, and ratified by the Cabinet and the Parliament from July to August 1975. It was based on the rationale that there were imminent internal and external threats to the Indian state.

Indira Gandhi declared the General Election to surprise the opposition, with the understanding that the opposition will not have sufficient time to get united and campaign for the election against her. But the people across

India were so unhappy about the excesses carried out during emergency, that not much campaigning was required for the Opposition to get the results in their favor. Although this proved bad for Indira Gandhi, it helped reinstall democracy in India.

1977 Indian general election

General elections were held in India between 16 and 20 March 1977 to elect the members of the 6th Lok Sabha. The elections took place during the Emergency period, which expired on 21 March 1977, shortly before the final results were announced.

The election resulted in a heavy defeat for the Indian National Congress (INC), with the incumbent Prime Minister and INC party leader Indira Gandhi losing her seat in Rae Bareli, while her son Sanjay lost his seat in Amethi. The call for restoration of democracy by revoking the Emergency is considered to be a major reason for the sweeping victory for the opposition Janata Alliance, whose leader Morarji Desai was sworn in as the fourth Prime Minister of India on 24 March. At 81, Desai became the oldest man to be elected Prime Minister of India.

Background

This sixth general elections, which were conducted for 542 seats in single-member constituencies, represented 27 Indian states and union territories. These 542 constituencies remained same until 2004 Indian general elections for the 14th Lok Sabha.

The Emergency declared by the Indira Gandhi led Congress government was the core issue in the 1977 elections. Civil liberties were suspended during the national emergency from 25 June 1975 to 21 March 1977 and Prime Minister Indira Gandhi assumed vast powers.

Gandhi had become extremely unpopular for her decision and paid for it during the elections. On 18 January, Gandhi called for fresh elections and released some political prisoners. Many remained in prison until she was ousted from office and a new Prime Minister took over. On 20 January, four opposition parties, the Indian National Congress (Organisation), the Bharatiya Jana Sangh, the Bharatiya Lok Dal and the

Praja Socialist Party, decided to fight the elections under a single banner called the Janata alliance. The alliance used the symbol allocated to Bhartiya Lok Dal as their symbol on the ballot papers.

The Janata Alliance reminded voters of the excesses and human rights violations during the Emergency, like compulsory sterilisation and imprisonment of political leaders. The Janata campaign said the elections would decide whether India would have "democracy or dictatorship." The Congress looked jittery. Agriculture and Irrigation Minister Babu Jagjivan Ram quit the party in the first week of February; other notable Congress stalwarts who crossed the floor with Jagjivan Ram before the election were Hemvati Nandan Bahuguna and Nandini Satpathy.

1979 Machchhu dam failure

The Machchhu dam failure or Morbi disaster is a dam-related flood disaster which occurred on 11 August 1979. The Machchu-2 dam, situated on the Machchhu river, failed, sending a wall of water through the town of Morbi (now in the Morbi district) of Gujarat, India. Estimates of the number of people killed vary greatly ranging from 1,800 to 25,000 people.

The Machchu II dam

The first dam on the Machchhu river, named Machchhu I, was built in 1959, having a catchment area of 730 square kilometres (280 sq mi). The Machchhu II dam was constructed downstream of Machchhu I in 1972, and has a catchment area of 1,929 square kilometres (745 sq mi).

It was an earthfill dam. The dam was meant to serve an irrigation scheme. Considering the long history of drought in Saurashtra region, the primary consideration at the time of design was water supply, not flood control. It consisted of a masonry spillway of 206 metres (676 ft) consisting 18 sluice gates across the river section and long earthen embankments on both sides. The spillway capacity provided for 5,663 cubic metres per second (200,000 cu ft/s). The embankments were of 2,345 metres (7,694 ft) and 1,399 metres (4,590 ft) of length on left and right side respectively. The embankments had a 6.1 m top width, with upstream and downstream slopes 1:3 (V:H) and 1:2 respectively; and a clay core extending through alluvium to bedrock. The upstream face consisted of 61 cm small gravel and a 61 cm hand packed rip-rap. The dam stood 22.6 metres (74 ft) above the river bed and its overflow section was 164.5 metres (540 ft) long. The reservoir had a storage capacity of 101,020 cubic decametres (81,900 acre-feet).

Failure

The failure was caused by excessive rain and massive flooding leading to the disintegration of the earthen walls of the four kilometre long Machchhu-2 dam. The actual observed flow following the intense rainfall reached 16,307 m3/s, thrice what the dam was designed for, resulting in its collapse. 762 metres (2,500 ft) of the left and 365 metres (1,198 ft) of the right embankment of the dam collapsed. Within 20 minutes the floods of 12 to 30 ft (3.7 to 9.1 m) height inundated the low-lying areas of Morbi industrial town located 5 km below the dam.

Around 3.30 pm the tremendous swirling flow of water struck Morbi. Water level rose to 30 feet (9.1 m) within the next 15 minutes and some low lying areas of city were under 20 feet (6.1 m) of water for the next 6 hours.

The Morbi dam failure was listed as the worst dam burst in the Guinness Book of Records. There was great economic loss. The flood damaged farmland, leading to a decrease in productivity of crops.

The book by Wooten and Sandesara gives vivid first person accounts of many survivors. It narrates how people scrambled for rooftops, hilltops, and other safe grounds in order to save themselves. Over a hundred people took shelter in Vajepar Ram Mandir but later the deluge submerged them with the temple. Women were compelled to drop their babies into the furious surge in order to save themselves and people lost their loved ones in a flash.

During reconstruction of the dam the capacity of the spillway was increased by four times and fixed at about 21,000 m3/s.

Janata Party

The Janata Party (abbreviated as JP, lit. People's Party) was a political party that was founded as an amalgam of Indian political parties opposed to the

Emergency that was imposed between 1975 and 1977 by Prime Minister Indira Gandhi of the Indian National Congress. In the 1977 general election, the party defeated the Congress and Janata leader Morarji Desai became the first non-Congress prime minister in independent modern India's history.

Raj Narain, a socialist leader, had filed a legal writ alleging electoral malpractice against Indira Gandhi in 1971. On 12 June 1975, Allahabad High Court found her guilty of using corrupt electoral practices in her 1971 election victory over Narain in the Rae Bareli constituency. She was barred from contesting any election for the next six years. Economic problems, corruption and the conviction of Gandhi led to widespread protests against the Congress (R) government, which responded by imposing a State of Emergency. The rationale was that of preserving national security. However, the government introduced press censorship, postponed elections and banned strikes and rallies. Opposition leaders such as Jivatram Kripalani, Jayaprakash Narayan, Anantram Jaiswal, Chandra Shekhar, Biju Patnaik, Atal Bihari Vajpayee, L. K. Advani, Raj Narain, Satyendra Narayan Sinha, Ramnandan Mishra and Morarji Desai were imprisoned, along with thousands of other political activists. When the State of Emergency was lifted and new elections called in 1977, opposition political parties such as the Congress (O), Bharatiya Jana Sangh, Bharatiya Lok Dal as well as defectors from the Indian National Congress joined to form the Janata party, which won a sweeping majority in the Indian Parliament. Narain defeated Gandhi at Rae Bareli in those elections.

The new Janata-led government reversed many Emergency-era decrees and opened official investigations into Emergency-era abuses. Although several major foreign policy and economic reforms were attempted, continuous in-fighting and ideological differences made the Janata government unable to effectively address national problems. By mid-1979, Prime Minister Morarji Desai was forced to resign and his successor Chaudhary Charan Singh failed to sustain a parliamentary majority as alliance partners withdrew support. Popular disenchantment with the political in-fighting and ineffective government led to the resurgence of Gandhi and her new Congress (I) party, which won the general election called in 1980. Although the original Janata Party fragmented and dissolved, modern political parties continue to invoke its legacy.

Very immature behavior of Janata-led Govt leaders led to their downfall.

India at the 1980 Summer Olympics

India competed at the 1980 Summer Olympics in Moscow, USSR and won Gold Medal in Men's Field Hockey.

PAKISTAN

Yahya Khan

Agha Muhammad Yahya Khan (4 February 1917 – 10 August 1980) was a Pakistani military officer who served as the third president of Pakistan from 1969 to 1971. He also served as the commander-in-chief of the Pakistan Army from 1966 to 1971. Along with Tikka Khan, he is considered the chief architect of the 1971 Bangladesh genocide.

Yahya Khan's presidency oversaw martial law by suspending the constitution in 1969. Holding the country's first general election in 1970, he delayed the power transition to the victorious Sheikh Mujibur Rahman from East Pakistan. In March 1971, Khan ordered Operation Searchlight in an effort to suppress Bengali nationalism. This led to the Bangladesh Liberation War in March 1971. Yahya Khan was central to the perpetration of Bangladesh genocide, in which around 300,000–3,000,000 Bengalis were killed, and between 200,000 to 400,000 women were raped. In December 1971, Pakistan carried out pre-emptive strikes against the Bengali-allied Indian Army, culminating in the start of the Third India–Pakistan War. The wars resulted in the surrender of Pakistan, and East Pakistan seceded as Bangladesh. After Pakistan's surrender, Khan resigned from the military command and transferred the presidency to Zulfikar Ali Bhutto. Khan remained under house surveillance prior to 1979 when he was released by Fazle Haq. Khan died the following year in Rawalpindi and was buried in Peshawar.

Khan's short regime is regarded as the leading cause of the breakup of Pakistan. He is viewed negatively in both Bangladesh, being considered the chief-architect of the genocide, and in Pakistan.

Presidency (1969–1971)

A sustained anti-regime mass movement began in the fall of 1968 in West Pakistan. The uprising spread to East Pakistan and gathered strength. President Ayub Khan tried to quell the revolt by making concessions to the opposition, but demonstrations continued. Rather than resigning and allowing a constitutional transfer of power, Ayub Khan requested that Yahya Khan, Commander-in-Chief of the Army, utilize the military's supra-constitutional authority to declare martial law and take power. On 25 March 1969, Yahya did so.

When Yahya Khan assumed the office on 25 March 1969, he inherited a two-decade constitutional problem of inter-provincial ethnic rivalry between the Punjabi-Pashtun-Mohajir dominated West Pakistan and the ethnically-Bengali Muslim East Pakistan. In addition, Yahya also inherited an 11-year problem of transforming a country essentially ruled by one man to a democratic country, which was the ideological basis of the anti-Ayub movement of 1968–69. As an army chief, Yahya had all the capabilities, qualifications and potential, but he inherited an extremely-complex problem and was forced to perform the multiple roles of caretaker head of the country, drafter of a provisional constitution, resolving the One Unit question, satisfying the frustrations and the sense of exploitation and discrimination successively created in the East Wing by a series of government policies since 1948.

Zulfikar Ali Bhutto

Zulfikar Ali Bhutto (5 January 1928 – 4 April 1979) was a Pakistani barrister, politician and statesman who served as the fourth president of Pakistan from 1971 to 1973, and later as the ninth prime minister of Pakistan from 1973 to 1977. He was the founder of the Pakistan People's Party (PPP) and served as its chairman until his execution.

As president, Bhutto recovered 93,000 prisoners of war and five thousand square miles (13,000 km2) of Indian-held territory after signing the Simla Agreement. He strengthened ties with China and Saudi Arabia, recognized Bangladesh, and hosted the second Organisation of the Islamic Conference in Lahore in 1974. His government drafted the current constitution of Pakistan, in 1973, upon which he appointed Fazal Ilahi Chaudhry president and switched to the newly empowered office of prime minister. Bhutto played an integral role in initiating the country's nuclear programme. However, Bhutto's nationalisation of much of Pakistan's fledgling industries, healthcare, and educational institutions was met with economic stagnation. After dissolving provincial feudal governments in Balochistan was met with unrest, Bhutto also ordered an army operation in the province in 1973, causing thousands of civilian casualties. Despite civil disorder, the People's Party won the 1977 parliamentary elections by a wide margin. However, the opposition alleged widespread vote rigging, and violence escalated across the country. On 5 July that same year, Bhutto was deposed in a military coup by his appointed army chief Muhammad Zia-ul-Haq, before being controversially tried and executed by the Supreme Court of Pakistan in 1979 for authorising the murder of a political opponent, Muhammad Ahmad Kasuri.

Bhutto's legacy remains contentious; he is hailed by supporters for his nationalism and secular internationalist agenda. He is denounced by critics for political repression, impoverished economy, and human rights abuses in Balochistan. Bhutto is often considered one of Pakistan's greatest leaders, and his party, the PPP, remains among Pakistan's largest, with his daughter Benazir Bhutto being twice elected Prime Minister, while his son-in-law and Benazir's husband, Asif Ali Zardari, served as president.

Presidency (1971–1973)

A Pakistan International Airlines flight was sent to fetch Bhutto from New York, who at that time was presenting Pakistan's case before the United Nations Security Council on the East Pakistan Crises. Bhutto returned home on 18 December 1971. On 20 December, he was taken to the President House in Rawalpindi, where he took over two positions from Yahya Khan, one as president and the other as first civilian Chief Martial Law Administrator. Thus, he was the first civilian Chief Martial Law Administrator of the dismembered Pakistan. By the time Bhutto had assumed control of what remained of Pakistan, the nation was completely isolated, angered, and demoralized. Bhutto addressing the nation through radio and television said:

My dear countrymen, my dear friends, my dear students, labourers, peasants… those who fought for Pakistan… We are facing the worst crisis in our country's life, a deadly crisis. We have to pick up the pieces, very small pieces, but we will make a new Pakistan, a prosperous and progressive Pakistan, a Pakistan free of exploitation, a Pakistan envisaged by the Quaid-e-Azam.

As president, Bhutto faced mounting challenges on both internal and foreign fronts. The trauma was severe in Pakistan, a psychological setback and emotional breakdown for Pakistan. The two-nation theory— the theoretical basis for the creation of Pakistan—lay discredited, and Pakistan's foreign policy collapsed when no moral support was found anywhere, including long-standing allies such as the U.S. and China. However this is disputed even by Bangladeshi academics who insist that the two-nation theory was not discredited. Since her creation, the physical and moral existence of Pakistan was in great danger. On the internal front, Baloch, Sindhi, Punjabi, and Pashtun nationalisms were at their peak, calling for their independence from Pakistan. Finding it difficult to keep Pakistan united, Bhutto launched full-fledged intelligence and military operations to stamp out any separatist movements. By the end of 1978, these nationalist organizations were brutally quelled by Pakistan Armed Forces.

Bhutto placed Yahya Khan under house arrest, brokered a ceasefire and ordered the release of Sheikh Mujib, who was held prisoner by the Pakistan Army. To implement this, Bhutto reversed the verdict of Mujib's earlier court-martial trial, in which Brigadier-General Rahimuddin Khan had sentenced Mujib to death. Appointing a new cabinet, Bhutto appointed Lieutenant-General Gul Hasan as Chief of Army Staff. On 2 January 1972 Bhutto announced the nationalisation of all major industries, including iron and steel, heavy engineering, heavy electricals, petrochemicals, cement and public utilities. A new labour policy was announced increasing workers' rights and the power of trade unions. Although he came from a feudal background himself, Bhutto announced his first reforms in 1972 which is also called Martial Law Regulation (MLR-115). As Bhutto came as Populist leader, his charismatic politics was evident. Consequently, he put ceiling on land ownership wherein no one can hold more than 200 acres irrigated and more than 300 acres non-irrigated land. Bhutto also dismissed the military chiefs on 3 March after they refused orders to suppress a major police strike in Punjab. He appointed General Tikka Khan as the new Chief of the Army Staff in March 1972 as he felt the general would not interfere in political matters and would concentrate on rehabilitating the Pakistan Army. Bhutto convened the National Assembly on 14 April, rescinded martial law on 21 April and charged the legislators with writing a new constitution.

Nuclear weapons program

Zulfiqar Ali Bhutto was the founder of Pakistan's atomic bomb programme, and due to his administration and aggressive leadership of this programme, he is often known as the Father of Nuclear deterrence programme. Bhutto's interest in nuclear technology was said to have begun during his college years in the United States when Bhutto attended a course in political science, discussing the political impact of the U.S.'s first nuclear test, Trinity, on global politics. While at Berkeley, Bhutto witnessed the public panic when the Soviet Union first exploded their bomb, codename First Lightning in 1949, prompting the U.S. government to launch their research on 'hydrogen' bombs. However, long before in 1958, as Minister for Fuel, Power, and National Resources, Bhutto played a key role in setting up the Pakistan Atomic Energy Commission (PAEC) administrative research bodies and institutes. Soon, Bhutto offered a technical post to Munir Ahmad Khan in PAEC in 1958, and lobbied for Abdus Salam to be appointed as Science Adviser in 1960. Before being elevated to Foreign Minister, Bhutto directed the funds for key research in nuclear weapons and related science.

After India's nuclear test – codename **Smiling Buddha**—in May 1974, Bhutto sensed and saw this test as final anticipation for Pakistan's death. In a press conference, held shortly after India's nuclear test,

Bhutto said, "India's nuclear program is designed to intimidate Pakistan and establish *"hegemony in the subcontinent"*. Despite Pakistan's limited financial resources, Bhutto was so enthusiastic about the nuclear energy project, that he is reported to have said *"Pakistanis will eat grass but make a nuclear bomb."*

Prime Minister of Pakistan

Bhutto was sworn in as the prime minister of the country on 14 August 1973, after he had secured 108 votes in a house of 146 members. Fazal Ilahi Chaudhry was elected as the president under the new constitution. During his five years of government, the Bhutto government made extensive reforms at every level of government. Pakistan's capital and Western reforms that were begun and built in 1947 throughout the 1970s, were transformed and replaced with socialist system. His policies were seen as people-friendly but did not produce long-lasting effects as the civil disorder against Bhutto began to take place in 1977.

Bhutto is considered the main architect of 1973 constitution as part of his vision to put Pakistan to road to parliamentary democracy. One of the major achievements in Bhutto's life was drafting of Pakistan's first ever consensus constitution to the country. Bhutto supervised the promulgation of 1973 constitution that triggered an unstoppable constitutional revolution through his politics wedded to the emancipation of the downtrodden masses, by first giving people a voice in the Parliament, and introducing radical changes in the economic sphere for their benefit.

During his period in office the government carried out seven major amendments to the 1973 Constitution. The First Amendment led to Pakistan's recognition of and diplomatic ties with Bangladesh. The Second Amendment in the constitution declared the Ahmadis as non-Muslims, and defined the term non-Muslim. The rights of the detained were limited under the Third Amendment while the powers and jurisdiction of the courts for providing relief to political opponents were curtailed under the Fourth Amendment. The Fifth Amendment passed on 15 September 1976, focused on curtailing the power and jurisdiction of the Judiciary. This amendment was highly criticised by lawyers and political leaders. The main provision of the Sixth Amendment extended the term of the Chief Justices of the Supreme Court and the High Courts beyond the age of retirement. This Amendment was made in the Constitution to favour the then Chief Justice of the Supreme Court who was supposed to be a friend of Bhutto.

Industrial reforms

The Bhutto government carried out a number of reforms in the industrial sector. His reforms were twofold: nationalization, and the improvement of workers' rights. In the first phase, basic industries like steel, chemical and cement were nationalized. This was done in 1972. The next major step in nationalization took place on 1 January 1974, when Bhutto nationalised all banks. The last step in the series was the nationalization of all flour, rice and cotton mills throughout the country. This nationalisation process was not as successful as Bhutto expected. Most of the nationalized units were small businesses that could not be described as industrial units, hence making no sense for the step that was taken. Consequently, a considerable number of small businessmen and traders were ruined, displaced or rendered unemployed. In the concluding analysis, nationalisation caused colossal loss not only to the national treasury but also to the people of Pakistan.

Bhutto is credited for establishing the world class Quaid-e-Azam University and Allama Iqbal Open University in Islamabad in 1974, as well as establishing Gomal University Dera Ismail Khan in 1973.

As part of his investment policies, Bhutto founded the National Development Finance Corporation (NDFC). In July 1973, this financial institute began operation with an initial government investment of 100 million PRs.

Banking reforms were introduced to provide more opportunities to small farmers and business such as forcing banks to ensure 70% of institutional lending should be for small land holders of 12.5 acres or less, which was a revolutionary idea at a time when banks only clients were the privileged classes. The number of bank branches rose by 75% from December 1971 to November 1976, from 3,295 to 5,727. It was one of the most radical move made by Bhutto, and the Bank infrastructure was expanded covering all towns and villages with a population of 5,000 in accordance with targets set after the nationalisation of banks.

Balochistan

Military operation

Following the secession of East Pakistan, calls for the independence of Balochistan by Baloch nationalists grew immensely. Surveying the political instability, Bhutto's central government sacked two provincial governments within six months, arrested the two chief ministers, two governors and forty-four MNAs and MPAs, obtained an order from the Supreme Court banning the National People's Party on the recommendation of Akbar Bugti, and charged everyone with high treason to be tried by a specially constituted Hyderabad tribunal of hand-picked judges.

In January 1973, Bhutto ordered the Pakistan Armed Forces to suppress a rising insurgency in the province of Balochistan. He dismissed the governments in Balochistan and the North-West Frontier Province once more. Following the alleged discovery of Iraqi arms in Islamabad in February 1973, Bhutto dissolved the Provincial Assembly of Balochistan. The operation, under General Tikka Khan, soon took shape in a five-year conflict with the Baloch separatists. The sporadic fighting between the insurgency and the army started in 1973 with the largest confrontation taking place in September 1974. Later on, Pakistan Navy, under Vice-Admiral Patrick Julius Simpson, also jumped in the conflict as it had applied naval blockades to Balochistan's port. The Navy began its separate operations to seize the shipments sent to aid Baloch separatists. Pakistan Air Force also launched air operations, and with the support of navy and army, the air force had pounded the mountainous hidden havens of the Separatists. The Iranian military, also fearing a spread of the greater Baloch resistance in Iran, aided the Pakistani military as well. Among Iran's contribution were 30 Huey cobra attack helicopters and $200 million in aid.

Bhutto began facing considerable criticism and increasing unpopularity as his term progressed.

On 3 July 1977, military general Khalid Mahmud Arif secretly met Bhutto, revealing that the planning of a coup had been taking place in the General Combatant Headquarters (GHQ).

Bhutto had good intelligence within the Army, and officers such as Major-General Tajamül Hussain Malik were loyal to him until the end. However, General Zia-ul-Haq ordered a training programme with the officers from Special Air Service (SAS). General Zia-ul-Haq ordered many of Bhutto's loyal officers to attend the first course. However, classes for senior officers were delayed until the midnight. None of the officers were allowed to leave until late in the evening before the coup. During this time, arrangements for the coup were made.

General Zia announced that martial law had been imposed, the constitution suspended and all assemblies dissolved and promised elections within ninety days. Zia also ordered the arrest of senior PPP and PNA leaders but promised elections in October. Bhutto was released on 29 July and was received by a large crowd of supporters in his hometown of Larkana. He immediately began touring across Pakistan, delivering speeches to very large crowds and planning his political comeback. Bhutto was arrested again on 3 September before being released on bail on 13 September. Fearing yet another arrest, Bhutto named his wife, Nusrat, president of the Pakistan People's Party. Bhutto was imprisoned on 16 September and a large number of PPP leaders, notably Dr. Mubashir Hassan and activists were arrested and disqualified from contesting the elections. Observers noted that when Bhutto was removed from power in July 1977, thousands of Pakistanis cheered and were delighted.

On 5 July 1977 the military, led by General Muhammad Zia-ul-Haq, staged a coup. Zia relieved prime minister Bhutto of power, holding him in detention for a month. He was released but on 3 September, the Army arrested Bhutto again on charges of authorising the murder of a political opponent in March 1974. Bhutto's defence team fought the case efficiently and challenged the prosecution with evidence from an army logbook the prosecution had submitted. On 18 March 1978, Bhutto was declared guilty of murder, and was sentenced to death. The court granted a stay of execution while it studied the petition. By 24 February 1979 when the next court hearing began, appeals for clemency arrived from many heads of state. Zia said that the appeals amounted to "trade union activity" among politicians. On 24 March 1979 the Supreme Court dismissed the appeal. Zia upheld the death sentence. Bhutto was hanged at Central Jail Rawalpindi, on 4 April 1979, and was buried at his family mausoleum in Garhi Khuda Baksh.

Fazal Ilahi Chaudhry

Fazal Ilahi Chaudhry (1 January 1904 – 2 June 1982) was a Pakistani politician who served as the fifth president of Pakistan from 1973 to 1978 prior to the martial law led by Chief of Army Staff General Zia-ul-Haq. He also served as the deputy speaker of the National Assembly of Pakistan from 1965 to 1969 and the eighth speaker of the National Assembly of Pakistan from 1972 to 1973.

He contested the Presidential Elections of 1973 against Khan Amirzadah Khan of NAP and all opposition parties, and was elected President in 1973 (receiving 139 votes against Khan's 45), when the head of the PPP, Zulfiqar Ali Bhutto was made Prime Minister. He was the first Punjabi President of Pakistan.

Chaudhry was largely a figurehead, and was the first Pakistani President with less power than the Prime Minister. This was due to the new constitution of 1973 that gave more powers to the Prime Minister. Previously, the President had been the chief executive of Pakistan and had the power to appoint Prime Minister. After Operation Fair Play - a codename of the operation to remove Zulfikar Ali Bhutto from power - Chaudhry continued his presidency but had no influence in the government operations or the military and national affairs.

After contentious relations with the military, Chaudhry decided to resign from his post despite the urging of the Chief of Army Staff and Chairman of Joint Chiefs of Staff. On 16 September 1978, Chaudhry handed the charge of the presidency to ruling military general Zia-ul-Haq who succeeded him as the sixth president, in addition to being the Chief Martial Law Administrator and the Chief of Army Staff.

Death

Chaudhry died of a heart ailment on 2 June 1982 at the age of 78.

Muhammad Zia-ul-Haq

Muhammad Zia-ul-Haq (12 August 1924 – 17 August 1988) was a Pakistani military officer and politician who served as the sixth president of Pakistan from 1978 until his death. He also served as the second chief of the army staff from 1976 until his death.

Assumption of the post of President of Pakistan

Despite the dismissal of most of the Bhutto government, president Fazal Ilahi Chaudhry was persuaded to continue in office as a figurehead. After completing his term, and despite Zia's insistence to accept an extension as President, Chaudhry resigned, and Zia took the office of President of Pakistan on 16 September 1978.

Political structural changes

Formation of Majlis-e-Shoora

Although ostensibly only holding office until free elections could be held, General Zia, like the previous military governments, disapproved of the lack of discipline and orderliness that often accompanies multiparty "parliamentary democracy." He preferred a "presidential" form of government and a system of decision making by technical experts, or "technocracy". His first replacement for the parliament or National Assembly was a Majlis-e-Shoora, or "consultative council." After banning all political parties in 1979 he disbanded Parliament and at the end of 1981 set up the majlis, which was to act as a sort of board of advisors to the President and assist with the process of Islamization. The 350 members of the Shoora were to be nominated by the President and possessed only the power to consult with him, and in reality served only to endorse decisions already taken by the government. Most members of the Shoora were intellectuals, scholars, ulema, journalists, economists, and professionals in different fields.

Zia's parliament and his military government reflect the idea of "military-bureaucratic technocracy" (MBT) where professionals, engineers, and high-profile military officers were initially part of his military government. His antipathy for the politicians led the promotion of bureaucratic-technocracy which was seen a strong weapon of countering the politicians and their political strongholds. Senior statesman and technocrats were included physicist-turned diplomat Agha Shahi, jurist Sharifuddin Perzada, corporate leader Nawaz Sharif, economist Mahbub ul Haq, and senior statesman Aftab Kazie, Roedad Khan, and chemist-turned diplomat Ghulam Ishaq Khan were a few of the leading technocratic figures in his military government.

1984 referendum

After Bhutto's execution, momentum to hold elections began to mount both internationally and within Pakistan. But before handing over power to elected representatives, Zia-ul-Haq attempted to secure his position as the head of state. A referendum was held on 19 December 1984 with the option being to elect or reject the General as the future President, the wording of the referendum making a vote against Zia appear to be a vote against Islam. According to official figures 97.8% of votes were cast in favour of Zia, however only 20% of the electorate participated in the referendum.

After holding the 1984 referendum, Zia succumbed to international pressure and gave permission to election commission to hold nation wide general elections but without political parties in February 1985. Most of the major opposing political parties decided to boycott the elections but election results showed that many victors belonged to one party or the other. Critics complained that ethnic and sectarian mobilisation filled the void left by banning political parties (or making elections "non-partisan"), to the detriment of national integration.

The General worked to give himself the power to dismiss the Prime Minister dissolve the National Assembly, appoint provincial governors and the chief of the armed forces. His prime minister Muhammad Khan Junejo was known as an unassuming and soft-spoken Sindhi.

Before handing over the power to the new government and lifting the martial law, Zia got the new legislature to retroactively accept all of

Zia's actions of the past eight years, including his coup of 1977. He also managed to get several amendments passed, most notably the Eighth Amendment, which granted "reserve powers" to the president to dissolve the Parliament. However, this amendment considerably reduced the power he'd previously granted himself to dissolve the legislature, at least on paper. The text of the amendment permitted Zia to dissolve the Parliament only if the government had been toppled by a vote of no confidence and it was obvious that no one could form a government or the government could not function in a constitutional manner.

In general Zia gave economic development and policy a fairly low priority (aside from Islamization) and delegating its management to technocrats such as Ghulam Ishaq Khan, Aftab Qazi and Vaseem Jaffrey. However, between 1977 and 1986, the country experienced an average annual growth in the GNP of 6.8%—the highest in the world at that time—thanks in large part to remittances from the overseas workers, rather than government policy. The first year of Zia's government coincided with a dramatic rise in remittances, which totalled $3.2 billion/year for most of the 1980s, accounted for 10 percent of Pakistans's GDP; 45 percent of its current account receipts, and 40 percent of total foreign exchange earnings.

United States sponsorship

The United States, notably the Ronald Reagan administration, was an ardent supporter of Zia's military regime and a close ally of Pakistan's conservative-leaning ruling military establishment. The Reagan administration declared Zia's regime as the "front line" ally of the United States in the fight against the threat of Communism. American legislators and senior officials most notable were Zbigniew Brzezinski, Henry Kissinger, Charlie Wilson, Joanne Herring, and the civilian intelligence officers Michael Pillsbury and Gust Avrakotos, and senior US military officials General John William Vessey, and General Herbert M. Wassom, had been long associated with the Zia military regime where they had made frequent trips to Pakistan advising on expanding the idea of establishment in the political circle of Pakistan. Nominally, the American conservatism of Ronald Reagan's Republican Party influenced Zia to adopt his idea of Islamic conservatism as the primary line of his military government, forcefully enforcing the Islamic and other religious practices in the country.

Foreign affairs

Soviet–Afghan War

On 25 December 1979, the Soviet Union invaded Afghanistan. Following this invasion, Zia chaired a meeting and was asked by several cabinet members to refrain from interfering in the war, owing to the vastly superior military power of the USSR. Zia, however, was ideologically opposed to the idea of communism taking over a neighbouring country, supported by the fear of Soviet advancement into Pakistan, particularly Balochistan, in search of warm waters, and made no secret about his intentions of monetarily and militarily aiding the Afghan resistance (the Mujahideen) with major assistance from the United States.

American president Jimmy Carter offered $400 million aid package to Pakistan; Zia ridiculed the offer as "peanuts". Zia ultimately succeeded in winning an increased aid of $3.2 billion provided by Carter's successor Ronald Reagan.

This US help assisted Pakistan to a great extent to start Proxy war (Terrorist attacks) on India.

During this meeting, the Director-General of the Directorate for Inter-Services Intelligence (ISI) then-Lieutenant-General Akhtar Abdur Rahman advocated for a covert operation in Afghanistan by arming Islamic Extremists. After this meeting, Zia authorised this operation under General Rahman, and it was later merged with Operation Cyclone, a programme funded by the United States and the Central Intelligence Agency (CIA).

In November 1982, Zia travelled to Moscow to attend the funeral of Leonid Brezhnev, the late General Secretary of the Communist Party of the Soviet Union. Soviet Foreign Minister Andrei Gromyko and new Secretary General Yuri Andropov met with Zia there. Andropov expressed indignation over Pakistan's support of the Afghan resistance against the Soviet Union and its satellite state, Socialist Afghanistan. Zia took his hand and assured him, "General Secretary, believe me, Pakistan wants nothing but very good relations with the Soviet Union". According to Gromyko, Zia's sincerity convinced them, but Zia's actions didn't live up to his words.

Zia reversed many of Bhutto's foreign policy initiatives by first establishing stronger links with the United States, Japan, and the Western world. Zia broken off relations with the Socialist state and State capitalism became his major economic policy. US politician Charlie Wilson claims that he worked with Zia and the CIA to channel Soviet weapons that Israel captured from the PLO in Lebanon to fighters in Afghanistan. Wilson claims that Zia remarked to him: "Just don't put any stars of David on the boxes".

1980's was the most important period from the point of view of India & Pakistan in the fast changing world politics.

Iran-Iraq War

On 22 September 1980, the Iraqi invasion of Iran initiated a nearly eight-year long war between Iran and Iraq. In an effort to end the war and maintain unity of the Islamic world, Zia visited Tehran on 27 September and Baghdad on 29 September. Despite declaring neutrality, Zia maintained close relations with Iran and Pakistan sold weapons to Iran, which proved to be a main factor for the Iranian victory in the Tanker War.

Consolidation of atomic bomb program

One of the earliest initiatives taken by Zia in 1977, was to militarize the integrated atomic energy program which was founded by Zulfiqar Ali Bhutto in 1972. During the first stages, the program was under the control of Bhutto and the Directorate for Science, under Science Advisor Dr. Mubashir Hassan, who was heading the civilian committee that supervised the construction of the facilities and laboratories. This atomic bomb project had no boundaries with Munir Ahmad Khan and Dr. Abdul Qadeer Khan leading their efforts separately and reported to Bhutto and his science adviser Dr. Hassan who had little interest in the atomic bomb project. Major-General Zahid Ali Akbar, an engineering officer, had little role in the atomic project; Zia responded by taking over the program under military control and disbanded the civilian directorate when he ordered the arrest of Hassan. This whole giant nuclear energy project was transferred into the administrative hands of Major-General Akbar who was soon made the Lieutenant-General and Engineer-in-Chief of the Pakistan Army Corps of Engineers to deal with the authorities whose co-operation was required. Akbar consolidated the entire project by placing the scientific research under military control, setting boundaries and goals. Akbar proved to be an extremely capable officer in the matters of science and technology when he aggressively led the development of nuclear weapons under Munir Ahmad Khan and Abdul Qadeer Khan in a matter of five years.

By the time, Zia assumed control, the research facilities became fully functional and 90% of the work on atom bomb project was completed. Both the Pakistan Atomic Energy Commission (PAEC) and the Khan Research Laboratories (KRL) had built the extensive research infrastructure started by Bhutto. Akbar's office was shifted to Army's General Headquarters (GHQ) and Akbar guided Zia on key matters of nuclear science and atomic bomb production. He became the first engineering officer to have acknowledge Zia about the success of this energy project into a fully matured program. On the recommendation of Akbar, Zia approved the appointment of Munir Ahmad Khan as the scientific director of the atomic bomb project, as Zia was convinced by Akbar that civilian scientists under Munir Khan's directorship were at their best to counter international pressure.

Unlike Bhutto, who faced rogue criticism and a heated diplomatic war with the United States throughout the 1970s, Zia took different diplomatic approaches to counter the international pressure. From 1979 to 1983, the country was made a subject of attack by international organization for not signing the Nuclear Non-Proliferation Treaty (NPT); Zia deftly neutralized international pressure by tagging Pakistan's nuclear weapons program to the nuclear designs of the neighboring Indian nuclear program. Zia, with the help of Munir Ahmad Khan and Agha Shahi, Foreign Minister, drew a five-point proposal as a practical rejoinder to world pressure on Pakistan to sign the NPT; the points including the renouncing of the use of nuclear weapons. He also escalated Pakistan's atomic bomb project, and instituted industrialization and deregulation, helping Pakistan's economy become the fastest-growing in South Asia, overseeing the highest GDP growth in the country's history.

Islamization of Pakistan

The "primary" policy or "centerpiece" of Zia's government was "Sharization" or "Islamization".

In 1977, prior to the coup, the drinking and selling of wine by Muslims, along with nightclubs, and horse racing was banned by Prime Minister Bhutto in an effort to stem the tide of street Islamization. Zia went much further, committing himself to enforce Nizam-e-Mustafa ("Rule of the prophet" or Islamic System, i.e. establishing an Islamic state and sharia law), a significant turn from Pakistan's predominantly secular law, inherited from the British.

In his first televised speech to the country as head of state Zia declared that Pakistan which was created in the name of Islam will continue to survive only if it sticks to Islam. That is why I consider the introduction of [an] Islamic system as an essential prerequisite for the country.

In the past he complained, "Many a ruler did what they pleased in the name of Islam."

Zia established "Sharia Benches" in each High Court (later the Federal Sharia Court) to judge legal cases using the teachings of the Quran and the Sunna, and to bring Pakistan's legal statutes into alignment with Islamic doctrine. Zia bolstered the influence of the ulama (Islamic clergy) and the Islamic parties. 10,000s of activists from the Jamaat-e-Islami party were appointed to government posts to ensure the continuation of his agenda after his passing. Conservative ulama (Islamic scholars) were added to the Council of Islamic Ideology.

Islamization was a sharp change from Bhutto's original philosophical rationale captured in the slogan, "Food, clothing, and shelter". In Zia's view, socialist economics and a secular-socialist orientation served only to upset Pakistan's natural order and weaken its moral fiber. General Zia defended his policies in an interview in 1979 given to British journalist Ian Stephens:

The basis of Pakistan was Islam. … Muslims of the subcontinent are a separate culture. It was on the Two-Nation Theory that this part was carved out of the Subcontinent as Pakistan…. Mr. Bhutto's way of flourishing in this Society was by eroding its moral fiber. … by pitching students against teachers, children against their parents, landlord against tenants, workers against mill owners. [Pakistan has economic difficulties] because Pakistanis have been made to believe that one can earn without working. … We are going back to Islam not by choice but by the force of circumstances. It is not I or my government that is imposing Islam. It was what 99 percent of people wanted; the street violence against Bhutto reflected the people's desire …

– General Zia-ul-Haq,

Hudood Ordinance

In one of his first and most controversial measures to Islamize Pakistani society was the replacement of parts of the Pakistan Penal Code (PPC) with the 1979 "Hudood Ordinance." (Hudood meaning limits or restrictions, as in limits of acceptable behavior in Islamic law.) The Ordinance added new criminal offences of adultery and fornication to Pakistani law, and new punishments of whipping, amputation, and stoning to death.

For theft or robbery, the PPC punishments of imprisonment or fine, or both, were replaced by amputation of the right hand of the offender for theft, and amputation of the right hand and left foot for robbery. For Zina (extramarital sex) the provisions relating to adultery were replaced by the Ordinance with punishments of flogged 100 lashes for those unmarried offenders, and stoning to death for married offenders.

All these punishments were dependent on proof required for hadd being met. In practice the Hudd requirement—four Muslim men of good repute testifying as witness to the crime—was seldom met. As of 2014, no offenders have been stoned or had limbs amputated by the Pakistani judicial system. To be found guilty of theft, zina, or drinking alcohol by less strict tazir standards—where the punishment was flogging and/or imprisonment—was common, and there have been many floggings.

Islamic Law

Under Zia, the order for women to cover their heads while in public was implemented in public schools, colleges and state television. Women's participation in sports and the performing arts was severely restricted. Following Sharia law, women's legal testimony was given half the weight of a man's, according to critics.

In 1981 interest payments were replaced by "profit and loss" accounts (though profit was thought to be simply interest by another name). Textbooks were overhauled to remove un-Islamic material, and un-Islamic books were removed from libraries.

Blasphemy ordinances

To outlaw blasphemy, the Pakistan Penal Code (PPC) and the Criminal Procedure Code (CrPC) were amended through ordinances in 1980, 1982 and 1986. The 1980 law prohibited derogatory remarks against Islamic personages, and carried a three-year prison sentence. In 1982 the small Ahmadiyya religious minority were prohibited from saying or implying they were Muslims. In 1986 declaring anything implying disrespect to the Islamic prophet Muhammad, Ahl al-Bayt (family members of Muhammad), Sahabah (companions of Muhammad) or Sha'ar-i-Islam (Islamic symbols) was made a cognisable offence, punishable with imprisonment or fine, or both.

This is the Law which is largely used even today against the minorities to eliminate them in Pakistan.

Madrassa expansions

Traditional religious madrassas in Pakistan received state sponsorship for the first time, under the General Zia-ul-Haq's administration, their number grew from 893 to 2,801. Most were Deobandi in doctrinal orientation, while one quarter of them were Barelvi. They received funding from Zakat councils and provided free religious training, room and board to impoverished Pakistanis. The schools, which banned televisions and radios, have been criticised by authors for stoking sectarian hatred both between Muslim sects and against non-Muslims.

In a 1979 address to the nation, Zia decried the Western culture and music in the country. Soon afterwards, PTV, the national television network ceased playing music videos and only patriotic songs were broadcast. New taxes were levied on the film industry and most of the cinemas in Lahore were shut down. New tax rates were introduced, further decreasing cinema attendances.

On 29 May 1988, Zia dissolved the National Assembly and removed the Prime Minister under article 58(2)b of the amended Constitution. Apart from many other reasons, Prime Minister Junejo's decision to sign the Geneva Accord against the wishes of Zia, and his open declarations of removing any military personnel found responsible for an explosion at a munitions dump at Ojhri Camp, on the outskirts of army headquarters in Rawalpindi, earlier in the year, proved to be some of the major factors responsible for his removal. Relations with India worsened amid the Siachen conflict and accusations that Pakistan was aiding the Khalistan movement.

Zia promised to hold elections in 1988 after the dismissal of Junejo government. He said that he would hold elections within the next 90 days. The late Zulfikar Ali Bhutto's daughter Benazir Bhutto had returned from exile earlier in 1986, and had announced that she would be contesting the elections. With Bhutto's popularity somewhat growing, and a decrease in international aid following the Soviet withdrawal from Afghanistan, Zia was in an increasingly difficult political situation.

Zia died in a plane crash on 17 August 1988. After witnessing a US M1 Abrams tank demonstration in Bahawalpur, Zia had left the city in the Punjab province by C-130B Hercules aircraft. The aircraft departed from Bahawalpur Airport and was expected to reach Islamabad International Airport. Shortly after a smooth takeoff, the control tower lost contact with the aircraft. Witnesses who saw the plane in the air afterward claim it was flying erratically, then nosedived and exploded on impact. In addition to Zia, 31 others died in the plane crash, including chairman Joint Chiefs of Staff Committee General Akhtar Abdur Rahman, close associate of Zia, Brigadier Siddique Salik, the American ambassador to Pakistan Arnold Lewis Raphel and General Herbert M. Wassom, the head of the US military aid mission to Pakistan. Ghulam Ishaq Khan, the

Senate chairman announced Zia's death on radio and TV. Conditions surrounding his death have given rise to many conspiracy theories. There is speculation that Israel's Mossad, the United States, India, the Soviet Union (in retaliation for Pakistani support of the mujahideen in Afghanistan) or an alliance of them and internal groups within Zia's military were behind the incident.

A board of inquiry was set up to investigate the crash. It concluded 'the most probable cause of the crash was a criminal act of sabotage perpetrated in the aircraft'. It also suggested that poisonous gases were released which incapacitated the passengers and crew, which would explain why no Mayday signal was given. There was also speculation into other facts involving the details of the investigation. A flight recorder (black box) was not located after the crash even though previous C-130 aircraft did have them installed.

Maj. Gen. (retd) Mahmud Ali Durrani, who was suspected by many circles within Pakistan and also by then United States ambassador to India, John Gunther Dean, for being "extraordinarily insistent" with President Zia to visit the demonstration, is considered to be the prime suspect in the incident. He claimed later that reports of Israeli and Indian involvement in Zia's plane crash were only speculations.

Prime Ministers

Muhammad Junejo

Muhammad Khan Junejo (18 August 1932–18 March 1993) was a Pakistani politician and statesman who served as the tenth prime minister of Pakistan from 1985 to 1988 under president Muhammad Zia-ul-Haq.

In January 1985, President Zia-ul-Haq announced to hold nationwide general elections that would be based on non-partisanism– there have been political rumors that the U.S. President Ronald Reagan had a subsequent political role in such regards.

Junejo was successful in defending his constituency from the Sanghar District and was known to be a religiopolitical missionary of Pir Pagara who had been leading his own political faction in Sindh. President Zia considered three names for the appointment of the Prime Minister that included: Ghulam Mustafa Jatoi, Liaquat Ali Jatoi and Junejo– all were from Sindh. After consulting with Pir Pagara, President Zia hand-picked and appointed Junejo as Prime Minister through an invitation to form the civilian government in accordance to the revival of constitution.

His mindset reflected a conservatism and was a powerful feudalist whom President Zia considered him to be ineffective in leading towards the decision-making processes and after securing votes in the Parliament through the Vote of Confidence (VoC), he met with President Zia and reportedly asking him about the ending of the martial law.

The martial law was eventually lifted on his repeated instances and announced his cabinet which saw the ouster of many of President Zia's military members in the civilian cabinet. He kept two ministerial departments of defence and interior.

Prime Minister Junejo's social policies led to the political independence when he was appointed as the President of Pakistan Muslim League. His policy also included the freedom of the press despite the opposition he faced from President Zia in this issue. He gained popularity for his daring stance and disagreement with Zia over a number of issues.

On the economic front, he took the austerity measures and ultimately halted the Islamization of Economy process ran under the Zia regime, which put him at odds with President Zia.

In 1986–87, his political relations with President Zia began to deteriorate over the control of foreign policy. Against Zia's wishes Junejo authorized his Foreign Minister Yakob Ali Khan to ratify the Geneva Accords that allowed the Russian retreat from Afghanistan.

Prime Minister Junejo also stalled the fundamentalist legislation in an attempt to keep leverage on President Zia. Following the massive explosion near the hidden Ojhri camp facility in Rawalpindi Cantonment that resulted in more than 100 lives lost, Prime Minister Junejo announced to call for a parliamentary inquiry to overlook the incident.

On 28 May 1988, DG ISPR Brigadier Siddique Salik informed Prime Minister Junejo of President Zia holding the press conference the next day in this regard, terming it "very important." On 29 May 1988, President Zia appeared on PTV News and surprisingly announced to have dissolved the Parliament, using the Eighth Amendment.

During the general elections held in 1988, he was unsuccessful for defending his constituency but was elected for the National Assembly general elections held in 1990 and remained head of the PML.

In 1993, he was diagnosed with leukemia and went to the United States for the treatment where he was treated at the Johns Hopkins Hospital in Baltimore, Maryland, United States, where he died the same year. He was brought and buried in his locality.

His widow, Begum Junejo, died in Karachi on July 13, 2003, at the age of 60.

Benazir Bhutto

Benazir Bhutto (21 June 1953 – 27 December 2007) was a Pakistani politician and stateswoman who served as the 11th and 13th prime minister of Pakistan from 1988 to 1990 and again from 1993 to 1996. She was the first woman elected to head a democratic government in a Muslim-majority country. Ideologically a liberal and a secularist, she chaired or co-chaired the Pakistan People's Party (PPP) from the early 1980s until her assassination in 2007.

Bhutto's first cabinet was the largest in Pakistan's history. She appointed herself as the new treasury minister, with her mother as a senior minister without portfolio, and her father-in-law as chairman of the parliamentary public accounts committee, quashing hopes that her administration would depart from the entrenched systems of cronyism in the country. Most of those in the administration had little political experience. Various members of the PPP old guard, including Mumtaz Ali Bhutto, left the party in frustration at the pro-capitalist direction she had taken.

Among the problems facing Pakistan when Bhutto took the Premiership was soaring high unemployment. The Pakistani government was bankrupt, with Zia having borrowed at high-interest rates to pay government wages. Many of the policy promises she had made in her election campaign were not delivered because the Pakistani state was unable to finance them; she had claimed that a million new homes would be built each year and that universal free education and healthcare would be introduced, none of which was economically feasible for her government to deliver. The country also faced a growing problem with the illegal narcotics trade, with Pakistan being among the world's largest heroin exporters and the drug's use rapidly increasing domestically. Bhutto pledged that she would take tough action on the powerful drug barons.

In April 1989, opposition parties organised a parliamentary no-confidence vote in Bhutto's leadership, but it was defeated by 12 votes. Bhutto claimed that many National Assembly voters had been bribed to vote against her, with $10 million having been supplied for this by a Saudi Salafi cleric, Osama bin Laden, who sought to overthrow her government and replace it with an Islamic theocracy. Her conservative critics continued to claim it was un-Islamic for a woman to govern, and unsuccessfully tried to have Pakistan suspended from the international Organisation of Islamic Cooperation on this basis.

During her first premiership, Bhutto went on a number of foreign trips, enhancing her image as the first female Prime Minister in the Islamic world. In these, she sought to attract foreign investment and aid for Pakistan. She also made efforts to cultivate good relationships with the leaders of Islamic countries who also had good relationships with her father, including Libya's Gaddafi, Abu Dhabi's Sheikh Zayed, and the Saudi royal family. In 1989, she attended the Commonwealth Heads of Government Meeting in Kuala Lumpur, where Pakistan was re-admitted to the Commonwealth of Nations. In January 1989, she made a second pilgrimage to Mecca, and in June visited the U.S. to address both houses of Congress and giving the commencement speech at Harvard.

As Premier, Bhutto was reluctant to challenge the ISI's support for the Islamist mujahideen forces in Afghanistan which were then engaged in a civil war against the country's Marxist–Leninist government. The U.S. was funneling money to these mujahedeen through Pakistan, although preferred to deal directly with Beg, Gul, and Ishaq Khan rather than through Bhutto. In April 1989, Gul led an invasion of Afghanistan with the purpose of seizing Jalalabad, which was then to be formed into a capital from which the country's anti-Soviet, Islamist-dominated opposition forces could operate. When the operation failed and the Pakistanis were driven out by the Afghan Army, Gul blamed Bhutto's administration for the failure, claiming that someone in her entourage had leaked details of the mission to the Afghan government. Gul was too powerful for Bhutto to force him into retirement, but in May 1989 she transferred him from the ISI to another section of the military, placing a more trusted military figure in his role.

India and the nuclear bomb

Bhutto initially attempted to improve relations with neighbouring India, withdrawing Zia's offer of a no-war pact and announcing the 1972 Simla Agreement as the basis of future relations. She invited Indian Prime Minister Rajiv Gandhi and his wife Sonia as her guests for a three-day visit in Islamabad following the South Asian Association for Regional Cooperation summit. Rajiv returned on a bilateral visit six months later. She pleased him by revoking Zia's offer of the Nishan-e-Pakistan award to the former Indian leader Morarji Desai. The two countries agreed to reduce their military levels along the border and agreed not to attack their respective nuclear installations. Bhutto claimed that she terminated support for Sikh separatists active in India, something which Zia had encouraged to destabilise Indian control in their half of the Punjab. This warming of relations angered many domestic Islamist and conservative forces; they alleged that she was secretly an Indian agent, and also placed renewed emphasis on the fact that Bhutto's paternal grandmother had been born to a Hindu family.

After accusations of being too conciliatory towards India, Bhutto took a harder line against them, particularly on the Kashmir conflict. In 1990, Major General Pervez Musharraf proposed a military invasion of Kargil as part of an attempt to annex Kashmir; Bhutto refused to back the plan, believing that the international condemnation would be severe.

After Bhutto became Prime Minister, President Khan and the military were reluctant to tell her about Pakistan's nuclear program, and it remains unknown how much Bhutto knew about the issue during her first term in office. She later related that to find out more she contacted key scientists in the program, such as A. Q. Khan, herself, bypassing the president and military hierarchy. On her trip to the United States, she told Congress that "we do not possess, nor do we intend to make, a nuclear device". While in Washington D.C., she met with CIA director William Webster, who showed her a mock-up of the Pakistani nuclear weapon and stated his opinion that research the project it had reached a crescendo in the final years of Zia's government. William's revelations came as a shock to Bhutto, who was unaware of how advanced Pakistan's nuclear development had become. The United States wanted to prevent Pakistan from creating such a device, and President George H. W. Bush informed her that U.S. military aid to the country would cease unless Pakistan refrained from producing nuclear bomb cores, the final step in creating the weapon. Between January and March 1989, she authorised cold tests of nuclear weaponry, without fissionable material, although this did not satisfy the military authorities. In 1990, shortly before leaving office, the American Ambassador Robert Oakley informed her that information obtained by U.S. satellites indicated that her commitment to not produce weapons-grade uranium had been breached at the Kahuta enrichment plant.

Tales of corruption in public-sector industries began to surface, which undermined the credibility of Bhutto. The unemployment and labour strikes began to take place which halted and jammed the economic wheel of the country, and Bhutto was unable to solve these issues due to the cold war with the President. In August 1990, Khan dismissed Bhutto's government under the Eighth Amendment of the constitution. He claimed that this was necessary owing to her government's corruption and inability to maintain law and order. A caretaker government under the control of former PPP member Ghulam Mustafa Jatoi was sworn in, with Khan declaring a state of national emergency.

The proxy war started by Pakistan against India was the starting of Terrorist activities all over the world on a large scale. Pakistan has always been in a denial mode disowning the terrorists. These terrorist groups had different names, like LeT. If the group was black listed, the name of the group will be changed. Pak and LeT are two sides of the same coin. Similarly Hizbollah and Iran. (Two sides of the same coin), and many more.

Pakistan at the 1972 Summer Olympics

Pakistan competed at the 1972 Summer Olympics in Munich, West Germany. **The men's hockey team won a silver medal.**

Pakistan at the 1976 Summer Olympics

Pakistan competed at the 1976 Summer Olympics in Montreal, Canada. **The men's hockey team won a bronze medal.**

4

(1980-1990)

INDIA - 1983 Cricket World Cup - Assassination of Indira Gandhi - Bhopal disaster - Air India Flight 182 hijacking - Mohd. Ahmed Khan v. Shah Bano Begum Case - Bofors scandal - Rajiv Gandhi - Mufti Mohammad Sayeed - Kashmiri Pandits

PAKISTAN – Presidents - Ghulam Ishaq Khan - Wasim Sajjad (acting) - Farooq Leghari - Muhammad Rafiq Tarar - Prime Ministers - Nawaz Sharif - 1984 Summer Olympics - 1988 Summer Olympics

INDIA

1983 Cricket World Cup

The 1983 Cricket World Cup (officially the Prudential Cup '83) was the 3rd edition of the Cricket World Cup tournament. It was held from 9 to 25 June 1983 in England and Wales and was won by India. Eight countries participated in the event. England, India, Pakistan and West Indies qualified for the semi-finals. The preliminary matches were played in two groups of four teams each, and each country played the others in its group twice. The top two teams in each group qualified for the semi-finals.

The matches consisted of 60 overs per innings and were played in traditional white clothing and with red balls. They were all played during the day.

Indian Team was considered as a black horse and not considered as champions by any of the experts in the beginning of tournament. Even when the final match started between West Indies and India no body was willing to accept or consider India as the Winner of the World Cup.

Assassination of Indira Gandhi

Indian Prime Minister Indira Gandhi was assassinated at 9:30 a.m. on 31 October 1984 at her residence in Safdarjung Road, New Delhi. She was killed by her bodyguards Satwant Singh and Beant Singh in the aftermath of Operation Blue Star, an Indian military action carried out between 1 and 8 June 1984 ordered by Indira Gandhi to remove Jarnail Singh Bhindranwale and his followers from the Golden Temple of Harmandir Sahib in Amritsar, Punjab. The collateral damage included the death of many pilgrims, as well as damage to the Akal Takht. The military action on the sacred temple was criticized both inside and outside India.

Operation Blue Star

Operation Blue Star was a large Indian military operation carried out between 1 and 8 June 1984, ordered by Indira Gandhi to remove leader Jarnail Singh Bhindranwale and his militant Sikh followers from the buildings of the Harmandir Sahib complex in Amritsar, Punjab. The Indian Army suffered around 83 casualties with 700 injuries, and 450–500 Sikh rebels were killed during the operation. The handling of the operation, damage to the holy shrine, and loss of military and civilian life on both sides led to widespread criticism of the Indian government.

The perceived threat to Gandhi's life increased after the operation. Accordingly, Sikhs were removed from her personal bodyguard detail by the Intelligence Bureau for fear of assassination. Gandhi thought that this would reinforce her anti-Sikh image among the public, however, and she ordered the Delhi Police to reinstate her Sikh bodyguards, including Beant Singh, who was reported to be her personal favorite.

Assassination

At about 9:20 a.m. Indian Standard Time, on 31 October 1984, Gandhi was on her way to be interviewed by British actor Peter Ustinov, who was filming a documentary for Irish television. She was accompanied by Constable

Narayan Singh, personal security officer Rameshwar Dayal and Gandhi's personal secretary, R. K. Dhawan. She was walking through the garden of the Prime Minister's Residence at No. 1 Safdarjung Road in New Delhi towards the neighboring 1 Akbar Road office.

Gandhi passed a wicket gate guarded by Satwant and Beant Singh, and the two men opened fire. Beant fired three rounds into her abdomen from his .38 (9.7 mm) revolver; then Satwant fired 30 rounds from his Sterling sub-machine gun after she had fallen to the ground. Both men then threw down their weapons and Beant said, "I have done what I had to do. You do what you want to do." In the next six minutes, Border Police officers Tarsem Singh Jamwal and Ram Saran captured and killed Beant, while Satwant was arrested by Gandhi's other bodyguards and an accomplice trying to escape; he was seriously wounded. Satwant Singh was tried, convicted, and sentenced to death for killing Gandhi. He was hanged in 1989, along with accomplice Kehar Singh.

Salma Sultan gave the first news of the assassination of Gandhi on Doordarshan's evening news on 31 October 1984, more than ten hours after she was killed. It is alleged by the Indian government that Gandhi's secretary R. K. Dhawan overruled intelligence and security officials who had ordered the removal of policemen as a security threat, including her assassins.

Gandhi was taken to the All India Institute of Medical Sciences, New Delhi at 9:30 a.m. Doctors operated on her. She was declared dead at 2:20 p.m. The postmortem examination was conducted by a team of doctors headed by Tirath Das Dogra, who stated that 30 bullets had struck Gandhi from a Sterling sub-machine gun and a revolver. The assailants had fired 33 bullets at her, of which 30 had hit; 23 had passed through her body, while seven remained inside. Dogra extracted bullets to establish the identity of the weapons and to correlate each weapon with the bullets recovered by ballistic examination. The bullets were matched to the weapons at CFSL Delhi.

The Indian government ordered a national mourning from November 1 to November 12 with flags half-masted and canceled entertainment and cultural events and offices closed for several days. Pakistan declared three days of mourning and Bulgaria declared a day of national mourning.

Funeral

Gandhi's body was taken in a gun carriage through Delhi roads on the morning of 1 November to Teen Murti Bhavan, where her father stayed and where she lay in state. She was cremated with full state honors on 3 November near Raj Ghat, a memorial to Mahatma Gandhi, at an area named Shakti Sthal. Her elder son and successor, Rajiv Gandhi, lit the pyre.

Prime Minister Indira Gandhi's death was a great shock to the nation.

Bhopal disaster

The Bhopal disaster or Bhopal gas tragedy was a chemical accident on the night of 2–3 December 1984 at the Union Carbide India Limited (UCIL) pesticide plant in Bhopal, Madhya Pradesh, India. Considered the world's worst industrial disaster, over 500,000 people in the small towns around the plant were exposed to the highly toxic gas methyl isocyanate (MIC). Estimates vary on the death toll, with the official number of immediate deaths being 2,259. In 2008, the Government of Madhya Pradesh paid compensation to the family members of 3,787 victims killed in the gas release, and to 574,366 injured victims. A government affidavit in 2006 stated that the leak caused 558,125 injuries, including 38,478 temporary partial injuries and approximately 3,900 severely and permanently disabling injuries. Others estimate that 8,000 died within two weeks, and another 8,000 or more have since died from gas-related diseases.

The owner of the factory, UCIL, was majority owned by the Union Carbide Corporation (UCC) of the United States, with Indian government-controlled banks and the Indian public holding a 49.1 percent stake. In 1989, UCC paid $470 million (equivalent to $907 million in 2021) to settle litigation stemming from the disaster. In 1994, UCC sold its stake in UCIL to Eveready Industries India Limited (EIIL), which subsequently merged with McLeod Russel (India) Ltd. Eveready ended clean-up on the site in 1998, when it terminated its 99-year lease and turned over control of the site to the state government of Madhya Pradesh. Dow Chemical Company purchased UCC in 2001, seventeen years after the disaster.

Civil and criminal cases filed in the United States against UCC and Warren Anderson, chief executive officer of the UCC at the time of the disaster, were dismissed and redirected to Indian courts on multiple occasions between 1986 and 2012, as the US courts focused on UCIL being a standalone entity of India. Civil and criminal cases were also filed in the District Court of Bhopal, India, involving UCC, UCIL, and Anderson. In June 2010, seven Indian nationals who were UCIL employees in 1984, including the former UCIL chairman Keshub Mahindra, were convicted in Bhopal of causing death by negligence and sentenced to two years' imprisonment and a fine of about $2,000 each, the maximum punishment allowed by Indian law. All were released on bail shortly after the verdict.

Air India Flight 182

Air India Flight 182 was an Air India flight operating on the Montreal–London–Delhi–Bombay route. On 23 June 1985, it was operated using Boeing 747-237B registered VT-EFO. It disintegrated in mid-air en route from Montreal to London, at an altitude of 31,000 feet (9,400 m) over the Atlantic Ocean, as a result of an explosion from a bomb. The remnants of the airliner fell into the ocean approximately 190 kilometres (120 miles) off the coast of Ireland, killing all 329 people aboard, including 268 Canadian citizens, 27 British citizens, and 24 Indian citizens. The bombing of Air India Flight 182 is the worst terrorist attack in Canadian history, the deadliest aviation incident in the history of Air India, and was the world's deadliest act of aviation terrorism until the September 11 attacks in 2001.

According to investigators, the bombing of Air India Flight 182 was part of a larger transnational terrorist plot which included a plan to bomb two Air India planes. The first bomb was meant to explode aboard Air India Flight 301, which was scheduled to take off from Narita International Airport, Japan, but it exploded before it was loaded onto the plane. This bomb detonated early, killing two baggage handlers, because perpetrators failed to take into account that Japan does not observe daylight saving time. The second bomb planted aboard Air India Flight 182 in Canada was successful. It was later revealed that both the conspiracy and the bombs, which were stashed inside luggage, originated in Canada. The plan's execution had transnational consequences and involved citizens and governments from five nation states. The Babbar Khalsa separatist group was implicated in the bombings.

Mohd. Ahmed Khan v. Shah Bano Begum Case

In 1932, Shah Bano, a Muslim woman, was married to Mohammed Ahmad Khan, an affluent and well-known advocate in Indore, Madhya Pradesh, and had five children from the marriage. After 14 years, Khan took a younger woman as his second wife. Then after years of living with both wives, he divorced Shah Bano when she was 62 years old. In April 1978, when Khan stopped giving her the ₹200 per month he had apparently promised, claiming that she had no means to support herself and her children, she filed a criminal suit at a local court in Indore, against her husband under section 125 of the Code of Criminal Procedure, asking him for a maintenance amount of ₹500 for herself and her children. In November 1978 her husband gave an irrevocable talaq (divorce) to her which was his prerogative under Islamic law and took up the defence that hence Bano had ceased to be his wife and therefore he was under no obligation to provide maintenance for her as except prescribed under the Islamic law which was in total ₹5,400. In August 1979, the local court directed Khan to pay a sum of ₹25 per month to Bano by way of maintenance. On 1 July 1980, on a revisional application of Bano, the High Court of Madhya Pradesh enhanced the amount of maintenance to ₹179.20 per month. Khan then filed a petition to appeal before the Supreme Court claiming that Shah Bano is not his responsibility anymore because Mr. Khan had a second marriage which is also permitted under Islamic Law.

Opinion of Supreme Court

On 3 February 1981, the two judge bench composed of Justice Murtaza Fazal Ali and A. Varadarajan who first heard the matter, in light of the earlier decisions of the court which had held that section 125 of the Code applies to Muslims also, referred Khan's appeal to a larger Bench. Muslim bodies All India Muslim Personal Law Board and Jamiat Ulema-e-Hind joined the case as intervenor. The matter was then heard by a five-judge bench composed of Chief Justice Chandrachud, Rangnath Misra, D. A. Desai, O. Chinnappa Reddy, and E. S. Venkataramiah. On 23 April 1985, Supreme Court in a unanimous decision, dismissed the appeal and confirmed the judgment of the High Court.

Supreme Court concluded that "there is no conflict between the provisions of section 125 and those of the Muslim Personal Law on the question of the Muslim husband's obligation to provide maintenance for a divorced wife who is unable to maintain herself." After referring to the Quran, holding it to the greatest authority on the subject, it held that there was no doubt that the Quran imposes an obligation on the Muslim husband to make provision for or to provide maintenance to the divorced wife. Shah Bano approached the courts for securing maintenance from her husband. When the case reached the Supreme Court of India, seven years had elapsed. The Supreme Court invoked Section 125 of Code of Criminal Procedure, which applies to everyone regardless of caste, creed, or religion. It ruled that Shah Bano be given maintenance money, similar to alimony.

The Court also regretted that article 44 of the Constitution of India in relation to bringing of Uniform Civil Code in India remained a dead letter and held that a common civil code will help the cause of national integration by removing disparate loyalties to laws which have conflicting ideologies.

Movement against the judgment

The Shah Bano judgment, as claimed, became the centre of raging controversy, with the press turning it into a major national issue. The Shah Bano judgment elicited a protest from many sections of Muslims who also took to the streets against what they saw, and what they were led to believe, was an attack on their religion and their right to their own religious personal laws. Some Muslims felt threatened by what they perceived as an encroachment on the Muslim Personal Law, and protested loudly at the judgment. The spokesmen for some were the Barelvi leader Obaidullah Khan Azmi and Syed Kazi. At the forefront was All India Muslim Personal Law Board, an organization formed in 1973 devoted to upholding what they saw as Sharia (Muslim Personal Law).

Dilution of the effect of the judgment

In the 1984 Indian general election, Indian National Congress had won absolute majority in the parliament. After the Shah Bano judgment, many leaders in the Indian National Congress suggested to the Prime Minister of India, Rajiv Gandhi that if the government did not enact a law in Parliament overturning the Supreme Court judgement, the Congress would face decimation in the polls ahead.

In 1986, the Parliament of India passed an act titled The Muslim Women (Protection of Rights on Divorce) Act, 1986, that nullified the Supreme Court's judgment in the Shah Bano judgment. Diluting the Supreme Court judgment, the act allowed maintenance to a divorced woman only during the period of iddat, or till 90 days after the divorce, according to the provisions of Islamic law. This was in stark contrast to Section 125 of the Code. The 'liability' of husband to pay the maintenance was thus restricted to the period of the iddat only."

The "Statement of Objects and Reasons" of the act stated that "the Shah Bano decision had led to some controversy as to the obligation of the Muslim husband to pay maintenance to the divorced wife and hence opportunity was therefore taken to specify the rights which a Muslim divorced woman is entitled to at the time of divorce and to protect her interests."

Reactions to the act

The law received severe criticism from several sections of the society. The Opposition called it another act of "appeasement" towards the minority community by the Indian National Congress. The All India Democratic Women's Association (AIDWA) organised demonstrations of Muslim women against the move to deprive them of rights that they had hitherto shared with the Hindus.

The Bharatiya Janata Party regarded it as an 'appeasement' of the Muslim community and discriminatory to non-Muslim men and saw it as a "violation of the sanctity of the country's highest court". The 'Muslim Women (Protection of Rights on Divorce) Act' was seen as discriminatory as it denied divorced Muslim women the right to basic maintenance which women of other faiths had access to under secular law. Lawyer and former law minister of India, Ram Jethmalani has termed the act as "retrogressive obscurantism for short-term minority populism". Rajiv

Gandhi's colleague Arif Mohammad Khan who was INC member and a minister in Gandhi's cabinet resigned from the post and party in protest.

Critics of the Act point out that while divorce is within the purview of personal laws, maintenance is not, and thus it is discriminatory to exclude Muslim women from a civil law. Exclusion of non-Muslim men from a law that appears inherently beneficial to men is also pointed out by them. Hindu nationalists have repeatedly contended that a separate Muslim code is tantamount to preferential treatment and demanded a uniform civil code.

To deprive the divorced Muslim woman from getting any financial help legally from her husband by making a law with retrospective effect was the greatest blunder of the Govt and is clearly seen as an appeasement effort towards Muslims to maintain Congress Party's vote bank.

Bofors scandal

The Bofors scandal was a major weapons-contract political scandal that occurred between India and Sweden during the 1980s and 1990s, initiated by Indian National Congress politicians and implicating the Indian prime minister, Rajiv Gandhi, and several other members of the Indian and Swedish governments who were accused of receiving kickbacks from Bofors AB, an arms manufacturer principally financed by the Wallenberg family's Skandinaviska Enskilda Banken, for winning a bid to supply to India their 155 mm field howitzer. The scandal relates to illegal kickbacks paid in a US$1.4-billion deal between the Swedish arms manufacturer Bofors with the government of India for the sale of 410 field howitzer guns, and a supply contract almost twice that amount. It was the biggest arms deal ever in Sweden, and money marked for development projects was diverted to secure this contract at any cost. The investigations revealed flouting of rules and bypassing of institutions.

On 16 April 1987, a Swedish radio station broke out a story based on a whistleblower in the Swedish police, alleging that the reputed Swedish artillery manufacturer Bofors had paid kickbacks to people in several countries, including Sweden and India, to secure a ₹15 billion (equivalent to ₹200 billion or US$2.5 billion in 2023) contract. This had been done the previous year for a deal to supply 410 155 mm calibre howitzer guns for the Indian army. However, none of the newspapers in India were aware of this. In May 1987, a broadcast by a Swedish radio station revealed that bribes of ₹600 million (equivalent to ₹8.1 billion or US$100 million in 2023) had been paid by Bofors to Indian politicians, members of the Congress party and bureaucrats. This was picked up by a young journalist from The Hindu, Chitra Subramaniam, who happened to be in Sweden at that time, covering another story. The scale of the corruption was far worse than any that Sweden and India had seen before and directly led to the defeat of Gandhi's ruling Indian National Congress party in the November 1989 general elections. The Swedish company paid ₹640 million (US$8.0 million) in kickbacks to top Indian politicians and key defence officials.

The case came into light during Vishwanath Pratap Singh's tenure as defence minister, and was revealed through investigative journalism tipped off by a Reuters news revelation on Swedish radio, followed up by a team led by N. Ram of the newspaper The Hindu. The journalist who secured the over 350 documents that detailed the payoffs was Chitra Subramaniam reporting for The Hindu. Later the articles were published in The Indian Express and The Statesman when The Hindu stopped publishing stories about the Bofors scandal under immense government pressure and Chitra Subramaniam moved to the two newspapers. In an interview with her, published in The Hoot in April 2012 on the 25th anniversary of the revelations, Sten Lindström, former chief of Swedish police, discussed why he leaked the documents to her and the role of whistle-blowers in a democracy.

Rajiv Gandhi

Rajiv Gandhi (20 August 1944 – 21 May 1991) was an Indian politician who served as the 6th Prime Minister of India from 1984 to 1989. He took office after the assassination of his mother, then–prime minister Indira Gandhi, to become the youngest Indian prime minister at the age of 40. During his tenure, Gandhi introduced several initiatives and policies aimed at modernising India and promoting economic development. He emphasised technology, computerisation, and telecommunications, launching the "Vision 2020" program to transform India into a technologically advanced nation.

Gandhi was not related to the world-famous Mahatma Gandhi. Instead, he was from the politically powerful Nehru–Gandhi family, which had been associated with the Indian National Congress party. For much of his childhood, his maternal grandfather Jawaharlal Nehru was prime minister. Gandhi attended the elite all-boys' boarding The Doon School, Dehradun, and the University of Cambridge in the United Kingdom. He returned to India in 1966 and became a professional pilot for the state-owned Indian Airlines. In 1968, he married Sonia Maino; the couple settled in Delhi for a domestic life with their children Rahul and Priyanka. For much of the 1970s, his mother was prime minister and his brother Sanjay an MP; despite this, Gandhi remained apolitical. After Sanjay died in a plane crash in 1980, Gandhi reluctantly entered politics at the behest of his mother. The following year he won his brother's Parliamentary seat of Amethi and became a member of the Lok Sabha— the lower house of India's Parliament. As part of his political grooming, Rajiv was made general secretary of the Congress party and given significant responsibility in organising the 1982 Asian Games.

On the morning of 31 October 1984, his mother (the then prime minister) was assassinated by her two Sikh bodyguards Satwant Singh and Beant Singh in the aftermath of Operation Blue Star, an Indian military action to remove Sikh separatist activists from the Golden temple of the Harmandir Sahib. Later that day, Gandhi was appointed prime minister. His leadership was tested over the next few days as organised mobs of Congress supporters rioted against the Sikh community, resulting in anti-Sikh massacres in Delhi. Sources estimate the number of Sikh deaths at about 8,000–17,000. That December, the Congress party won the largest Lok Sabha majority to date, 411 seats out of 542. Gandhi's period in office was mired in controversies; perhaps the greatest crises were the Bhopal disaster, Bofors scandal and Mohd. Ahmed Khan v. Shah Bano Begum. Soon after the installation of Gul Shah as chief minister in Jammu and Kashmir, the 1986 Kashmir riots erupted. In 1988, he reversed the coup in Maldives, antagonising militant Tamil groups such as PLOTE, intervening and then sending peacekeeping troops to Sri Lanka in 1987, leading to open conflict with the Liberation Tigers of Tamil Eelam (LTTE). In mid-1987, the Bofors scandal damaged his corruption-free image and resulted in a major defeat for his party in the 1989 election.

Gandhi remained Congress president until the elections in 1991. While campaigning for the elections, he was assassinated by a suicide bomber from the LTTE. His widow Sonia became the president of the Congress party in 1998 and led the party to victory in the 2004 and 2009 parliamentary elections. His son Rahul was a Member of Parliament until being disqualified in March 2023 after being convicted in a criminal defamation case and was the President of the Indian National Congress till 2019. In 1991, the Indian government posthumously awarded Gandhi the Bharat Ratna, the country's highest civilian award. At the India Leadership Conclave in 2009, the "Revolutionary Leader of Modern India" award was conferred posthumously on Gandhi.

Rajiv Gandhi was in West Bengal on 31 October 1984 when his mother, Prime Minister Indira Gandhi, was assassinated by two of her Sikh bodyguards, Satwant Singh and Beant Singh, to avenge the military attack on the Golden Temple during Operation Blue Star. Sardar Buta Singh and President Zail Singh pressed Rajiv to succeed his mother as prime minister within hours of her murder. Commenting on the anti-Sikh riots in Delhi, Rajiv Gandhi said, "When a giant tree falls, the earth below shakes"; a statement for which he was widely criticised. Many Congress politicians were accused of orchestrating the violence.

Soon after assuming office, Gandhi asked President Singh to dissolve Parliament and hold fresh elections, as the Lok Sabha had completed its five-year term. Gandhi officially became the president of the Congress party, which won a landslide victory with the largest majority in history of the Indian Parliament, giving Gandhi absolute control of government. He benefited from his youth and a general perception of being free of a background in corrupt politics. Gandhi took his oath on 31 December 1984; at 40, he was the youngest prime minister of India. Historian Meena Agarwal writes that even after taking the Prime Ministerial oath, he was a relatively unknown figure, "novice in politics" as he assumed the post after being an MP for three years.

Rajiv Gandhi's last public meeting was on 21 May 1991, at Sriperumbudur, a village approximately 40 km (25 mi) from Madras (present-day Chennai), where he was assassinated while campaigning for the Sriperumbudur Lok Sabha Congress candidate. At 10:10 pm, a woman later identified as Thenmozhi Rajaratnam – a member of the Liberation Tigers of Tamil Eelam – approached Gandhi in public and greeted him. She then bent down to touch his feet and detonated a belt laden with 700 g (1.5 lb) of RDX explosives tucked under her dress.

The explosion killed Gandhi, Rajaratnam, and at least 14 other people. The assassination was captured by a 21-year-old local photographer, whose camera and film were found at the site. The cameraman, named Haribabu, died in the blast but the camera remained intact. Gandhi's mutilated body was airlifted to the All India Institute of Medical Sciences in New Delhi for post-mortem, reconstruction and embalming.

A state funeral was held for Gandhi on 24 May 1991; it was telecast live and was attended by dignitaries from over 60 countries. He was cremated at Vir Bhumi, on the banks of the river Yamuna near the shrines of his mother Indira Gandhi, brother Sanjay Gandhi, and grandfather Jawaharlal Nehru.

Indo-Sri Lanka Accord

The Indo-Sri Lanka Peace Accord was an accord signed in Colombo on 29 July 1987, between Indian Prime Minister Rajiv Gandhi and Sri Lankan President J. R. Jayewardene. The accord was expected to resolve the Sri Lankan Civil War by enabling the thirteenth Amendment to the Constitution of Sri Lanka and the Provincial Councils Act of 1987. Under the terms of the agreement, Colombo agreed to a devolution of power to the provinces, the Sri Lankan troops were to be withdrawn to their barracks in the north and the Tamil rebels were to surrender their arms.

Importantly however, the Tamil groups, notably the Liberation Tigers of Tamil Eelam (LTTE) (which at the time was one of the strongest Tamil forces), had not been made party to the talks and initially agreed to surrender their arms to the Indian Peace Keeping Force (IPKF) only reluctantly. Within a few months however, this flared into an active confrontation. The LTTE declared their intent to continue the armed struggle for an independent Tamil Eelam and refused to disarm. The IPKF found itself engaged in a bloody police action against the LTTE. Further complicating the return to peace, a Marxist insurgency began in the south of the island.

Sending IPKF was a blunder on the part of Indian Govt. Our forces were fighting LTTE who were Tamil people. This enraged Tamils in India which ultimately resulted in the assassination of PM Rajiv Gandhi.

Great Coincidences in Indian Politics

Rajiv Gandhi had a total of 181 rallies in his entire life. In which Sonia Gandhi was also with him in 180, just not with him on the day when the last rally of Rajiv Gandhi's life took place.

The Supreme Court judgement, by Justice K. T. Thomas, confirmed that Gandhi was killed because of personal animosity by the LTTE chief Prabhakaran arising from his sending the Indian Peace Keeping Force (IPKF) to Sri Lanka and the IPKF atrocities against Sri Lankan Tamils. The Gandhi administration had already antagonised other Tamil militant organisations like PLOTE for reversing the 1988 military coup in Maldives. The judgement further cites the death of Thileepan in a hunger strike and the suicide by 12 LTTE cadres in a vessel in Oct 1987.

In the Jain Commission report, various people and agencies are named as suspects in the murder of Rajiv Gandhi. Among them, the cleric Chandraswami was suspected of involvement, including financing the assassination. Nalini Sriharan, the only surviving member of the five-member squad behind the assassination of Rajiv Gandhi, is serving life imprisonment. Arrested on 14 June 1991, she and 25 others were sentenced to death by a special court on 28 January 1998. The court confirmed the death sentences of four of the convicts, including Nalini, on 11 May 1999. Nalini was a close friend of an LTTE operative known as Sriharan alias Murugan, another convict in the case who has been sentenced to death. Nalini later gave birth to a girl, Harithra, in prison. Nalini's death sentence was commuted to life imprisonment in April 2000. Rajiv's widow, Sonia Gandhi, intervened and asked for clemency for Nalini on the grounds of the latter being a mother. Later, it was reported that Gandhi's daughter, Priyanka Gandhi Vadra, had met Nalini at Vellore Central Prison in March 2008. Nalini regrets the killing of Gandhi and said the real conspirators have not been caught yet.

The report of the Jain Commission created controversy when it accused the Tamil Nadu chief minister Karunanidhi of a role in the assassination, leading to Congress withdrawing its support for the I. K. Gujral government and fresh elections in 1998. LTTE spokesman Anton Balasingham told the Indian television channel NDTV the killing was a "great tragedy, a monumental historical tragedy which we deeply regret". A memorial called Vir Bhumi was constructed at the place of Gandhi's cremation in Delhi. In 1992, the Rajiv Gandhi National Sadbhavana Award was instituted by the Indian National Congress Party.

Since his death, 21 May has been declared Anti-Terrorism Day in India.

Mufti Mohammad Sayeed

Mufti Mohammad Sayeed (12 January 1936 – 7 January 2016) was an Indian politician who served twice as the Chief Minister of Jammu and Kashmir, during November 2002–November 2005 and March 2015–January 2016. He was also Minister of Tourism in Rajiv Gandhi's cabinet and Home Minister of India in V. P. Singh's cabinet. He started in the wing of the National Conference led by G. M. Sadiq, which later merged into the Indian National Congress. He switched to Janata Dal in 1987, eventually founding his own regional party, People's Democratic Party (PDP). The PDP continues to be a political force in Jammu and Kashmir, currently led by his daughter Mehbooba Mufti.

In 1972, Sayeed became a cabinet minister and, the president of the state Congress unit. He is said to have brought about the downfall of the Jammu & Kashmir National Conference government, which was led by Farooq Abdullah, in 1984. He joined the Rajiv Gandhi government in 1986 as Minister of Tourism. In 1987, he quit the Congress party to join V. P. Singh's Jan Morcha, which led to his becoming the first Muslim Minister for Home Affairs in the Union Cabinet of India for one year, from 1989 to 1990.

He rejoined the Congress under P. V. Narasimha Rao, which he left in 1999 along with daughter Mehbooba Mufti to form his own party, the Jammu and Kashmir Peoples Democratic Party.

Union Minister for Home Affairs

In 1989, within few days of taking office as the Union Minister for Home Affairs, his third daughter, Rubaiya, was kidnapped. She was released in exchange for the release of five terrorist. During his tenure as Home Minister of India the Exodus of Kashmiri Hindus took place.

Kashmiri Pandits

The Kashmiri Pandits (also known as Kashmiri Brahmins) are a group of Kashmiri Hindus and a part of the larger Saraswat Brahmin community of India. They belong to the Pancha Gauda Brahmin group from the Kashmir Valley, a mountainous region located within the Indian union territory of Jammu and Kashmir. Kashmiri Pandits are Hindu Kashmiris native to the Kashmir Valley, and the only remaining Hindu Kashmiris after the large-scale of conversion of the Valley's population to Islam during the medieval times. Prompted by the growth of Islamic militancy in the valley, large numbers left in the exodus of the 1990s. Even so, small numbers remain.

Exodus from Kashmir (1989–1995)

The Kashmiri Pandits had been a favoured section of the population of the valley during Dogra rule (1846–1947). 20 per cent of them left the valley as a consequence of the 1950 land reforms, and by 1981 the Pandit population amounted to 5 per cent of the total.

They began to leave in much greater numbers in the 1990s during the eruption of militancy, following persecution and threats by radical Islamists and militants. The events of 19 January 1990 were particularly vicious. On that day, mosques issued declarations that the Kashmiri Pandits were Kafirs and that the males had to leave Kashmir, convert to Islam or be killed. Those who chose to the first of these were told to leave their women behind. The Kashmiri Muslims were instructed to identify Pandit homes so they could be systematically targeted for conversion or killing.

According to a number of authors, approximately 100,000 of the total Kashmiri Pandit population of 140,000 left the valley during the

1990s. The nature of the planned exodus has remain controversial, with the involvement of then Governor Jagmohan in organising a clandestine exodus been a subject of controversy. Many of the refugee Kashmiri Pandits have been living in abject conditions in refugee camps of Jammu. The government has reported on the terrorist threats to Pandits still living in the Kashmir region.

Some Hindus across India tried to help the Pandits. Bal Thackeray from Maharashtra got seats reserved in engineering colleges for the children of these Pandits. He was one of the first persons to help them after which Punjab also followed suit.

PAKISTAN

Presidents

Ghulam Ishaq Khan

Ghulam Ishaq Khan (20 January 1915 – 27 October 2006), commonly known by his initials GIK, was a Pakistani bureaucrat, politician and statesman who served as the seventh president of Pakistan from 1988 to 1993. He previously served as Chairman of the Senate from 1985 to 1988 under president Muhammad Zia-ul-Haq, and was sworn in shortly after Zia's death.

The oldest person to serve as president, Ghulam Ishaq Khan played a hawkish role against Communist Afghanistan, while relations with the United States deteriorated following the Pressler amendment. Domestically, Khan's term faced challenges: ethnic riots flared in Karachi, and Prime Minister Benazir Bhutto accused him of frustrating her government as part of an alliance with conservative opposition leader Nawaz Sharif and the post-Zia military establishment. Khan invoked the Eighth Amendment and dismissed Benazir's government after just 20 months, on charges of rampant corruption and misgovernance. Sharif was elected Prime Minister in 1990, but Khan dismissed his government on similar charges three years later. The Supreme Court overturned the dismissal, but the gridlock ultimately led to both men resigning in 1993. He was the founder of his namesake Ghulam Ishaq Khan Institute.

Retiring from public service, Khan served as rector of the GIK Institute of Engineering Sciences and Technology in his native province, dying from pneumonia in 2006. He is viewed contentiously by Pakistani historians; he is credited with personal austerity, but criticized for wielding an autocratic presidency that ousted two governments.

Dismissal of Bhutto and Sharif governments

As economic and law and order crises deepened, Khan used the Eighth Amendment to the Constitution of Pakistan to dismiss Prime Minister Benazir Bhutto's government over corruption charges and deteriorating law and order situation and called fresh elections. After holding the general elections in 1993, he supported Nawaz Sharif as the Prime Minister and his IDA government.

Problems with Sharif arose with the issue of reversing the Eighth Amendment when Sharif tried to pass the bill. Eventually, he used the same Amendment to dismiss Sharif's government on similar charges. However, Sharif retaliated by bringing a lawsuit against him in the Supreme Court of Pakistan. President Khan's attempt to use the Eighth Amendment was deemed illegal by the Court and Sharif was reinstated as the Prime Minister. The political deadlock persisted and after the joint intervention of the judiciary and the military, both Khan and Sharif were forced to resign.

Philanthropy, retirement and death

In 1988, Khan founded the Ghulam Ishaq Khan Institute of Engineering Sciences and Technology, which runs programmes in engineering, science and technology. The university was established with the financial support from the BCCI. He invited A Q Khan who took the professorship of physics and delegated Asghar Qadir, a PAEC mathematician, to take professorship in mathematics.

He again negotiated with the PPP for the presidency but eventually dropped as a candidate in favour of Farooq Leghari in general elections held in 1993. He retired from the national politics and avoided contact with international and domestic news media. He died on 27 October 2006, after a bout of pneumonia.

Wasim Sajjad

Wasim Sajjad (born 30 March 1941) is a Pakistani conservative politician and lawyer who served as the acting president of Pakistan for two non-consecutive terms and as the Chairman of the Senate between 1988 and 1999.

Farooq Leghari

Farooq Ahmad Khan Leghari (29 May 1940 – 20 October 2010), was a Pakistani politician who served as the eighth president of Pakistan from 14 November 1993 until resigning on 2 December 1997. He was the first Baloch to be elected as President.

His credentials and "clean reputation" as opposed to politicians accused of mass corruption and white collar crimes won him the support from Prime Minister Bhutto and Pakistan Peoples Party (PPP). He accepted the nomination and ran in the presidential elections against Wasim Sajjad, the Acting President and PML(N) nominee by Nawaz Sharif.

In 1994–95, a major scandal was revealed by the sting operation led by the FIA that gained national attention. Known as the Mehrangate, Leghari's and Bhutto's name was implicated in the corruption scandal in news media. However, the PPP forcefully suppressed the FIA's investigations and judicial inquires as well as media coverage. Leghari supported the Bhutto administration's internal and foreign policies and staunchly backed Prime Minister Bhutto's initiatives at the national level. Leghari met with Indian Prime Minister Narasimha Rao and Queen Elizabeth when she paid a state visit to Pakistan during his tenure as president.

His political relations with Benazir Bhutto drifted apart over on policy issues concerning the internal politics and judicial nominations for the Supreme Court of Pakistan in 1996. In 1993, Leghari confirmed the nomination of Justice Sajjad Ali Shah as Chief Justice of Pakistan who was known to be closer to the PPP's ideology. In 1994, Prime Minister Bhutto nominated 20 senior judges for the appointment to the Supreme Court; of which, 13 had political relations with the PPP. Some of the nominated judges had not been practised judges and controversial reputations in the law circles. The PPP government began pressuring Chief Justice Shah to dissuade him from taking up to appeals against the nominations. President Leghari backed Chief Justice Shah over the appointment and confirmations that created problems with the Prime Minister Bhutto who saw this as a conspiracy being hatched by the Chief Justice Shah. Notoriety over the confirmations of additional judges in the High Courts further maligned Leghari's image as the appointments were seen as "inappropriate."

The situation with Prime Minister Bhutto further escalated when President Leghari raised issue of senior ministers' involvement in corruption and Asif Ali Zardari's appointment as Investment Minister. Leghari also suspected Benazir Bhutto and Asif Zardari involvement in controversial murder of Murtaza Bhutto that occurred in 1996, despite Prime Minister Bhutto hinted Leghari's involvement. On October–November 1996, there were several meetings between President Leghari and Prime Minister Bhutto to resolve the issue but the two sides used the intelligence community against each other. The economic recession further escalated the situation and President Leghari surprisingly dismissed the Benazir's administration using the Eighth Amendment to the Constitution on charges of corruption, economic recession, lawlessness and extra judicial killings.

Resignation and post-presidency

A caretaker set-up was formed under Acting Prime Minister Malik Meraj Khalid and general elections were held in 1997 that witnessed the return of Nawaz Sharif with a heavy mandate in all over the country. Prime Minister Sharif decisively removed the Eighth Amendment by approving the Thirteenth Amendment and oversaw its complete effect that ultimately made President Leghari as figurehead. Leghari seek the nomination for the second term but the chances of his re-election were diminished due to PPP's dilution in the Parliament.

Problems between Chief Justice Shah and Prime Minister Sharif further escalated when Chief Justice Shah decided to listen to appeals against the Fourteenth and Fifteenth Amendment bills and the PML(N) partisan attacked the Shah's court in 1997. President Leghari intervened in the matter in support of Chief Justice Shah but this only made it worse for Leghari when Prime Minister Sharif decided to bring the impeachment movement against President Leghari. On 2 December 1997, President Leghari resigned from the presidency to avoid the possible impeachment which also resulted in the resignation of the Chief Justice Shah, also the same year.

His post-presidency marked with his active involvement in politics when he found the Millat Party which entered into a coalition of seven parties, known as the National Alliance, to participate in the general elections held in 2002. The National Alliance won enough seats in the National Assembly to form government as a coalition with the PML(Q) that was supported by President Pervez Musharraf. In 2004, he left his own party and joined the PML(Q) and supported his son, Awais Leghari, becoming the cabinet member. His elder son, Jamal Leghari, was elected as member of Senate on PML(Q) platform.

Muhammad Rafiq Tarar

Muhammad Rafiq Tarar (2 November 1929 – 7 March 2022) was a Pakistani politician and jurist who served as the ninth President of Pakistan from January 1998 until his resignation in June 2001, and prior to that as a senator from Punjab in 1997. Before entering politics, Tarar served as senior justice of the Supreme Court of Pakistan from 1991 to 1994 and as the 28th Chief Justice of Lahore High Court from 1989 to 1991.

After Farooq Leghari's resignation in 1997, he was nominated as a candidate for the President of Pakistan. On 31 December 1997, in an indirect election, Tarar was elected by a huge margin, getting 374 of 457 votes of the Electoral College against Aftab Mirani of PPP (a PML(N)'s rival) who got 31 votes, and Muhammad Khan Shirani of JUI(S) who got 22 votes. This was the largest margin in such elections. On his appointment former Prime Minister Benazir Bhutto delivered a speech in London to the Commonwealth Ethnic Bar Association and criticized his appointment. She accused him of being dishonest by saying "A former judge [Tarar] who dishonestly legitimized the overthrow of my first government was elected President of Pakistan. This same man stands accused by a former

President Farooq Leghari of "taking briefcases of money" to bribe other judges in the famous 1997 case. The Election Commission rejected Justice Tarar's nomination for the presidency. Justice Qayyum, on leave for his mother's funeral, rushed back to grant a stay. And Tarar was elected. As for the bribery charges, Tarar, as a former judge, like former generals, is immune to prosecution in real terms."

Upon becoming President, Tarar was an unassuming and merely ceremonial figurehead who kept a low profile, and avoided news media, and he remained a devoted servant and loyalist of the Sharif family. He readily signed the Thirteenth, Fourteenth, and Fifteenth amendments to the Constitution of Pakistan that limited the powers of the presidency.

The President of Pakistan's powers had thus been slowly removed over the years, culminating in the 1997 Thirteenth Amendment to the Constitution of Pakistan which removed virtually all remaining reserve powers, making the office almost entirely symbolic in nature as per the true spirit of the Pakistani constitution.

Tarar did not endorse the 1999 Pakistani coup d'état by the Pakistani military which elevated General Pervez Musharraf, Chairman Joint Chiefs of Staff Committee, since he was an appointee of the Nawaz Sharif. The Pakistani military thus decided not to retain Tarar as the President for his full term of five years, given his partisan attitude. On 21 June 2001, General Musharraf who acted as Chief Executive in capacity, enforced the Legal Framework Order, 2002; Musharraf removed Tarar as he read the paragraph: "Mr. Muhammad Rafiq Tarar has ceased to hold the office of the President with immediate effect."

Tarar retired from politics and settled in Lahore, where he died after a long illness on 7 March 2022, at the age of 92.

Prime Ministers

Nawaz Sharif

Mian Muhammad Nawaz Sharif (born 25 December 1949) is a Pakistani businessman and politician who has served as the Prime Minister of Pakistan for three non-consecutive terms. He is the longest-serving prime minister of Pakistan, having served a total of more than 9 years across three tenures. Each term has ended in his ousting.

Born into the upper-middle-class Sharif family in Lahore, Nawaz is the son of Muhammad Sharif, the founder of Ittefaq and Sharif groups. He is the elder brother of Shehbaz Sharif, who also became the prime minister of Pakistan in 2022. According to the Election Commission of Pakistan, Nawaz is one of the wealthiest men in Pakistan, with an estimated net worth of at least Rs. 1.75 billion (equivalent to Rs. 8.9 billion or US$31 million in 2021). Most of his wealth originates from his businesses in steel construction.

First term as prime minister (1990–1993)

The conservatives first came to power in a democratic Pakistan under Nawaz's leadership. Nawaz Sharif became the 12th prime minister of Pakistan on 1 November 1990, succeeding Benazir Bhutto. He also became head of IJI. Sharif had a majority in the assembly and ruled with considerable confidence, having disputes with three successive army chiefs.

Nawaz had campaigned on a conservative platform and vowed to reduce government corruption. Nawaz introduced an economy based on privatisation and economic liberalisation to reverse the nationalisation by Zulfikar Bhutto, notably for banks and industries. He legalised foreign money exchange to be transacted through private money exchangers. His privatisation policies were continued by both Benazir Bhutto in the mid-1990s and Shaukat Aziz in the 2000s. He also improved the nation's infrastructure and spurred the growth of digital telecommunication.

Nawaz continued the simultaneous Islamization and conservatism of Pakistan society, a policy begun by Zia. Reforms were made to introduce fiscal conservatism, supply-side economics, bioconservatism and religious conservatism in Pakistan.

Nawaz intensified Zia's controversial Islamization policies, and introduced Islamic laws such as the Shariat Ordinance and Bait-ul-Maal (to help poor orphans, widows, etc.) to drive the country on the model of an Islamic welfare state. Moreover, he gave tasks to the Ministry of Religion to prepare reports and recommendations for steps taken toward Islamization. He ensured the establishment of three committees:

+ Ittehad-e-bain-ul-Muslemeen (English: Unity of Muslims Bloc)

+ Nifaz-e-Shariat Committee (English: Sharia Establishment Committee)

+ Islamic Welfare Committee

Nawaz extended membership of Economic Cooperation Organization (ECO) to all Central Asian Muslim countries, to unite them into a Muslim Bloc. Nawaz included environmentalism in his government platform, and established the Environmental Protection Agency in 1997.

Conflicts

Following the imposition and passing of Resolution 660, 661, and 665, Nawaz sided with the United Nations on the Iraqi invasion of Kuwait. Nawaz's government criticised Iraq for invading the fellow Muslim country, which strained Pakistan's relationships with Iraq. This continued as Pakistan sought to strengthen its relations with Iran. This policy continued under Benazir Bhutto and Pervez Musharraf until the removal of Saddam Hussein in 2003. Nawaz raised the issue of Kashmir in international forums and worked toward a peaceful transfer of power in Afghanistan to curb the rampant trading of illicit drugs and weapons across the border.

Nawaz challenged former Chief of Army Staff General Mirza Aslam Beg over the 1991 Gulf War. Under the direction of Beg, Pakistan Armed Forces participated in Operation Desert Storm and the Army Special Service Group and the Naval Special Service Group were deployed to Saudi Arabia to provide security for the Saudi royal family.

Nawaz faced difficulty working with the PPP and the Mutahidda Qaumi Movement (MQM), a potent force in Karachi. The MQM and the PPP opposed Nawaz due to his focus on beautifying Punjab and Kashmir while neglecting Sindh, and the MQM also opposed Nawaz's conservatism. Although the MQM had formed the government with Nawaz, the political tensions between liberalism and conservatism erupted into conflict by renegade factions in 1992.

To end the fighting between PML-N and MQM, Nawaz's party passed a resolution to launch a paramilitary operation under command of Chief of Army Staff General Asif Nawaz Janjua. Violence erupted in Karachi in 1992 and brought the economy to a halt. During this time, Benazir Bhutto and the centre-left PPP remained neutral, but her brother Murtaza Bhutto exerted pressure which suspended the operation. The period of 1992–1994 is considered the bloodiest in the history of the city, with many people missing.

Industrialization and privatisation

Nawaz had campaigned on a conservative platform and after assuming office announced his economic policy under the National Economic Reconstruction Programme (NERP). This programme introduced an extreme level of the Western-styled capitalist economics.

Unemployment had limited Pakistan's economic growth and Nawaz believed that only privatisation could solve this problem. Nawaz introduced an economy based on privatisation and economic liberalisation, notably for banks and industries. According to the US Department of State, this followed a vision of "turning Pakistan into a [South] Korea by encouraging greater private saving and investment to accelerate economic growth."

The privatisation programme reversed the nationalisation by Zulfikar Ali Bhutto and the PPP in the 1970s. By 1993, around 115 nationalised industries were opened to private ownership, including the National Development Finance Corporation, Pakistan National Shipping Corporation, National Electric Power Regulatory Authority, Pakistan International Airlines (PIA), Pakistan Telecommunication Corporation, and Pakistan State Oil. This boosted the economy but a lack of competition in bidding allowed the rise of business oligarchs and further widened the wealth gap, contributing to political instability. Former science advisor Dr. Mubashir Hassan called Nawaz's privatisation "unconstitutional". The PPP held that nationalisation policy was given constitutional status by parliament, and that privatisation policies were illegal and had taken place without parliamentary approval.

While privatising industry, Nawaz took steps for intense government control of science in Pakistan, and placed projects under his authorisation. In 1991, Nawaz founded and authorised the Pakistan Antarctic Programme under the scientific directions of National Institute of Oceanography (NIO), with the Pakistan Navy's Weapons Engineering Division, and first established the Jinnah Antarctic Station and Polar Research Cell. In 1992, Pakistan became an associate member of the Scientific Committee on Antarctic Research.

On 28 July 1997, Nawaz declared 1997 a year of science in Pakistan and personally allotted funds for the 22nd INSC College on Theoretical Physics. In 1999, Nawaz signed the executive decree, declaring 28 May as the National Science Day in Pakistan.

Nuclear policy

Nawaz made the nuclear weapons and energy programme one of his top priorities. He expanded the nuclear energy program, and continued an atomic programme while following a policy of deliberate nuclear ambiguity.

This resulted in a nuclear crisis with the United States which tightened its embargo on Pakistan in December 1990 and reportedly offered substantial economic aid to halt the country's uranium enrichment programme. Responding to US embargo, Nawaz announced that Pakistan had no atomic bomb, and would sign the Nuclear Nonproliferation Treaty if India did as well. The embargo blocked plans for a French-built nuclear power plant, so Nawaz's advisors intensively lobbied the International Atomic Energy Agency (IAEA), which allowed China to establish CHASNUPP-I nuclear power plant and upgrade KANUPP-I.

Nawaz's nuclear policy was considered less aggressive towards India with its focus on public usage through nuclear power and medicine, viewed as a continuation of the US Atoms for Peace programme. In 1993, Nawaz established the Institute of Nuclear Engineering (INE) to promote his policy for the peaceful use of nuclear energy.

Co-operatives societies scandal

Nawaz suffered a major loss of political support from the co-operatives societies scandal. These societies accept deposits from members and can legally make loans only to members for purposes to the benefit of the membership. However, mismanagement led to a collapse affecting millions of Pakistanis in 1992. In Punjab and Kashmir, around 700,000 people lost their savings, and it was discovered that billions of rupees had been granted to the Ittefaq Group of Industries – Nawaz's steel mill. Although the loans were hurriedly repaid, Nawaz's reputation was severely damaged.

Constitutional crisis and resignation

Nawaz had developed serious issues of authority with conservative President Ghulam Ishaq Khan, who had raised Nawaz to prominence during the Zia dictatorship. On 18 April, ahead of the 1993 Parliamentary election, Khan used his reserve powers to dissolve the National Assembly, and with the support of the army appointed Mir Balakh Sher as interim prime minister. Nawaz refused to accept this act and raised a challenge at the Supreme Court of Pakistan. On 26 May, the Supreme Court ruled 10–1 that the presidential order was unconstitutional, that the president could dissolve the assembly only if a constitutional breakdown had occurred and that the government's incompetence or corruption was irrelevant.

Issues of authority continued. In July 1993, under pressure from the armed forces, Nawaz resigned under an agreement that also removed President Khan from power. Chairman of the Joint Chiefs of Staff Committee General Shamim Allam and the Chief of Army Staff General Abdul Vahied Kakar forced Khan to resign from the presidency and ended the political standoff. Under the close scrutiny of the Pakistan Armed Forces, an interim and transitional government was formed and new parliamentary election was held after three months.

Pakistan at the 1984 Summer Olympics

Pakistan competed at the 1984 Summer Olympics in Los Angeles, United States. The nation returned to the Games after participating in the American-led boycott of the 1980 Summer Olympics. **Pakistan won the gold medal in the men's hockey team competition.**

Pakistan at the 1988 Summer Olympics

Pakistan competed at the 1988 Summer Olympics in Seoul, South Korea.

Medalists

Medal	Name	Sport	Event
Bronze	Hussain Shah	Boxing	Middleweight

5

(1991-2000)

<u>INDIA</u> - 1991 Indian economic crisis - Economic liberalisation in India - 1992 Indian stock market scam – Demolition of the Babri Masjid - Miss Universe & Miss World -1996 Summer Olympics - Pokhran-II - Kargil War - Indian Airlines Flight 814 hijacking - World Chess Champion - 2000 Summer Olympics

<u>PAKISTAN</u> – Presidents - Farooq Ahmad Khan Leghari - Muhammad Rafiq Tarar - 1993 Pakistani general election – Prime Minister Benazir Bhutto (2nd Term) – Nawaz Shariff (2nd Term) - 1992 Summer Olympics - 1992 Cricket World Cup

<u>INDIA</u>

1991 Indian economic crisis

The 1991 Indian economic crisis was an economic crisis in India resulting from a balance of payments deficit due to excess reliance on imports and other external factors. India's economic problems started worsening in 1985 as imports swelled, leaving the country in a twin deficit: the Indian trade balance was in deficit at a time when the government was running on a huge fiscal deficit.

The fall of the Eastern Bloc, which had trade relations with India and allowed for rupee exchange, posed significant issues. Towards the end of 1990, leading up to the Gulf War, the situation became dire. India's foreign exchange reserves were not enough to finance three weeks' worth of imports. Additionally, the Iraq-Kuwait conflict caused a significant shift in the trade deficit as India relied on these nations for crude oil. The surge in crude oil prices further exacerbated the imbalance in India's balance of payments. Meanwhile, the government was on the brink of defaulting on its financial obligations. In July of that year, the rupee experienced a sharp depreciation/devaluation due to the low reserves, which further worsened the twin deficit problem.

In February 1991, the Chandrasekhar government was unable to pass the budget after Moody's downgraded India's bond ratings. The ratings declined further due to the unsuccessful passage of the budget, making it increasingly challenging and expensive for India to borrow money from international capital markets. This placed additional pressure on the country's economy. The International Monetary Fund (IMF) suspended its loan program to India, and the World Bank also discontinued its assistance. These actions limited the government's options to address the crisis and forced it to take drastic measures to avoid defaulting on its payments.

To address the economic crisis, the government implemented various measures, including the pledge of a significant portion of India's gold reserves to the Bank of England and the Union Bank of Switzerland as collateral. The aim of this move was to secure much-needed foreign exchange to meet India's debt obligations and stabilize the economy. However, this decision was not without controversy and was seen by some as a drastic and desperate move. Critics viewed the decision to mortgage the country's gold as a sign of the government's limited options and inability to manage the crisis effectively.

The economic crisis created a situation where India had to accept the conditions imposed by the World Bank and IMF loan, which included structural reforms. As a result, the Indian economy was opened up to foreign participation in various sectors, including state-owned enterprises. This move towards liberalization was seen by some as necessary to secure much-needed funds and prevent default on loan payments. However, it also led to concerns about the impact of foreign entities on India's economy and the potential loss of control over vital industries.

In mid-1991, India's exchange rate was subjected to a severe adjustment. This event began with a slide in the value of the Indian rupee leading up to mid-1991. The authorities at the Reserve Bank of India took partial action, defending the currency by expanding international reserves and slowing the decline in value. However, in mid-1991, with foreign reserves nearly depleted, the Indian government permitted a sharp devaluation that took place in two steps within three days (1 July and 3 July 1991) against major currencies.

Government of India's immediate response was to secure an emergency loan of $2.2 billion from the International Monetary Fund by pledging 67 tons of India's gold reserves as collateral security. The Reserve Bank of India had to airlift 47 tons of gold to the Bank of England and 20 tons of gold to the Union Bank of Switzerland to raise $600 million. During the transport of the gold reserves to the airport, the van experienced a tyre burst and caused panic. The government, in the midst of the 1991 Indian General Elections, conducted the airlift with secrecy. The news of the government pledging the entire gold reserves against the loan outraged national sentiments and caused a public outcry. The gold was transported to London via a chartered plane from May 21 to May 31, 1991. The Chandra Shekhar government, which authorised the airlift, had collapsed a few months later. This move was seen as prioritising the balance of payment crisis over the welfare of the Indian people and kick-started P.V. Narasimha Rao's economic reform process.

Economic liberalisation in India

Liberalisation of 1991

The collapse of the Chandra Shekhar government in the midst of the crisis and the assassination of Rajiv Gandhi led to the election of a new Congress government led by P. V. Narasimha Rao. He selected Amar Nath Verma to be his Principal Secretary and Manmohan Singh to be finance minister and gave them complete support in doing whatever they thought was necessary to solve the crisis. Verma helped draft the New Industrial Policy alongside Chief Economic Advisor Rakesh Mohan, and it laid out a plan to foster Indian industry in five points.

- Firstly, it abolished the License Raj by removing licensing restrictions for all industries except for 18 that "related to security and strategic concerns, social reasons, problems related to safety and overriding environmental issues."

- To incentivise foreign investment, it laid out a plan to pre-approve all investment up to 51% foreign equity participation, allowing foreign companies to bring modern technology and industrial development. To further incentivise technological advancement, the old policy of government approval for foreign technology agreements was scrapped.

- The fourth point proposed to dismantle public monopolies by floating shares of public sector companies and limiting public sector growth to essential infrastructure, goods and services, mineral exploration, and defense manufacturing.

- Finally the concept of an MRTP company, where companies whose assets surpassed a certain value were placed under government supervision, was scrapped.

Meanwhile, Manmohan Singh worked on a new budget that would come to be known as the Epochal Budget. The primary concern was getting the fiscal deficit under control, and he sought to do this by curbing government expenses. Part of this was the disinvestment in public sector companies, but accompanying this was a reduction in subsidies for fertilizer and abolition of subsidies for sugar. He also dealt with the depletion of foreign exchange reserves during the crisis with a 19 per cent devaluation of the rupee with respect to the US dollar, a change which sought to make exports cheaper and accordingly provide the necessary foreign exchange reserves. The devaluation made petroleum more expensive to import, so Singh proposed to lower the price of kerosene to benefit the poorer citizens who depended on it while raising petroleum prices for industry and fuel. On 24 July 1991, Manmohan Singh presented the budget alongside his outline for broader reform. During the speech he laid out a new trade policy oriented towards promoting exports and removing import controls. Specifically, he proposed limiting tariff rates to no more than 150 percent while also lowering rates across the board, reducing excise duties, and abolishing export subsidies.

In August 1991, the Reserve Bank of India (RBI) Governor established the Narasimham Committee to recommend changes to the financial system. Recommendations included reducing the statutory liquidity ratio (SLR) and cash reserve ratio (CRR) from 38.5% and 15% respectively to 25% and 10% respectively, allowing market forces to dictate interest rates instead of the government, placing banks under the sole control of the RBI, and reducing the number of public sector banks. The government heeded some of these suggestions, including cutting the SLR and CRR rates, liberalizing interest rates, loosening restrictions on private banks, and allowing banks to open branches free from government mandate.

On 12 November 1991, based on an application from the Government of India, World Bank sanctioned a structural adjustment loan/credit that consisted of two components – an IBRD loan of $250 million to be paid over 20 years, and an IDA credit of SDR 183.8 million (equivalent to $250 million) with 35 years maturity, through India's ministry of finance, with the President of India as the borrower. The loan was meant primarily to support the government's program of stabilization and economic reform. This specified deregulation, increased foreign direct investment, liberalisation of the trade regime, reforming domestic interest rates, strengthening capital markets (stock exchanges), and initiating public enterprise reform (selling off public enterprises). As part of a bailout deal with the IMF, India was forced to pledge 20 tonnes of gold to Union Bank of Switzerland and 47 tonnes to the Bank of England and Bank of Japan.

The reforms drew heavy scrutiny from opposition leaders. The New Industrial Policy and 1991 Budget was decried by opposition leaders as "command budget from the IMF" and worried that withdrawal of subsidies for fertilizers and hikes in oil prices would harm lower and middle-class citizens. Critics also derided devaluation, fearing it would worsen runaway inflation that would hit the poorest citizens the hardest while doing nothing to fix the trade deficit. In the face of vocal opposition, the support and political will of the prime minister was crucial in order to see through the reforms. Rao was often referred to as Chanakya for his ability to steer tough economic and political legislation through the parliament at a time when he headed a minority government.

Impact

Reforms in India in the 1990s and 2000s aimed to increase international competitiveness in various sectors, including auto components, telecommunications, software, pharmaceuticals, biotechnology, research and development, and professional services. These reforms included reducing import tariffs, deregulating markets, and lowering taxes, which led to an increase in foreign investment and high economic growth. From 1992 to 2005, foreign investment increased by 316.9%, and India's GDP grew from $266 billion in 1991 to $2.3 trillion in 2018.

According to one study, wages rose on the whole, as well as wages as the labor-to-capital relative share. GDP, however, has been criticized by some to be flawed as it doesn't show inequality or living standards.

Extreme poverty reduced from 36 percent in 1993–94 to 24.1 percent in 1999–2000. However, these poverty figures have been criticised as not representing the true picture of poverty. According to one report, the wealthiest one percent of the country earns between 5 and 7 percent of the national income, while approximately 15 percent of the working population earns less than ₹ 5,000 (about $64) per month.

The liberalisation policies have also been criticised for increasing income inequality, concentrating wealth, worsening rural living standards, causing unemployment, and leading to an increase in farmer suicides.

India also increasingly integrated its economy with the global economy. The ratio of total exports of goods and services to GDP in India approximately doubled from 7.3 percent in 1990 to 14 percent in 2000. This rise was less dramatic on the import side but was significant, from 9.9 percent in 1990 to 16.6 percent in 2000. Within 10 years, the ratio of total goods and services trade to GDP rose from 17.2 percent to 30.6 percent. India, however, continues to have a trade deficit, relying on foreign capital to maintain its balance of payments and as such, makes it vulnerable to external shocks.

Foreign investment in India in form of foreign direct investment, portfolio investment, and investment raised on international capital markets increased significantly, from US$132 million in 1991–92 to $5.3 billion in 1995–96.

However, the liberalization did not benefit all parts of India equally, with urban areas benefiting more than rural areas. Additionally, some states with pro-worker labor laws saw slower industry expansion than those with pro-employer labor laws.

After the reforms, life expectancy and literacy rates continued to increase at roughly the same rate as before the reforms. For the first 10 years after the 1991 reforms, GDP also continued to increase at roughly the same rate as before the reforms.

1992 Indian stock market scam

The 1992 Indian stock market scam was a market manipulation carried out by Harshad Shantilal Mehta with other bankers and politicians on the Bombay Stock Exchange. The scam caused significant disruption to the stock market of India, defrauding investors of over ten million USD.

Techniques used by Mehta involved having corrupt officials signing fake cheques, misusing market loopholes, and fabrication to drive the prices of stocks up to 40 times their original price. Stock traders making good returns as a result of the scam were able to fraudulently obtain unsecured loans from banks. When the scam was discovered in April 1992, the Indian stock market collapsed, and the same banks suddenly found themselves holding millions of Indian rupees (INR) in now useless debt.

1992 Scandal

Overview

The scam was the biggest money market scam ever committed in India, amounting to approximately ₹ 5,000 crores. The main perpetrator of the scam was a stock and money market broker Harshad Mehta. It was a systematic stock scam using fake bank receipts and stamp paper that caused the Indian stock market to crash. The scam exposed the inherent loopholes of the Indian financial systems and resulted in a completely reformed system of stock transactions, including an introduction of online security systems.

Security frauds refer to the idea of diversion of funds from the banking system to various stockholders or brokers. The 1992 scam was a systematic fraud committed by Mehta in the Indian stock market which led to the complete collapse of security systems. He committed a scam of over 1 billion from the banking system to buy stocks on the Bombay Stock Exchange. This impacted the entire exchange system as the security system collapsed and investors lost hundreds of thousands of rupees in the exchange system. The scope of the scam was so large that the net value of the stocks was higher than the combined health and education budget of India. The scam was orchestrated in such a way that Mehta secured securities from the State Bank of India against forged cheques signed by corrupt officials and failed to deliver the securities. Mehta made the prices of the stocks soar high through fictitious practices and sold the stocks that he owned in these companies. The impact of the scam had many consequences, which included the losses incurred by lakhs of families and the immediate crash of the stock market. The index fell from 4500 to 2500 representing a loss of ₹ 1000 billion in market capitalization. The 1992 scam raised many questions involving bank officials responsible for being in collusion with Mehta. An interview with Montek Singh Ahluwalia (Secretary, economic affairs at the Ministry of Finance) revealed that many top bank officials were involved.

Mehta used forged BR's to gain unsecured loans, and used several small banks to issue BRs on demand. Since these banks were small, Mehta held on to the receipts as long as he wanted. The cheques in favour of both the banks were credited into the brokers' accounts which was the account of Mehta. As a result, banks made heavy investments in BOK and MCB as they showed positive signs of growth. Using the BR scam, Mehta took the price of ACC from ₹200 to ₹9000 in a short span of time. This 4400% percent increase was seen in several other stocks and as he sold the stocks, the market crashed.

This went on as long as the stock prices kept going up, and no one had a clue about Mehta's operations. Once the scam was exposed, though, a lot of banks were left holding BRs which did not have any value – the banking system had been swindled of a whopping ₹4,000 crore (equivalent to ₹310 billion or US$3.8 billion in 2023). They knew that they would be accused if their involvement in issuing cheques to Mehta was discovered. Subsequently, it transpired that Citibank, brokers like Pallav Sheth and Ajay Kayan, industrialists like Aditya Birla, Hemendra Kothari, a number of politicians, and the RBI Governor S.Venkitaramanan all had played a role in allowing or facilitating Mehta's rigging of the share market.

Realization of scam and market crash

The scam first became apparent in late April 1992, when it became clear that Mehta was a disproportionately large investor in government securities. At the time, Mehta was doing more than a third of the total securities business in India. When the public realized that Mehta's investments were illegitimate and that his stocks were likely worthless, it set off a selling frenzy of Mehta's stocks. The banks that had loaned money to Mehta were suddenly holding hundreds of millions in unsecured loans. The combination of the selling frenzy and the fact that numerous banks been defrauded crashed the Indian stock market, with prices dropping 40% immediately. Stocks eventually dropped 72%, and a bear market lasted for about 2 years.

Subsequent reforms

The first reform was the formation of the National Stock Exchange of India (NSE). It was followed by the development of the CII Code for Desirable Corporate Governance by Rahul Bajaj. The CII Code commanded the formation of two major committees headed by Kumar Mangalam Birla and N. R. Narayana Murthy, and overseen by the Securities and Exchange Board of India (SEBI). The objective was to monitor corporate governance and prevent future scams. The SEBI were to monitor the NSE and the National Securities Depository. For the equity market, the government introduced ten acts of parliament and one constitutional amendment based upon the principles of economic reform and legislative changes. The introduction of online trading by NSE changed the dynamics of stock buying and selling. The financial market opened up nationally rather than being confined to Bombay (now, Mumbai).

Changes in the financial structure of India

The 1992 scam collapsed the Indian stock market; around 40% of the market value or ₹1,000 billion was wiped out. It led the authorities to reconsider existing financial systems and restructure it. The first structural change was to record payments made for purchasing investments in reconciled bank receipts and subsidiary general ledgers to prevent fraudulent transactions. On the advice of the Janakiraman Committee, a committee was established to oversee the Securities and Exchange Board of India. The primary recommendation of the committee was to limit ready forward and double ready forward deals to government securities only. All banks were made custodians rather than principals in transactions. Banks were to have a separate audit system for portfolios, and it were to be monitored by the Reserve Bank of India (RBI).

Demolition of the Babri Masjid

The demolition of the Babri Masjid was carried out on 6 December 1992 by a large group of activists of the Vishva Hindu Parishad and allied organisations. The 16th-century Babri Masjid in the city of Ayodhya, in Uttar Pradesh, India, had been the subject of a lengthy socio-political dispute, and was targeted after a political rally organised by Hindu nationalist organisations turned violent.

In Hindu tradition, the city of Ayodhya is the birthplace of Rama. In the 16th century a Mughal general, Mir Baqi, had built a mosque, known as the Babri Masjid at a site identified by some Hindus as Ram Janmabhoomi, or the birthplace of Rama. The Archaeological Survey of India states that the mosque was built on land where a non-Islamic structure had previously existed. In the 1980s, the Vishva Hindu Parishad (VHP) began a campaign for the construction of a temple dedicated to Rama at the site, with the Bharatiya Janata Party (BJP) as its political voice. Several rallies and marches were held as a part of this movement, including the Ram Rath Yatra led by L. K. Advani.

On 6 December 1992 the VHP and the BJP organised a rally at the site involving 150,000 people. The rally turned violent, and the crowd overwhelmed security forces and tore down the mosque. A subsequent inquiry into the incident found 68 people responsible, including several leaders of the BJP and the VHP. The demolition resulted in several months of intercommunal rioting between India's Hindu and Muslim communities, causing the death of at least 2,000 people. Retaliatory violence against Hindus also occurred in Pakistan and Bangladesh.

Background

In Hinduism the birthplace of the deity Rama, known as "Ram Janmabhoomi", is considered a holy site. This site is often believed to be at the place where the Babri Masjid stood in the city of Ayodhya in Uttar Pradesh: historical evidence to support this belief is scarce. There is a rough scholarly consensus that in 1528, following the Mughal conquest of the region, a mosque was built at the site by the Mughal general Mir Baqi, and named the "Babri Masjid" after the Mughal emperor Babur. Popular belief holds that Baqi demolished a temple of Rama to build the mosque; historical basis for the belief is debated. Archaeological evidence has been found of a structure pre-dating the mosque. This structure has been variously identified as a Hindu temple and a Buddhist structure.

For at least four centuries, the site was used for religious purposes by both Hindus and Muslims. The claim that the mosque stood on the site of a temple was first made in 1822, by an official of the Faizabad court. The Nirmohi Akhara sect cited this statement in laying claim to the site later in the 19th century, leading to the first recorded incidents of religious violence at the site in 1855. In 1859 the British colonial administration set up a railing to separate the outer courtyard of the mosque to avoid disputes. The status quo remained in place until 1949, when idols of Rama were surreptitiously placed inside the mosque, allegedly by Hindu Mahasabha activists. This led to an uproar, with both parties filing civil suits laying claim to the land. The placement of the idols was seen as a desecration by the users of the Masjid. The site was declared to be in dispute, and the gates to the Masjid were locked.

In the 1980s, the Vishva Hindu Parishad (VHP) began a campaign for the construction of a temple dedicated to Rama at the site, with the Bharatiya Janata Party (BJP) as its political voice. The movement was bolstered by the decision of a district judge, who ruled in 1986 that the gates would be reopened and Hindus permitted to worship there. This decision was endorsed by Indian National Congress politician Rajiv Gandhi, then the Prime Minister of India, who sought to regain support from Hindus he had lost over the Shah Bano controversy. Nonetheless, the Congress lost the 1989 general election, and the BJP's strength in parliament grew from 2 members to 88, making its support crucial to the new government of V. P. Singh.

In September 1990, BJP leader L. K. Advani began a Rath Yatra, a political rally travelling across much of north India to Ayodhya. The yatra sought to generate support for the proposed temple, and also sought to unite Hindu votes by mobilizing anti-Muslim sentiment. Advani was arrested by the government of Bihar before he could reach Ayodhya. Despite this, a large body of Sangh Parivar supporters reached Ayodhya and attempted to attack the mosque. This resulted in a pitched battle with the paramilitary forces that ended with the death of several rioters. The BJP withdrew its support to the V. P. Singh ministry, necessitating fresh elections. The BJP substantially increased its tally in the union parliament, as well as winning a majority in the Uttar Pradesh assembly.

The then Prime Minister P. V. Narasimha Rao has been often criticized for his mishandling of the situation. Rao in his book Ayodhya 6 December 1992 wrote that the demolition was a "betrayal" by the then chief minister of Uttar Pradesh, Kalyan Singh, who repeatedly assured to the Congress government that the mosque would be protected.

Miss Universe & Miss World

Miss World and Miss Universe are the world's two most popular beauty pageants, the former having originated in the United Kingdom and the latter in the United States of America. Miss World commenced in the year 1951 and the first edition of Miss World pageant was held on 29th July 1951 when Kiki Håkansson of Sweden became the first ever Miss World. A year later, Miss Universe pageant started and the winner of the inaugural edition was Armi Kuusela of Finland.

Coincidentally, both the winners were from Nordic countries!

Well, looking at the history of the two pageants, there have been certain years (though not too many) when girls from the same country achieved the feat of winning both the titles in the very same year.

And finally, in the years 1994 and 2000 India accomplished the dual win. In 1994, Aishwarya Rai won the Miss World title and Sushmita Sen won the Miss Universe title. In the year 2000 again, India won both Miss World 2000 and Miss Universe 2000 titles and the winners were Priyanka Chopra and Lara Dutta respectively.

GREAT COINCIDENCES IN THE POLITICAL HISTORY OF INDIA

Giani Zail Singh was the former President. He announced, "Tomorrow I am going to reveal all the secrets of Bofors after reaching Chandigarh." Next day, on 29 November 1994, on the Delhi-Chandigarh road, a truck came roaring from the front and crushed Zail Singh's car. He died in the accident. No investigation took place.

India at the 1996 Summer Olympics

India competed at the 1996 Summer Olympics in Atlanta, United States. **Leander Paes' bronze in the men's tennis event was the only medal won by the country.** It had been 44 years since an Indian last won an individual medal at the Olympics (K. D. Jadhav earned bronze for freestyle bantamweight wrestling at the 1952 Summer Olympics, Helsinki). The medal was also India's first since their men's hockey team won gold at the 1980 Moscow Olympics. Subash Razdan, a prominent Indian American community leader in Atlanta was appointed Attache for India by the Indian Olympic Association. He also served as the acting chef-de-mission for the Indian contingent.

Pokhran-II

The Pokhran-II tests were a series of five nuclear bomb test explosions conducted by India at the Indian Army's Pokhran Test Range in May 1998. It was the second instance of nuclear testing conducted by India; the first test, code-named Smiling Buddha, was conducted in May 1974.

The tests achieved their main objective of giving India the capability to build fission and thermonuclear weapons with yields up to 200 kilotons. The then-Chairman of the Indian Atomic Energy Commission described each one of the explosions of Pokhran-II to be "equivalent to several tests carried out by other nuclear weapon states over decades". Subsequently, India established computer simulation capability to predict the yields of nuclear explosives whose designs are related to the designs of explosives used in this test.

Pokhran-II consisted of five detonations, the first of which was a fusion bomb while the remaining four were fission bombs. The tests were initiated on 11 May 1998, under the assigned code name Operation Shakti, with the detonation of one fusion and two fission bombs. On 13 May 1998, two additional fission devices were detonated, and the Indian government led by Prime Minister Atal Bihari Vajpayee shortly convened a press conference to declare India as a full-fledged nuclear state. The tests resulted in a variety of sanctions against India by a number of major countries including Japan and the United States.

Many names have been assigned to these tests; originally these were collectively called Operation Shakti–98, and the five nuclear bombs were designated Shakti-I through to Shakti-V. More recently, the operation as a whole has come to be known as Pokhran-II, and the 1974 explosion as Pokhran-I.

Post-Smiling Buddha

Responding to Smiling Buddha, the Nuclear Suppliers Group severely affected India's nuclear program. The world's major nuclear powers imposed technological embargo on India and Pakistan, which was on its own technological race to match India's achievement. The nuclear program struggled for years to gain credibility and its progress was crippled by the lack of indigenous resources and dependence on imported technology and technical assistance. Prime Minister Indira Gandhi declared to the IAEA that India's nuclear program was not for military purposes, despite authorising preliminary work on the hydrogen bomb design.

1998 Indian general elections

The BJP, came to power in 1998 general elections with an exclusive public mandate. BJP's political might had been growing steadily in strength over the past decade over several issues.

In Pakistan, the similar conservative force, the PML(N), was also in power with an exclusive mandate led by Prime Minister Nawaz Sharif who defeated the leftist PPP led by Benazir Bhutto in the general elections held in 1997. During the BJP campaign, Atal Bihari Vajpayee indulged in grandstanding— such as when he declared on 25 February that his government would "take back that part of Kashmir that is under Pakistan's control." Before this declaration, the BJP platform had clear intentions to "exercise the option to induct nuclear weapons" and "India should become an openly nuclear power to garner the respect on the world stage that India deserved." By 18 March 1998, Vajpayee publicly began lobbying for nuclear testing and declared that "there is no compromise on national security; all options including the nuclear options will be exercised to protect security and sovereignty."

Pokhran II

Consultation began between Prime Minister Vajpayee, Dr. Abdul Kalam, R. Chidambaram and officials of the Indian DAE on nuclear options. Chidambaram briefed Prime Minister Vajpayee extensively on the nuclear program; Abdul Kalam presented the status of the missile program. On 28 March 1998, Prime Minister Vajpayee asked the scientists to make preparations in the shortest time possible, and preparations were hastily made.

Pakistan, at a Conference on Disarmament, said it would offer a peace agreement with India for "an equal and mutual restraint in conventional, missile and nuclear fields." Pakistan's equation was later reemphasised on 6 April and the momentum in India for nuclear tests began to build up which strengthened Vajpayee's position to order the tests.

Extensive planning was done by a small group of scientists, senior military officers and senior politicians to ensure that the test preparations would remain secret, and even senior members of the Indian government did not know what was going on. The chief scientific adviser and the Director of Defence Research and Development Organisation (DRDO), Dr. Abdul Kalam, and Dr. R. Chidambaram, the director of the Department of Atomic Energy (DAE), were the chief coordinators of this test planning. The scientists and engineers of the Bhabha Atomic Research Centre (BARC), the Atomic Minerals Directorate for Exploration and Research (AMDER), and the Defence Research and Development Organisation (DRDO) were involved in the nuclear weapon assembly, layout, detonation and data collection. A small group of senior scientists were involved in the detonation process. All scientists were required to wear army uniforms to preserve the secrecy of the tests. Since 1995, the 58th Engineer Regiment had learned how to avoid satellite detection. Work was mostly done during night, and equipment was returned to the original place to give the impression that it was never moved.

Bomb shafts were dug under camouflage netting and the dug-out sand was shaped like dunes. Cables for sensors were covered with sand and concealed using native vegetation. Scientists would not depart for Pokhran in groups of two or three. They travelled to destinations other than Pokhran under pseudonyms, and were then transported by the army. Technical staff at the test range wore military uniforms, to prevent detection in satellite images.

Pakistan

The most vehement and strong reaction to India's nuclear explosion was from a neighbouring country, Pakistan. Great ire was raised in Pakistan, which issued a severe statement blaming India for instigating a nuclear arms race in the region. Prime Minister Nawaz Sharif vowed that his country would give a suitable reply to India. The day after the first tests, Foreign Minister Gohar Ayub Khan indicated that Pakistan was ready to conduct a nuclear test. He stated: "Pakistan is prepared to match India, we have the capability.... We in Pakistan will maintain a balance with India in all fields", he said in an interview. "We are in a headlong arms race on the subcontinent."

On 13 May 1998, Pakistan bitterly condemned the tests, and Foreign Minister Gohar Ayub was quoted as saying that Indian leadership seemed to "have gone berserk and was acting in a totally unrestrained way." Prime Minister Nawaz Sharif was much more subdued, maintaining ambiguity about whether a test would be conducted in response: "We are watching the situation and we will take appropriate action with regard to our security", he said. Sharif sought to mobilise the entire Islamic world in support of Pakistan and criticised India for nuclear proliferation.

Prime Minister Nawaz Sharif had been under intense pressure regarding the nuclear tests by US President Bill Clinton and Opposition leader Benazir Bhutto at home. Initially surprising the world, Prime Minister Nawaz Sharif authorised a nuclear testing program and the Pakistan Atomic Energy Commission (PAEC) carried out nuclear testing under the codename Chagai-I on 28 May 1998 and Chagai-II on 30 May 1998. These six underground nuclear tests at the Chagai and Kharan test site were conducted fifteen days after India's last test. The total yield of the tests was reported to be 40 kt (see codename: Chagai-I).

Pakistan's subsequent tests invited similar condemnation from the United States. American President Bill Clinton was quoted as saying "Two wrongs don't make a right", criticising Pakistan's tests as reactionary to India's Pokhran-II. The United States and Japan reacted by imposing economic sanctions on Pakistan. According to the Pakistan's science community, the Indian nuclear tests gave an opportunity to Pakistan to conduct nuclear tests after 14 years of conducting only cold tests.

Pakistan's leading nuclear physicist, Pervez Hoodbhoy, held India responsible for Pakistan's nuclear test experiments in Chagai.

United States

The United States issued a strong statement condemning India and promised that sanctions would follow. The American intelligence community was embarrassed as there had been "a serious intelligence failure of the decade" in detecting the preparations for the test.

In keeping with its preferred approach to foreign policy in recent decades, and in compliance with the 1994 anti-proliferation law, the United States imposed economic sanctions on India. The sanctions on India consisted of cutting off all assistance to India except humanitarian aid, banning the export of certain defence material and technologies, ending American credit and credit guarantees to India, and requiring the US to oppose lending by international financial institutions to India.

From 1998 to 1999, the United States held series of bilateral talks with India over the issue of India becoming a part of the CTBT and NPT. In addition, the United States also made an unsuccessful attempt of holding talks regarding the rollback of India's nuclear program. India took a firm stand against the CTBT and refusing to become a signatory of it despite under pressure by the US President Bill Clinton, and noted the treaty as it was not consistent with India's national security interest.

UN condemnation

The reactions from abroad started immediately after the tests were advertised. On 6 June, the UN Security Council adopted Resolution 1172, condemning the Indian and the Pakistani tests. China issued a vociferous condemnation calling upon the international community to exert pressure on India to sign the NPT and to eliminate its nuclear arsenal. With India joining the group of countries possessing nuclear weapons, a new strategic dimension had emerged in Asia, particularly in South Asia.

Kargil War

The Kargil War, also known as the Kargil conflict, was fought between India and Pakistan from May to July 1999 in the Kargil district of Jammu and Kashmir and elsewhere along the Line of Control (LoC). In India, the conflict is also referred to as Operation Vijay (Hindi: विजय, lit. 'Victory'), which was the codename of the Indian military operation in the region. The Indian Air Force acted jointly with the Indian Army to flush out the Pakistan Army and paramilitary troops from vacated Indian positions along the LoC, in what was designated as Operation Safed Sagar (ऑपरेशन सफेद सागर, lit. 'White Sea').

The conflict was triggered by the infiltration of Pakistani troops— disguised as Kashmiri militants—into strategic positions on the Indian side of the LoC, which serves as the de facto border between the two countries in the disputed region of Kashmir. During its initial stages, Pakistan blamed the fighting entirely on independent

Kashmiri insurgents, but documents left behind by casualties and later statements by Pakistan's Prime Minister and Chief of Army Staff showed the involvement of Pakistani paramilitary forces, led by General Ashraf Rashid. The Indian Army, later supported by the Indian Air Force, recaptured a majority of the positions on the Indian side of the LoC; facing international diplomatic opposition, Pakistani forces withdrew from all remaining Indian positions along the LoC.

The Kargil War is the most recent example of high-altitude warfare in mountainous terrain, and as such, posed significant logistical problems for the combatting sides. It also marks one of only two instances of conventional warfare between nuclear-armed states (alongside the Sino-Soviet border conflict). India had conducted its first successful test in 1974; Pakistan, which had been developing its nuclear capability in secret since around the same time, conducted its first known tests in 1998, just two weeks after a second series of tests by India.

Before the Partition of India in 1947, Kargil was a tehsil of Ladakh, a sparsely populated region with diverse linguistic, ethnic and religious groups, living in isolated valleys separated by some of the world's highest mountains. The Indo-Pakistani War of 1947-1948 concluded with the Line of Control bisecting the Ladakh district, with the Skardu tehsil going to Pakistan (now part of Gilgit-Baltistan). After Pakistan's defeat in the Indo-Pakistani War of 1971, the two nations signed the Simla Agreement promising not to engage in armed conflict with respect to that boundary.

The town of Kargil is located 205 km (127 mi) from Srinagar, facing the Northern Areas across the LOC. Like other areas in the Himalayas, Kargil has a continental climate. Summers are cool with frigid nights, while winters are long and chilly with temperatures often dropping to $-48\,°C$ ($-54\,°F$).

An Indian national highway (NH 1) connecting Srinagar to Leh cuts through Kargil. The area that witnessed the infiltration and fighting is a 160-kilometre (100 mi) long stretch of ridges overlooking this only road linking Srinagar and Leh. The military outposts on the ridges above the highway were generally around 5,000 m (16,000 ft) high, with a few as high as 5,485 m (17,995 ft). Apart from the district capital, Kargil, the populated areas near the front line in the conflict included the Mushkoh Valley and the town of Drass, southwest of Kargil, as well as the Batalik sector and other areas northeast of Kargil.

Kargil was targeted partly because the terrain was conducive to the preemptive seizure of several unoccupied military positions. With tactically vital features and well-prepared defensive posts atop the peaks, a defender on the high ground would enjoy advantages akin to that of a fortress. Any attack to dislodge a defender from high ground in mountain warfare requires a far higher ratio of attackers to defenders, and the difficulties would be exacerbated by the high altitude and freezing temperatures.

Kargil is just 173 km (107 mi) from the Pakistani-controlled town of Skardu, which was capable of providing logistical and artillery support to Pakistani combatants. A road between Kargil and Skardu exists, which was closed in 1949.

The New York Times

July 17. 1999

states "India buries soldiers that Pakistan won't claim."

Up and down some of the steepest peaks in the Himalayas are dozens of freshly dug graves of unknown soldiers, men who India insists are Pakistanis and whose nation dares not claim them.

The Indian Army buried five more bodies here today near the crown of a mountaintop 16,500 feet high, a spot recently re-named Gun Hill on military maps because of the intense mortar fire that has been lobbed from its rocky summit.

Just as they have with the bodies of others, the Indians offered them to Pakistan, but Pakistan, caught in what much of the world believes is an elaborate fiction, cannot accept the dead from an invasion force it has disavowed.

For two months Pakistan has insisted that the hundreds of invaders who had dug into mountaintop positions just inside Indian-controlled Kashmir were mujahedeen, Muslim holy warriors, though today its Army chief, Gen. Pervez Musharraf, told BBC that Pakistani troops occasionally engaged in "aggressive patrolling" on the Indian side. The Indians have from the beginning maintained that the infiltrators were largely Pakistani Army regulars, a view increasingly accepted by outsiders.

Indian Airlines Flight 814

Indian Airlines Flight 814, commonly known as IC 814, was an Indian Airlines Airbus A300 en route from Tribhuvan International Airport in Kathmandu, Nepal, to Indira Gandhi International Airport in Delhi, India, on Friday, 24 December 1999, when it was hijacked and flown to several locations before landing in Kandahar, Afghanistan.

Indian Airlines flight IC 814 took off from Kathmandu, Nepal, with Delhi, India as its intended destination. The flight left with 180 persons on board, including both the crew and the passengers. One of the passengers on board was Roberto Giori, the then-owner of De La Rue Giori, a company which controlled the majority of the world's currency-printing business at the time.

The aircraft was piloted by 37-year-old Captain Devi Sharan and first officer Rajinder Kumar, with 58-year-old flight engineer Anil Kumar Jaggia. The Airbus was hijacked by five masked Pakistani militants of the Harkat-ul-Mujahideen (HuM) shortly after it entered Indian airspace at about 17:30 IST. The hijackers ordered the aircraft to be flown to a series of locations: Amritsar, Lahore, and across the Persian Gulf to Dubai. The hijackers finally forced the aircraft to land in Kandahar, Afghanistan, which at the time was controlled by the Taliban. The hijackers released 27 of 176 passengers in Dubai but fatally stabbed one and wounded several others.

At that time, most of Afghanistan, including the Kandahar airport where the hijacked plane landed, was under Taliban control. Taliban militiamen fighters encircled the aircraft to prevent any Indian military intervention, which was found by current National Security Advisor Ajit Doval when he landed there. They also found two Inter-Services Intelligence (Pakistan) officers were on the apron and others soon joined them; one was a lieutenant colonel and the other a major. Doval said that if the hijackers did not have ISI support, India could have resolved the crisis.

The motive for the hijacking was to secure the release of Islamist terrorists held in prison in India – fellow HuM members Ahmed Omar Saeed Sheikh and Masood Azhar, and a Kashmiri militant, Mushtaq Ahmed Zargar. The hostage crisis lasted for seven days and ended after India agreed to release the three terrorists. The three have since been implicated in other terrorist actions, such as the 2001 Indian Parliament attack, 2002 kidnapping and murder of Daniel Pearl, 2008 Mumbai terror attacks, 2016 Pathankot attack and the 2019 Pulwama attack.

The hijacking has been seen as one of the millennium attack plots in late December 1999 and early January 2000 by al-Qaeda-linked terrorists.

The questions were raised particularly by USA about the security at Indian airports. But when 9/11 happened in 2001, no one dared to ask USA about how the terrorists carried the weapons through the high security checks at USA airports.

World Chess Champion

Viswanathan "Vishy" Anand (born 11 December 1969) is an Indian chess grandmaster and a former five-time World Chess Champion. He became the first grandmaster from India in 1988, and has the eighth highest peak FIDE rating of all-time. In 2022, he was elected the deputy president of FIDE.

Anand defeated Alexei Shirov in a six-game match to win the 2000 FIDE World Chess Championship, a title he held until 2002. He became the undisputed world champion in 2007 and defended his title against Vladimir Kramnik in 2008, Veselin Topalov in 2010, and Boris Gelfand in 2012. In 2013, he lost the title to challenger Magnus Carlsen, and he lost a rematch to Carlsen in 2014 after winning the 2014 Candidates Tournament.

In April 2006, Anand became the fourth player in history to pass the 2800 Elo mark on the FIDE rating list, after Kramnik, Topalov, and Garry Kasparov. He occupied the number one position for 21 months, the sixth-longest period on record.

Known for his rapid playing speed as a child, Anand earned the sobriquet "Lightning Kid"during his early career in the 1980s. He has since developed into a universal player, and many consider him the greatest rapid chess player of his generation. He won the FIDE World Rapid Chess Championship in 2003 and 2017, the World Blitz Cup in 2000, and numerous other top-level rapid and blitz events.

Anand was the first recipient of the Khel Ratna Award in 1991–92, India's highest sporting honour. In 2007, he was awarded India's second-highest civilian award, the Padma Vibhushan, making him the first sportsperson to receive the award.

India at the 2000 Summer Olympics

India competed at the 2000 Summer Olympics in Sydney, Australia.

India's Karnam Malleswari won Bronze medal in Weightlifting in Women's 69 kg category.

PAKISTAN

Presidents

Farooq Ahmad Khan Leghari

Farooq Ahmad Khan Leghari (29 May 1940 – 20 October 2010), was a Pakistani politician who served as the eighth president of Pakistan from 14 November 1993 until resigning on 2 December 1997. He was the first Baloch to be elected as President.

His credentials and "clean reputation" as opposed to politicians accused of mass corruption and white collar crimes won him the support from Prime Minister Bhutto and Pakistan Peoples Party (PPP). He accepted the nomination and ran in the presidential elections against Wasim Sajjad, the Acting President and PML(N) nominee by Nawaz Sharif.

As a result of indirect voting, Leghari received 274 votes in his favour against 168 votes for Wasim Sajjad. On 13 November 1993, Sardar Farooq Leghari was appointed the President of Pakistan for a term of five years. He vowed to repeal the Eighth Amendment to the Constitution of Pakistan and expressed his support for Prime Minister Benazir Bhutto. However, no bill was ever presented to repeal the Eighth Amendment to the Constitution. The law and order situation in the country worsen, especially in Karachi where the police operation resulted in various and unaccountable deaths.

In 1994–95, a major scandal was revealed by the sting operation led by the FIA that gained national attention. Known as the Mehrangate, Leghari's and Bhutto's name was implicated in the corruption scandal in news media. However, the PPP forcefully suppressed the FIA's investigations and judicial inquiries as well as media coverage. Leghari supported the Bhutto administration's internal and foreign policies and staunchly backed Prime Minister Bhutto's initiatives at the national level. Leghari met with Indian Prime Minister Narasimha Rao and Queen Elizabeth when she paid a state visit to Pakistan during his tenure as president.

His political relations with Benazir Bhutto drifted apart over on policy issues concerning the internal politics and judicial nominations for the Supreme Court of Pakistan in 1996. The situation with Prime Minister Bhutto further escalated when President Leghari raised issue of senior ministers' involvement in corruption and Asif Ali Zardari's appointment as Investment Minister. Leghari also suspected Benazir Bhutto and Asif Zardari involvement in controversial murder of Murtaza Bhutto that occurred in 1996, despite Prime Minister Bhutto hinted Leghari's involvement. On October–November 1996, there were several meetings between President Leghari and Prime Minister Bhutto to resolve the issue but the two sides used the intelligence community against each other. The economic recession further escalated the situation and President Leghari surprisingly dismissed the Benazir's administration using the Eighth Amendment to the Constitution on charges of corruption, economic recession, lawlessness and extra judicial killings.

Problems between Chief Justice Shah and Prime Minister Sharif further escalated when Chief Justice Shah decided to listen to appeals against the Fourteenth and Fifteenth Amendment bills and the PML(N) partisan attacked the Shah's court in 1997. President Leghari tried intervened in the matter in support of Chief Justice Shah but this only made it worse for Leghari when Prime Minister Sharif decided to bring the impeachment movement against President Leghari. On 2 December 1997, President Leghari resigned from the presidency to avoid the possible impeachment which also resulted in the resignation of the Chief Justice Shah, also the same year.

Muhammad Rafiq Tarar

Muhammad Rafiq Tarar (2November 1929 – 7 March 2022) was a Pakistani politician and jurist who served as the ninth President of Pakistan from January 1998 until his resignation in June 2001, and prior to that as a senator from Punjab in 1997. Before entering politics, Tarar served as senior justice of the Supreme Court of Pakistan from 1991 to 1994 and as the 28th Chief Justice of Lahore High Court from 1989 to 1991.

After Farooq Leghari's resignation in 1997, he was nominated as a candidate for the President of Pakistan. On 31 December 1997, in an indirect election, Tarar was elected by a huge margin.

Upon becoming President, Tarar was an unassuming and merely ceremonial figurehead who kept a low profile, and avoided news media, and he remained a devoted servant and loyalist of the Sharif family. He readily signed the Thirteenth, Fourteenth, and Fifteenth amendments to the Constitution of Pakistan that limited the powers of the presidency.

The President of Pakistan's powers had thus been slowly removed over the years, culminating in the 1997 Thirteenth Amendment to the Constitution of Pakistan which removed virtually all remaining reserve powers, making the office almost entirely symbolic in nature as per the true spirit of the Pakistani constitution.

Tarar did not endorse the 1999 Pakistani coup d'état by the Pakistani military which elevated General Pervez Musharraf, Chairman Joint Chiefs of Staff Committee, since he was an appointee of the Nawaz Sharif. The Pakistani military thus decided not to retain Tarar as the President for his full term of five years, given his partisan attitude. On 21 June 2001, General Musharraf who acted as Chief Executive in capacity, enforced the Legal Framework Order, 2002; Musharraf removed Tarar as he read the paragraph: "Mr. Muhammad Rafiq Tarar has ceased to hold the office of the President with immediate effect."

Tarar retired from politics and settled in Lahore, where he died after a long illness on 7 March 2022, at the age of 92.

1993 Pakistani general election

General elections were held in Pakistan on 6 October 1993 to elect the members of National Assembly. The elections took place after both the Prime Minister Nawaz Sharif and President Ghulam Ishaq Khan resigned to resolve a power struggle.

Prior to the elections, the ruling Islami Jamhoori Ittehad alliance was dissolved due to clashes between its member parties. The alliance's place in the two-party system (alongside the Pakistan Peoples Party) was taken up by Sharif's Pakistan Muslim League (N).

The elections were held under the caretaker government of Moeenuddin Ahmad Qureshi. Although the PML (N) received the most votes, the PPP won the most seats. After winning the support of minor parties and independents, Benazir Bhutto became Prime Minister for a second non-consecutive term. Voter turnout was 40%.

Results

The PPP won the most seats in the election at 86 but failed to gain a majority with the PML-N second with 73 seats. This was also the first election in Pakistan in which the party that won the popular vote, the PML-N, failed to win the most seats. The PPP performed strongly in Bhutto's native Sindh and rural Punjab, while the PML-N was strongest in industrial Punjab and the largest cities such as Karachi, Lahore and Rawalpindi. Islamic fundamentalist candidates did poorly in an election that was marked by a low turnout. Turnout in Pakistan's largest city, Karachi, was particularly low at 20% after one party MQM (A) boycotted the election. International observers from 40 countries reported no serious irregularities in an election which was seen as the most free and fair since 1970. One seat was not contested on election day due to the death of a candidate; it was subsequently won in a by-election by the People's Democratic Alliance.

After the IJI government of Prime Minister Nawaz Sharif was also dismissed on corruption charges, Bhutto led the PPP to victory in the 1993 elections. In her second term, she oversaw economic privatisation and attempts to advance women's rights. Her government was damaged by several controversies, including the assassination of her brother Murtaza, a failed 1995 coup d'état, and a further bribery scandal involving her and her husband Asif Ali Zardari; in response, President Farooq Leghari dismissed her government. The PPP lost the 1997 election and in 1998 she went into self-exile, living between Dubai and London for the next decade. A widening corruption inquiry culminated in a 2003 conviction in a Swiss court. Following the United States–brokered negotiations with President Pervez Musharraf, she returned to Pakistan in 2007 to compete in the 2008 elections; her platform emphasised civilian oversight of the military and opposition to growing Islamist violence. After a political rally in Rawalpindi, she was assassinated. The Salafi jihadi group al-Qaeda claimed responsibility, although the involvement of the Pakistani Taliban and rogue elements of the intelligence services was widely suspected. She was buried at her family mausoleum in Garhi Khuda Baksh.

Bhutto was a controversial figure who remains divisive. She was often criticised as being politically inexperienced, was accused of being corrupt, and faced much opposition from Pakistan's Islamist lobby for her secularist and modernising agenda. In the early years of her career, she was nevertheless domestically popular and also attracted support from Western nations, for whom she was a champion of democracy. Posthumously, she came to be regarded as an icon for women's rights due to her political success in a male-dominated society.

Nawaz Shariff (Second term as Prime Minister)

After being ousted in 1993, when President Ghulam Ishaq Khan dissolved the National Assembly, Nawaz served as the leader of the opposition to the government of Benazir Bhutto from 1993 to 1996. He returned to the premiership after the Pakistan Muslim League (N) (PML-N) was elected in 1997, and served until his removal in 1999 by military takeover and was tried in a plane hijacking case which was argued by Barrister Ijaz Husain Batalvi, assisted by Khawaja Sultan senior Advocate, Sher Afghan Asdi and Akhtar

Aly Kureshy Advocate. After being imprisoned and later exiled for more than a decade, he returned to politics in 2011 and led his party to victory for the third time in 2013.

Pakistan at the 1992 Summer Olympics

Pakistan competed at the 1992 Summer Olympics in Barcelona, Spain.

Won 1 Bronze medal in Men's Field Hockey.

1992 Cricket World Cup

The 1992 Cricket World Cup (known as the Benson & Hedges World Cup 1992 for sponsorship reasons) was the fifth Cricket World Cup, the premier One Day International cricket tournament for men's national teams, organised by the International Cricket Council (ICC). It was held in Australia and New Zealand from 22 February to 25 March 1992, and finished with Pakistan beating England by 22 runs in the final to become the World Cup champions for the first time. The tournament is remembered for the controversial "rain rule"; South Africa tried to take advantage of the rule in their semi-final against England, but the tactic ultimately cost them the match.

Pervez Musharraf

Pervez Musharraf (11 August 1943 – 5 February 2023) was a Pakistani army general and politician who served as the tenth president of Pakistan from 2001 to 2008. He also served as the 10th Chairman Joint Chiefs of Staff Committee from 1998 to 2001 and the 7th Chief of Army Staff from 1998 to 2007.

Kargil Conflict

The Pakistan Army originally conceived the Kargil plan after the Siachen conflict but the plan was rebuffed repeatedly by senior civilian and military officials. Musharraf was a leading strategist behind the Kargil Conflict. From March to May 1999, he ordered secret infiltration of forces into the Kargil district. After India discovered the infiltration, a fierce Indian offensive nearly led to a full-scale war. However, Sharif withdrew support for the insurgents in July because of heightened international pressure. Sharif's decision antagonised the Pakistan Army and rumours of a possible coup began emerging soon afterward. Sharif and Musharraf dispute on who was responsible for the Kargil conflict and Pakistan's withdrawal.

This strategic operation met with great hostility in the public circles and wide scale disapproval in the media who roundly criticised this operation. Musharraf had severe confrontation and became involved in serious altercations with his senior officers, chief of naval staff Admiral Fasih Bokhari, chief of air staff, Air Chief Marshal PQ Mehdi and senior lieutenant-general Ali Kuli Khan. Admiral Bokhari ultimately demanded a full-fledged joint-service court martial against General Musharraf, while on the other hand General Kuli Khan lambasted the war as "a disaster bigger than the East-Pakistan tragedy", adding that the plan was "flawed in terms of its conception, tactical planning and execution" that ended in "sacrificing so many soldiers." Problems with his lifelong friend, chief of air staff air chief marshal Pervez Mehdi also arose when air chief refrained to participate or authorise any air strike to support the elements of army operations in the Kargil region.

During the last meeting with the Prime minister, Musharraf faced grave criticism on results produced by Kargil infiltration by the principal military intelligence (MI) director lieutenant-general Jamshed Gulzar Kiani who maintained in the meeting: "(…) whatever has been written there is against logic. If you catch your enemy by the jugular vein he would react with full force… If you cut enemy supply lines, the only option for him will be to ensure supplies by air… (sic).. at that situation the Indian Army was unlikely to confront and it had to come up to the occasion. It is against wisdom that you dictate to the enemy to keep the war limited to a certain front...."

Nawaz Sharif has maintained that the Operation was conducted without his knowledge. However, details of the briefing he got from the military before and after the Kargil operation have become public. Before the operation, between January and March, Sharif was briefed about the operation in three separate meetings. In January, the army briefed him about the Indian troop movement along the LOC in Skardu on 29 January 1999, on 5 February at Kel, on 12 March at the GHQ, and finally on 17 May at the ISI headquarters. During the end of the June DCC meeting, a tense Sharif turned to the army chief and said "you should have told me earlier", Musharraf pulled out his notebook and repeated the dates and contents of around seven briefings he had given him since the beginning of January.

Chief Executive (1999–2002)

1999 coup

Military officials from Musharraf's Joint Staff Headquarters (JS HQ) met with regional corps commanders three times in late September in anticipation of a possible coup. To quieten rumours of a fallout between Musharraf and Sharif, Sharif officially certified Musharraf's remaining two years of his term on 30 September.

President Gen. Pervez Musharraf speaks during a press conference at the Pakistan Air Force base in Chaklala Pakistan.

Musharraf had left for a weekend trip to take part in Sri Lanka's Army's 50th-anniversary celebrations. When Pervez Musharraf was returning from an official visit to Colombo his flight was denied landing permissions to Karachi International Airport after orders were issued from the Prime Minister's office. Upon hearing the announcement of Nawaz Sharif, replacing Pervez Musharraf by Khwaja Ziauddin, the third replacement of the top military commander of the country in less than two years, local military commanders began to mobilise troops towards Islamabad from nearby Rawalpindi. The military placed Sharif under house arrest, but in a last-ditch effort Sharif privately ordered Karachi air traffic controllers to redirect Musharraf's flight to India. The plan failed after soldiers in Karachi surrounded the airport control tower. At 2:50 am on 13 October, Musharraf addressed the nation with a recorded message.

Musharraf met with President Rafiq Tarar on 13 October to deliberate on legitimising the coup. On 15 October, Musharraf ended emerging hopes of a quick transition to democracy after he declared a state of emergency, suspended the Constitution and assumed power as Chief Executive. He also quickly purged the government of political enemies, notably Ziauddin and national airline chief Shahid Khaqan Abbassi. On 17 October, he gave his second national address and established a seven-member military-civilian council to govern the country. He named three retired military officers and a judge as provincial administrators on 21 October. Ultimately, Musharraf assumed executive powers but did not obtain the office of the Prime minister. The Prime minister's secretariat (official residence of Prime minister of Pakistan) was closed by the military police and its staff was fired by Musharraf immediately.

There were no organised protests within the country to the coup, that was widely criticised by the international community. Consequently, Pakistan was suspended from the Commonwealth of Nations. Sharif was put under house arrest and later exiled to Saudi Arabia on his personal request and under a contract.

Sharif trial and exile

The Military Police held former prime minister Sharif under house arrest at a government guesthouse and opened his Lahore home to the public in late October 1999. He was formally indicted in November on charges of hijacking, kidnapping, attempted murder, and treason for preventing Musharraf's flight from landing at Karachi airport on the day of the coup. His trial began in early March 2000 in an anti-terrorism court, which is designed for speedy trials. He testified Musharraf began preparations of a coup after the Kargil conflict. Sharif was placed in Adiala Jail, infamous for hosting Zulfikar Ali Bhutto's trial, and his leading defence lawyer, Iqbal Raad, was shot dead in Karachi in mid-March. Sharif's defence team blamed the military for intentionally providing their lawyers with inadequate protection. The court proceedings were widely accused of being a show trial. Sources from Pakistan claimed that Musharraf and his military government's officers were in full mood to exercise tough conditions on Sharif, and intended to send Nawaz Sharif to the gallows to face a similar fate to that of Zulfikar Ali Bhutto in 1979. It was the pressure on Musharraf exerted by Saudi Arabia and the United States to exile Sharif after it was confirmed that the court is about to give its verdict on Nawaz Sharif over treason charges, and the court would sentence Sharif to death. Sharif signed an agreement with Musharraf and his military government and his family was exiled to Saudi Arabia in December 2000.

6

(2001-2010)

<u>**INDIA**</u> - 2001 Gujarat earthquake - September 11 attacks - 2001 Indian Parliament attack - Godhra train burning - Abdul Karim Telgi, Stamp Paper Scam - Kalpana Chawla - 2004 Summer Olympics - 2004 Indian general election - 2004 Indian Ocean earthquake and tsunami - Right to Information Act, 2005 - India–United States Civil Nuclear Agreement - Pratibha Patil - 2007 ICC World Twenty20 final - 2008 Mumbai attacks - Lehman crisis - 2008 Summer Olympics - 2009 Indian general election - Satyam Scam - Major overseas acquisitions by Tata group - Virender Sehwag - Yuvraj Singh - Strange deaths in Gandhi & Vadra Family

<u>**PAKISTAN**</u> - Pervez Musharraf - Nuclear scandals - Domestic politics - Fall from the presidency - Return of Benazir Bhutto and Nawaz Sharif - 2007 state of emergency - 2008 general elections - 2009 attack on the Sri Lanka national cricket team - Muhammad Mian Soomro - Asif Ali Zardari

INDIA

2001 Gujarat earthquake

The 2001 Gujarat earthquake, also known as the Bhuj earthquake, occurred on 26 January at 08:46 am IST. The epicentre was about 9 km south-southwest of the village of Chobari in Bhachau Taluka of Kutch (Kachchh) District of Gujarat, India.

The intraplate earthquake measured 7.6 on the moment magnitude scale and occurred at 17.4 km (10.8 mi) depth. It had a maximum felt intensity of X (Extreme) on the Mercalli intensity scale. The earthquake killed 13,805 to 20,023 people (including 18 in southeastern Pakistan), injured another 167,000 and destroyed nearly 340,000 buildings.

Tectonic setting

Gujarat lies 300–400 km from the plate boundary between the Indian Plate and the Eurasian Plate, but the current tectonics are still governed by the effects of the continuing continental collision along this boundary. During the break-up of Gondwana in the Jurassic, this area was affected by rifting with a roughly west–east trend. During the collision with Eurasia the area has undergone shortening, involving both reactivation of the original rift faults and development of new low-angle thrust faults. The related folding has formed a series of ranges, particularly in central Kutch.

September 11 attacks

The September 11 attacks, commonly known as 9/11, were four coordinated Islamist suicide terrorist attacks carried out by al-Qaeda against the United States on Tuesday, September 11, 2001. That morning, 19 terrorists hijacked four commercial airliners scheduled to travel from the New England and Mid-Atlantic regions of the East Coast to California. The hijackers crashed the first two planes into the Twin Towers of the World Trade Center in New York City, two of the world's five tallest buildings at the time, and aimed the next two flights toward targets in or near Washington, D.C., in an attack on the nation's capital. The third team succeeded in crashing into the Pentagon, the headquarters of the U.S. Department of Defense in Arlington County, Virginia, while the fourth plane crashed in rural Pennsylvania following a passenger revolt. The attacks killed nearly 3,000 people and instigated the multi-decade global war on terror.

When 9/11 happened, no one dared to ask US about how the terrorists carried the weapons through the high security checks at US airports.

This terrorist attack changed the political equations in the whole world. Till that point Pakistan was considered as a closest ally of US. The process of India - US ties becoming stronger slowly and steadily, started from this point onwards.

Osama bin Laden

Bin Laden orchestrated the attacks. He initially denied involvement, but later recanted his false statements. Al Jazeera broadcast a statement by him on September 16, 2001: "I stress that I have not carried out this act, which appears to have been carried out by individuals with their own motivation." In November 2001, U.S. forces recovered a videotape from a destroyed house in Jalalabad, Afghanistan. In the video, bin Laden is seen talking to Khaled al-Harbi and admits foreknowledge of the attacks. On December 27, 2001, a second bin Laden video was released. In the video, he said:

It has become clear that the West in general and America in particular have an unspeakable hatred for Islam. ... It is the hatred of crusaders. Terrorism against America deserves to be praised because it was a response to injustice, aimed at forcing America to stop its support for Israel, which kills our people. ... We say that the end of the United States is imminent, whether Bin Laden or his followers are alive or dead, for the awakening of the Muslim ummah [nation] has occurred. ... It is important to hit the economy (of the United States), which is the base of its military power...If the economy is hit they will become reoccupied.

– Osama bin Laden

but he stopped short of admitting responsibility for the attacks.

2001 Indian Parliament attack

The 2001 Indian Parliament attack was a terrorist attack on the Parliament of India in New Delhi, India on 13 December 2001. The perpetrators belonged to Lashkar-e-Taiba (LeT) and Jaish-e-Mohammed (JeM) - two Pakistan-raised militant organisations. The attack led to the deaths of six Delhi Police personnel, two Parliament Security Service personnel, and a gardener – in total 9 – and led to increased tensions between India and Pakistan, resulting in the 2001–2002 India–Pakistan standoff. The five militants were killed outside the parliament.

Attack

On 13 December 2001, five terrorists infiltrated the Parliament House in a car with Home Ministry and Parliament labels. While both the Rajya Sabha and Lok Sabha had been adjourned 40 minutes prior to the incident, many members of parliament (MPs) and government officials such as Home Minister LK Advani and Minister of State for Defence Harin Pathak were believed to have still been in the building at the time of the attack. More than 100 people, including major politicians, were inside the parliament building at the time. The gunmen used a fake identity sticker on the car they drove and thus easily breached the security deployed around the parliamentary complex. The terrorists carried AK-47 rifles, grenade launchers, pistols and grenades.

The gunmen drove their vehicle into the car of the Indian Vice President Krishan Kant (who was in the building at the time), got out, and began shooting. The Vice President's guards and security personnel shot back at the terrorists and then started closing the gates of the compound. A similar attack was carried out on the assembly of Srinagar, Jammu and Kashmir, in November 2001, killing 38 people.

Delhi Police officials said that gunmen received instructions from Pakistan and the operation was carried out under the guidance of Pakistan's Inter-Services Intelligence (ISI) agency.

A great Political Coincidence

Madhavrao Scindia died at the age of 56, in a plane crash in Motta village, which is on the outskirts of Mainpuri district of Uttar Pradesh, on 30 September 2001. The plane caught fire when it was above Bhainsrauli village.

Shrimant Madhavrao Shinde (Scindia) was the most popular and hardworking leader of the Congress before that Lok Sabha election. He was elected to the Lok Sabha for the ninth consecutive term and was also the Leader of the Opposition in the Lok Sabha. Congress leader told Uttar Pradesh Congress President - "I am coming to campaign!" The state president was fearless. He said - "You don't come. Send Madhavrao ji. Only he can get votes." There was no second thought after that. Madhavrao ji was told that you will not go by your personal plane but by this plane. An eyewitness farmer gave a statement - "First there was a bomb blast in the plane, then there was a fire." All eight people on board were killed but there was no investigation. After a short time, the Congress state president was also found dead. (Courtesy from the pen of Dr. Ishwar Chandra Karkare)

Godhra train burning

The Godhra train burning occurred on the morning of 27 February 2002: 59 Hindu pilgrims and karsevaks returning from Ayodhya were killed in a fire inside the Sabarmati Express near the Godhra railway station in the Indian state of Gujarat. The cause of the fire remains disputed. The Gujarat riots, in which Muslims were the targets of widespread and severe violence, occurred shortly afterward.

The Nanavati-Mehta commission, appointed by the state government in the immediate aftermath of the event, concluded in 2008 that the burning was a pre-planned arson committed by a thousand-strong Muslim mob. The Banerjee commission, instituted by the Ministry of Railways, characterized the fire as an accident in 2006 however, the Gujarat High Court found its appointment to be unconstitutional and quashed all findings.

In February 2011, the trial court convicted 31 Muslims for the burning, relying extensively on the Nanavati-Mehta Commission report as evidence. In October 2017, the Gujarat High Court upheld the convictions.

2002 Gujarat riots

The 2002 Gujarat riots, also known as the 2002 Gujarat violence, was a three-day period of inter-communal violence in the western Indian state of Gujarat. The burning of a train in Godhra on 27 February 2002, which caused the deaths of 58 Hindu pilgrims and karsevaks returning from Ayodhya, is cited as having instigated the violence. Following the initial riot incidents, there were further outbreaks of violence in Ahmedabad for three months; statewide, there were further outbreaks of violence against the minority Muslim population of Gujarat for the next year.

According to official figures, the riots ended with 1,044 dead, 223 missing, and 2,500 injured. Of the dead, 790 were Muslim and 254 Hindu. The Concerned Citizens Tribunal Report, estimated that as many as 1,926 may have been killed. Other sources estimated death tolls in excess of 2,000. Many brutal killings and rapes were reported on as well as widespread looting and destruction of property. Narendra Modi, then Chief Minister of Gujarat and later Prime Minister of India, was accused of condoning the violence, as were police and government officials who allegedly directed the rioters and gave lists of Muslim-owned properties to them.

In 2012, Modi was cleared of complicity in the violence by Special Investigation Team (SIT) appointed by the Supreme Court of India. The SIT also rejected claims that the state government had not done enough to prevent the riots. The Muslim community was reported to have reacted with anger and disbelief. In July 2013, allegations were made that the SIT had suppressed evidence. That December, an Indian court upheld the earlier SIT report and rejected a petition seeking Modi's prosecution. In April 2014, the Supreme Court expressed satisfaction over the SIT's investigations in nine cases related to the violence, and rejected a plea contesting the SIT report as "baseless".

What is a Scam 2003 Story? Know All About Abdul Karim Telgi

Abdul Karim Telgi was an Indian counterfeiter who was involved in a major counterfeit stamp paper scandal, said to be one of the biggest stamp scandals in India. He was born in 1961 and gained notoriety for operating a sophisticated counterfeit stamp paper racket in several Indian states. Telgi's scam involved the production and distribution of fake stamp papers, which are crucial for legal and financial transactions.

His counterfeit stamp paper racket caused significant financial losses to the Indian government and resulted in widespread legal and investigative actions. Telgi was arrested in 2001 and faced various charges related to counterfeiting, forgery, and other criminal activities. He was sentenced to prison for his involvement in the scam.

Abdul Karim Telgi Scam Amount

Abdul Karim Telgi's scam was worth about ₹300 billion (US$3.8 billion). He had 300 helpers who sold fake stamps to important places like banks, insurance companies, and stock firms. Even some police officers and government workers were involved with Telgi.

Kalpana Chawla

Kalpana Chawla (17 March 1962 – 1 February 2003) was an Indian-born American astronaut and aerospace engineer who was the first woman of Indian origin to fly to space. She first flew on Space Shuttle Columbia in 1997 as a mission specialist and primary robotic arm operator.

Chawla's second flight was on STS-107, the final flight of Columbia, in 2003. She was one of the seven crew members who died in the Space Shuttle Columbia disaster when the spacecraft disintegrated during its re-entry into the Earth's atmosphere on 1 February 2003. Chawla was posthumously awarded the Congressional Space Medal of Honor, and several streets, universities, and institutions have been named in her honor.

Second space mission and death

In 2000, Chawla was selected for her second flight as part of the crew of STS-107. This mission was repeatedly delayed due to scheduling conflicts and technical problems such as the July 2002 discovery of cracks in the shuttle engine flow liners. On 16 January 2003, Chawla finally returned to space aboard Space Shuttle Columbia on the ill-fated STS-107 mission. The crew performed nearly 80 experiments studying Earth and space science, advanced technology development, and astronaut health and safety.

During the launch of STS-107, Columbia's 28th mission, a piece of foam insulation broke off from the Space Shuttle external tank and struck the port wing of the orbiter. Previous shuttle launches had seen minor damage from foam shedding, but some engineers suspected that the damage to Columbia was more serious. NASA managers limited the investigation, reasoning that the crew could not have fixed the problem if it had been confirmed.

When Columbia re-entered the atmosphere of Earth, the damage allowed hot atmospheric gases to penetrate and destroy the internal wing structure, which caused the spacecraft to become unstable and break apart. After the disaster, Space Shuttle flight operations were suspended for more than two years, similar to the aftermath of the Challenger disaster. Construction of the International Space Station (ISS) was put on hold; the station relied entirely on the Russian Roscosmos State Corporation for resupply for 29 months until Shuttle flights resumed with STS-114 and 45 months for crew rotation.

Chawla died on 1 February 2003, in the Space Shuttle Columbia disaster, along with the other six crew members, when Columbia disintegrated over Texas during re-entry into the Earth's atmosphere, shortly before it was scheduled to conclude its 28th mission, STS-107. Her remains were identified along with those of the rest of the crew members and were cremated and scattered at Zion National Park in Utah in accordance with her wishes.

India at the 2004 Summer Olympics

India competed at the 2004 Summer Olympics in Athens, Greece, from 13 to 29 August 2004. The Indian Olympic Association sent a total of 73 athletes, 48 men, and 28 women, to compete in 14 sports. Men's field hockey was the only team-based sport in which India had its representation in these Olympic games. **As a pleasant surprise, the shooting team came successful with a silver medal, the winner being Capt. Rajyavardhan Singh Rathore. He was the first Indian to win an individual silver medal. (Men's Double Trap Event).**

Several Indian athletes came close to increasing the medal haul, finishing in fourth place, including Mahesh Bhupati and Leander Paes in tennis men's doubles and Kunjarani Devi in weightlifting women's 48 kg category.

Sanamacha Chanu originally finished fourth (women's weightlifting 53 kg category), but was disqualified after being tested positive for furosemide.

2004 Indian general election

General elections were held in India in four phases between 20 April and 10 May 2004. Over 670 million people were eligible to vote, electing 543 members of the 14ᵗʰ Lok Sabha. Seven states also held assembly elections to elect state governments. They were the first elections fully carried out with electronic voting machines.

On 13 May the Bharatiya Janata Party (BJP), the lead party of the National Democratic Alliance conceded defeat. The Indian National Congress, which had governed India for all but five years from independence until 1996, returned to power after a record eight years out of office. It was able to put together a comfortable majority of more than 335 members out of 543 with the help of its allies. The 335 members included both the Congress-led United Progressive Alliance, the governing coalition formed after the election, external support from the Bahujan Samaj Party (BSP), Samajwadi Party (SP), Kerala Congress (KC) and the Left Front.

The constitutional reason for Sonia Gandhi not becoming the PM in 2004

Subramanian Swamy opened up what he had written inside the letter in an interview and what turned into the "criminal snag" that prevented Sonia from being India's Prime Minister. The criminal bar changed into place due to a reciprocity the proviso to Section five of the Citizenship Act (now amended). Section five of the Act offers citizenship through registration.

Under Italian law, someone now no longer born in Italy can't turn out to be the Prime Minister of Italy. Therefore, on account that Sonia Gandhi changed into now no longer born in India, she should now no longer turn out to be the Prime Minister of India. This is the criminal hitch that in his letter impressed him. He additionally said if the appropriate order changed into now no longer issued, he could project the candidacy of Sonia Gandhi within side the Apex Court.

2004 Indian Ocean earthquake and tsunami

On 26 December 2004, at 07:58:53 local time, a major earthquake with a magnitude of 9.1–9.3 Mw struck with an epicentre off the west coast of northern Sumatra, Indonesia. The undersea megathrust earthquake, known by the scientific community as the Sumatra–Andaman earthquake, was caused by a rupture along the fault between the Burma Plate and the Indian Plate, and reached a Mercalli intensity up to IX in some areas.

A massive tsunami with waves up to 30 m (100 ft) high, known in some countries as the Boxing Day Tsunami after the Boxing Day holiday, devastated communities along the surrounding coasts of the Indian Ocean, killing an estimated 227,898 people in 14 countries in one of the deadliest natural disasters in recorded history. The direct results caused major disruptions to living conditions and commerce in coastal provinces of surrounded countries, including Aceh (Indonesia), Sri Lanka, Tamil Nadu (India) and Khao Lak (Thailand). Banda Aceh reported the largest number of deaths. It remains the deadliest natural disaster of the 21st century.

It was the most powerful earthquake ever recorded in Asia, the most powerful earthquake in the 21st century, and at least the third most powerful earthquake ever recorded in the world since modern seismography began in 1900. It had the longest duration of faulting ever observed, between eight and ten minutes. It caused the planet to vibrate as much as 10 mm (0.4 in), and also remotely triggered earthquakes as far away as Alaska. Its epicentre was between Simeulue and mainland Sumatra. The plight of the affected people and countries prompted a worldwide humanitarian response, with donations totalling more than US$14 billion.

Right to Information Act, 2005

The Right to Information (RTI) is an act of the Parliament of India which sets out the rules and procedures regarding citizens' right to information. It replaced the former Freedom of Information Act, 2002. Under the provisions of RTI Act, any citizen of India may request information from a "public authority" (a body of Government or "instrumentality of State") which is required to reply expeditiously or within thirty days. In case of matter involving a petitioner's life and liberty, the information has to be provided within 48 hours. The Act also requires every public authority to computerize their records for wide dissemination and to proactively publish certain categories of information so that the citizens need minimum recourse to request for information formally.

The RTI Bill was passed by Parliament of India on 15 June 2005 and came into force with effect from 12 October 2005. Every day on an average, over 4800 RTI applications are filed. In the first ten years of the commencement of the act, over 17,500,000 applications had been filed.

India–United States Civil Nuclear Agreement

The 123 Agreement signed between the United States of America and the Republic of India is known as the U.S.–India Civil Nuclear Agreement or Indo-US nuclear deal. The framework for this agreement was a July 18, 2005, joint statement by then Indian Prime Minister Manmohan Singh and then U.S. President George W. Bush, under which India agreed to separate its civil and military nuclear facilities and to place all its civil nuclear facilities under International Atomic Energy Agency (IAEA) safeguards and, in exchange, the United States agreed to work toward full civil nuclear cooperation with India. This U.S.-India deal took more than three years to come to fruition as it had to go through several complex stages, including amendment of U.S. domestic law, especially the Atomic Energy Act of 1954, a civil-military nuclear Separation Plan in India, an India-IAEA safeguards (inspections) agreement and the grant of an exemption for India by the Nuclear Suppliers Group, an export-control cartel that had been formed mainly in response to India's first nuclear test in 1974. In its final shape, the deal places under permanent safeguards those nuclear facilities that India has identified as "civil" and permits broad civil nuclear cooperation, while excluding the transfer of "sensitive" equipment and technologies, including civil enrichment and reprocessing items even under IAEA safeguards. On August 18, 2008, the IAEA Board of Governors approved, and on February 2, 2009, India signed an India-specific safeguards agreement with the IAEA. After India brought this agreement into force, inspections began in a phased manner on the 35 civilian nuclear installations India has identified in its Separation Plan.

The deal is seen as a watershed in U.S.-India relations and introduces a new aspect to international nonproliferation efforts. On August 1, 2008, the IAEA approved the safeguards agreement with India, after which the United States approached the Nuclear Suppliers Group (NSG) to grant a waiver to India to commence civilian nuclear trade. The 48-nation NSG granted the waiver to India on September 6, 2008, allowing it to access civilian nuclear technology and fuel from other countries. The implementation of this waiver made India the only known country with nuclear weapons which is not a party to the Non-Proliferation Treaty (NPT) but is still allowed to carry out nuclear commerce with the rest of the world.

The U.S. House of Representatives passed the bill to approve the deal on September 28, 2008. Two days later, India and France inked a similar nuclear pact making France the first country to have such an agreement with India. On October 1, 2008, the U.S. Senate also approved the civilian nuclear agreement allowing India to purchase nuclear fuel and technology from—and sell them to—the United States. U.S. president, George W. Bush, signed the legislation on the Indo-US nuclear deal, approved by the U.S. Congress, into law, now called the United States-India Nuclear Cooperation Approval and Non-proliferation Enhancement Act, on October 8, 2008. The agreement was signed by then Indian External Affairs Minister Pranab Mukherjee and his counterpart then Secretary of State Condoleezza Rice, on October 10.

Pratibha Patil

Prathibha Devisingh Patil (born 19 December 1934) is an Indian politician and lawyer who served as the 12th president of India from 2007 to 2012. She was the first woman to become the president of India. A member of the Indian National Congress, she previously served as the Governor of Rajasthan from 2004 to 2007, and was a member of the Lok Sabha from 1991 to 1996.

2007 ICC World Twenty20 final

The 2007 ICC World Twenty20 Final was a Twenty20 International cricket match played between India and Pakistan at the Wanderers Stadium, Johannesburg, South Africa. Administered by the International Cricket Council (ICC) it was the culmination of the 2007 ICC World Twenty20 which was the inaugural edition of the tournament. India won by defeating Pakistan by five runs. The teams had previously played each other in a Group-D match of the tournament, which was also won by India.

M S Dhoni

Mahendra Singh Dhoni (born 7 July 1981) is an Indian professional cricketer, who plays as a wicket-keeper-batsman. Widely regarded as one of the world's greatest wicket-keeper-batsmen and captains in the history of the sport, he is known for his explosive batting, wicket-keeping and leadership skills. He was the captain of the Indian national team in limited-overs formats from 2007 to 2017 and in Test cricket from 2008 to 2014. Dhoni is the first cricketer to be a winning captain of all three major ICC trophies, as under his captaincy, India won the 2007 ICC World Twenty20, the 2011 Cricket World Cup, and the 2013 ICC Champions Trophy, the most by any captain. He also led India to victory in the 2010 and 2016 Asia Cup. Additionally, under his leadership, India won the 2010 and 2011 ICC Test Mace and 2013 ICC ODI Championship. He plays for and captains Chennai Super Kings franchise in the Indian Premier League.

2008 Mumbai attacks

The 2008 Mumbai attacks (also referred to as 26/11 attacks or 26 November attacks) were a series of terrorist attacks that took place in November 2008, when 10 members of Lashkar-e-Taiba, a militant Islamist organisation from Pakistan, carried out 12 coordinated shooting and bombing attacks lasting four days across Mumbai. The attacks, which drew widespread global condemnation, began on Wednesday 26 November and lasted until Saturday 29 November 2008. A total of 175 people died, including nine of the attackers, with more than 300 injured.

Eight of the attacks occurred in South Mumbai: at Chhatrapati Shivaji Maharaj Terminus, the Oberoi Trident, the Taj Palace & Tower, the Leopold Cafe, the Cama Hospital, the Nariman House, the Metro Cinema, and in a lane behind the Times of India building and St. Xavier's College. There was also an explosion at Mazagaon, in Mumbai's port area, and in a taxi at Vile Parle. By the early morning of 28 November, all sites except for the Taj Hotel had been secured by the Mumbai Police and security forces. On 29

November, India's National Security Guards (NSG) conducted Operation Black Tornado to flush out the remaining attackers; it culminated in the death of the last remaining attackers at the Taj Hotel and ended the attacks.

Before his execution in 2012, Ajmal Kasab, the sole surviving attacker, disclosed that the attackers were members of the terrorist group Lashkar-e-Taiba, and were controlled from Pakistan, corroborating initial claims from the Indian Government. Pakistan later confirmed that the sole surviving perpetrator of the attacks was a Pakistani citizen. On 9 April 2015, the foremost ringleader of the attacks, Zakiur Rehman Lakhvi, was released on bail and disappeared; he was arrested again in Lahore on 2 January 2021. In 2018, former Pakistani prime minister Nawaz Sharif suggested that the Pakistani government played a role in the 2008 Mumbai attack. In 2022, one of the masterminds of the attack, Sajid Majeed Mir—who had been earlier claimed to be dead by the Pakistan Government—was convicted for funding terrorist activities by an anti-terrorism court in Pakistan.

Aftermath

The attacks are sometimes referred to in India as "26/11", after the date in 2008 that the attacks began. The Pradhan Inquiry Commission, appointed by the Maharashtra government, produced a report that was tabled before the legislative assembly more than a year after the events. The report said the "war-like" attack was beyond the capacity to respond of any police force, but also found fault with the Mumbai Police Commissioner Hasan Gafoor's lack of leadership during the crisis.

The Maharashtra government planned to buy 36 speed boats to patrol the coastal areas and several helicopters for the same purpose. It also planned to create an anti-terror force called "Force One" and upgrade all the weapons that Mumbai police currently have. Prime Minister Manmohan Singh on an all-party conference declared that legal framework would be strengthened in the battle against terrorism and a federal anti-terrorist intelligence and investigation agency, like the FBI, will be set up soon to co-ordinate action against terrorism. The government strengthened anti-terror laws with UAPA 2008, and the federal National Investigation Agency was formed.

Lehman crisis: Here's what it meant for India

On September 15, 2008, America's fourth-largest investment bank Lehman Brothers filed for bankruptcy. With total debts of $613 billion against total assets of $639 billion and 25,000 employees worldwide, Lehman's bankruptcy was said to be the largest in the history, surpassing that of Worldcom's and Enron's.

Lehman Brothers' crisis further led to global financial crisis that year with the development hitting several economies as global markets plummeted immediately. Several countries had to face the heat as the company's collapse pulled down confidence in banks across the world. This included India's then largest private lender ICICI Bank too.

On 3 March 2008, the Sensex fell by 900 points to settle at 16,677. On 17 March 2008, the BSE Sensex fell further to 14,809 - a fall of 951 points. On 24 October 2008, the BSE Sensex fell to 8701, a fall of 1070 points in a single day.

India at the 2008 Summer Olympics

India competed at the 2008 Summer Olympics in Beijing, People's Republic of China. India was represented by the Indian Olympic Association (IOA). A contingent of 57 athletes in 12 sports represented India, and had a support-staff of 42 officials.

For the first time since 1928, the men's national field hockey team was unable to take part in the Summer Olympics due to its failure to qualify. A two-year ban imposed by the International Weightlifting Federation after the 2006 Commonwealth Games doping scandal originally resulted in only one Olympic weightlifter, Monika Devi from India being scheduled to compete, but she withdrew from the competition after failing the drug test. On 9 August 2008, IWF declared that she was clean, but the event she was supposed to participate in, had already closed.

On 11 August 2008, Abhinav Bindra won the gold medal in the men's 10 m air rifle. It was a huge achievement for India at the Olympic games shooting event. In doing so, he won the first ever individual gold medal for India, and the first medal in any event for India at the Beijing Games.

The previous highest individual achievements for India were two silver medals won by Norman Pritchard, an Englishman born in India, at the 1900 Paris Olympics and one silver medal won by the 2008 flagbearer Rajyavardhan Rathore at the 2004 Athens Olympics. Sushil Kumar won the second ever wrestling medal for India, the first being the bronze earned by Khashaba Dadasaheb Jadhav in the 1952 Helsinki Olympics. Vijender Singh won a bronze medal in the middleweight boxing category, having lost in the semifinals. This was India's first-ever Olympic medal in boxing.

The 2008 Beijing Olympics saw the best ever performance by an Indian contingent, in terms of the number of medals. They won three medals in all (one gold and two bronze medals).

Medalists

Medals	Name	Sport	Event
Gold	Abhinav Bindra	Shooting	Men's 10 m air rifle
Bronze	Sushil Kumar	Wrestling	Men's freestyle 66 kg
Bronze	Vijender Singh	Boxing	Middleweight 75 kg

2009 Indian general election

Congress comes to power again.

General elections were held in India in five phases between 16 April 2009 and 13 May 2009 to elect the members of the fifteenth Lok Sabha. With an electorate of 716 million, it was the largest democratic election in the world until being surpassed by the 2014 general election.

By constitutional requirement, elections to the Lok Sabha must be held every five years or when Parliament is dissolved by the president. The previous elections were held in May 2004 and the term of the 14th Lok Sabha would have naturally expired on 1 June 2009. Elections are organised by the Election Commission of India (ECI) and are normally held in multiple phases to better handle the large electorate and security concerns. The 2009 elections were held in five phases. In February 2009,

Rs.11.20 billion ($200.5 million) was budgeted for election expenses by parliament.

A total of 8,070 candidates contested 543 seats elected in single-member constituencies using first-past-the-post voting. Voter turnout over all five phases was around 58%. The results of the election were announced within three days of phase five, on 16 May.

The United Progressive Alliance (UPA) led by the Indian National Congress formed the government after winning a majority of seats, with strong results in Andhra Pradesh, Kerala, Maharashtra, Rajasthan, Tamil Nadu, Uttar Pradesh and West Bengal. Manmohan Singh became the first Prime Minister since Jawaharlal Nehru in 1962 to be re-elected after completing a full five-year term. The UPA was able to put together a comfortable majority with support from 322 of the 543 elected members. External support was provided by the Bahujan Samaj Party (BSP), Samajwadi Party (SP), Janata Dal (Secular) (JD(S)), Rashtriya Janata Dal (RJD) and other minor parties.

Singh was sworn in as Prime Minister on 22 May 2009 at the Ashoka Hall of Rashtrapati Bhavan.

Satyam Scam

What is Satyam Scam?

Satyam scam means a huge corporate fraud committed in 2009 by Ramalinga Raju, the founder and chairman of Satyam Computer Services. He admitted to exaggerating sales, earnings, cash balances, and personnel numbers in the company's books. He also acknowledged siphoning off money from the firm for his personal use. The Satyam fraud was considered worth Rs. 7800 crores and was formerly regarded as India's largest business scandal.

The Satyam scam highlighted a lack of corporate governance, auditing standards, regulatory monitoring, and ethical behavior at one of India's largest IT firms. It also damaged the faith and confidence of Indian IT sector investors, consumers, workers, and stakeholders. The Satyam Computers scam had serious consequences for the corporation, its auditors, its board of directors, and its stockholders.

Understanding Satyam Scandal - India's Biggest Accounting Fraud

The Satyam Computers scam exemplifies one of India's most catastrophic scams, sending shockwaves across the business world. Ramalinga Raju, the founder and chairman of Satyam Computer Services, admitted to falsifying the company's accounting for many years in 2009. This disclosure surprised investors, workers, and regulators, ruining Satyam's and the Indian business community's image.

The Satyam scam was a methodically planned effort to defraud stakeholders. Raju and a small group of accomplices increased sales, earnings, and cash levels, providing a false sense of financial accomplishment. Forging bank statements, faking invoices, and inflating customer numbers were all part of the fraudulent operations. Auditors tasked with protecting shareholders' interests failed to discover the anomalies, showing the failure of corporate governance processes.

The results were devastating. Share prices fell precipitously, causing substantial capital destruction for investors. As the corporation fought to survive, thousands of workers faced uncertainty. The Satyam scandal damaged local and foreign investors' faith in India's business sector, generating concerns about transparency, accountability, and ethical standards. Following the incident, the Indian government intervened to avert Satyam's collapse and preserve stakeholders' interests. Tech Mahindra finally purchased the firm, kicking off a lengthy path to recovery. The episode was a wake-up call for Indian regulators, prompting substantial changes in corporate governance, accounting methods, and audit rules.

The Satyam controversy is a sharp reminder of the significance of strong regulatory supervision, ethical behavior, and good corporate governance in sustaining company confidence and integrity.

Major overseas acquisitions by Tata group

With the takeover of two British automobile marquees Jaguar and Land Rover, the $28.8 billion Tata group, with 98 companies in its fold, will add another prominent entry to its growing roster of global acquisitions.

Barely a year ago, it paid over $12 billion to acquire Anglo-Dutch steel maker Corus, in what remains the largest buy-out deal overseas by an Indian company till date.

And going by what senior executives of Tata Sons - the holding arm of the group that has 27 listed companies - maintain, the appetite for such mega mergers and acquisitions is only growing with each deal.

Tata Steel has made three major acquisitions worth some $13 billion in the past few years.

"A journey that began long ago is gathering pace," said chairman Ratan Tata on the overseas foray of the group that has interests in consumer goods, chemicals, energy, services, engineering, materials and IT systems and communications.

"From IT and tea to automobiles and steel, Tata companies are spreading their wings to find a place in the global sun," he says.

Here's a look at some notable acquisitions by the Tata group companies overseas in the past few years:

Tata Steel:

The company, which celebrated its centenary in August last year, wants to boost its annual output of 8.7 million tonnes to 15 million tonnes by 2010, and take it upwards to 30 million tonnes by 2030. More stunning moves on the mergers and acquisition front can definitely be expected, it says.

In January 2007, the group pulled off India's biggest ever takeover of an overseas company to buy Anglo-Dutch steel-maker Corus in a $12 billion deal that made it the combined entity the world's fifth largest producer of the commodity.

This came just over a year after it acquired Singapore's NatSteel, which also has a presence in Thailand, China, Malaysia, Vietnam, the Philippines and Australia followed by the acquisition of Thailand's Millennium Steel for a $421 million.

Tata Motors:

South Korea's Daewoo Commercial Vehicle Co was acquired by the company in March 2004 for $102 million and gained, in the process, a market share of 30 percent and access to markets where it had no prior presence.

This was followed by the acquisition of a 21 percent stake in Spanish bus maker Hispano Carrocera for $18 million with an option to pick up the remaining stake at a later date. This helped the company get technology to make top-end busses.

Another company in the fold - Tata Technologies, which provides automotive engineering and design, services - bought Britain's Incat International for $53 million.

Tata Consultancy Services:

This company, which was earlier a division of Tata Sons, has been among the most aggressive shoppers for companies overseas. It has acquired six companies in recent months, though the net value of the deals is no more than $100 million.

In the second half of 2005, following the merger of group company Tata Infotech into its fold, TCS acquired financial services company FNS of Australia for $26 million and then Chile's outsourcing major Comicrom for $23 million.

TCS, which has 160 offices in 30 countries, also entered into a structured deal with the British insurance major, the Pearl Group, which essentially called for the two entities to set up a subsidiary with TCS as the majority partner.

Videsh Sanchar Nigam Ltd:

The Tata group acquired the former state-run, international telecom carrier a few years ago. The company has made several overseas acquisitions since then with the aim of becoming a top-end services provider in the industry.

Some of the acquisitions include undersea cable company Tyco of the US for $130 million, Internet service provider Dishnet's India division for $64.28 million and international telecom service provider Teleglobe of US for $239 million.

Tata Chemicals:

Following its acquisition of Hindustan Lever Chemicals, Tata Chemicals was on the lookout for a steady supply of phosphoric acid for its newly acquired plant at Haldia.

It, accordingly, took over two overseas for a total value of $215 million - Indo Maroc Phosphore of Morocco in March 2005 and Brunner Mond Group of Britain in December last year. Morocco produces over 50 per cent of world's rock phosphate.

Tata Tea:

In 2000, Tata Tea bought British giant Tetley for a $407 million - in what was then the largest such deal by an Indian company - and started scouting for similar deals to become a global tea and related drinks brand.

Another acquisition has been a 33 per cent stake in South African Joekels Tea Packers for an undisclosed amount that was announced this month. It had earlier acquired the US-based Good Earth Corp for $32 million.

The company's other picks include Czech Republic's Jemca and 30 per cent stake in the US-based favoured water manufacturer Glaceau for $677 million.

Indian Hotels:

This company, which runs the Taj Group of hotels, acquired several hotels abroad for $121 million in the past few years. It has set aside $100 million for future acquisitions in Europe, the Middle East, Asia and the US.

In December 2006, it acquired W, a hotel at the Woolloomooloo Bay in Sydney, then it took over the management of The Pierre, a luxurious landmark hotel on New York's Fifth Avenue. India Hotels has 39 hotels in India and 18 worldwide.

Another acquisition was Campton Place Hotel in San Francisco

Tata AutoComp Systems:

This company - which makes auto components from 14 plants, three engineering centres and three export-oriented units for clients like General Motors, Ford and Toyota - acquired W, Weidinger of Germany for $7 million last year.

Virender Sehwag

Virender Sehwag (born 20 October 1978) is a former Indian cricketer who represented India from 1999 to 2013. Widely regarded as one of the most destructive openers and one of the greatest batsmen of his era, he played for Delhi Capitals in IPL and Delhi and Haryana in Indian domestic cricket. He played his first One Day International in 1999 and joined the Indian test side in 2001. In April 2009, Sehwag became the first Indian to be honoured as the Wisden Leading Cricketer in the World for his performance in 2008, subsequently becoming the first player of any nationality to retain the award for 2009. He worked as stand-in captain occasionally during absence of main captain of India, also worked as Vice-Captain for Indian squad. He is former captain of Delhi Daredevils and Delhi Ranji Team. During his time with India, Sehwag was a member of the team that was one of the joint winners of the 2002 ICC Champions Trophy, the winners of the 2007 T20 World Cup, and the winners of the 2011 Cricket World Cup. During the 2002 ICC Champions Trophy, Sehwag was the highest run scorer with 271 runs.

Sehwag holds multiple records including the highest score made by an Indian in Test cricket (319 against South Africa at M. A. Chidambaram Stadium in Chennai), which was also the fastest triple century in the history of international cricket (reached 300 off only 278 balls) as well as the fastest 250 by any batsman (in 207 balls against Sri Lanka on 3 December 2009 at the Brabourne Stadium in Mumbai). Sehwag also holds the distinction of being one of four batsmen in the world to have ever surpassed 300 twice in Test cricket. Sehwag has the highest strike rate in test matches among batsmen with 2000 or more test runs. Sehwag's career strike rate in test matches is 82.23. In March 2009, Sehwag smashed what was until then the fastest century ever scored by an Indian in ODI cricket, from 60 balls. On 8 December 2011, he hit his maiden double century in ODI cricket, against West Indies, becoming the second batsman after Sachin Tendulkar to reach the landmark. His score became the highest individual score in ODI cricket—219 off 149 balls which was later bettered by Rohit Sharma—264 off 173 balls on 13 November 2014. He is one of only two players in the world to score a double hundred in ODI and a triple hundred in Test Cricket, the other being Chris Gayle.

Yuvraj Singh

Yuvraj Singh (born 12 December 1981) is a former Indian international cricketer who played in all formats of the game. He is an all-rounder who batted left-handed in the middle order and bowled slow left-arm orthodox. He has won 7 Player of the Series awards in ODI cricket, which is joint 3rd highest by an Indian, shared with former Indian captain Sourav Ganguly. He is also the son of former Indian fast bowler and Punjabi actor Yograj Singh.

Yuvraj was a member of the Indian cricket team in One Day Internationals (ODIs) between 2000 and 2017 and played his first Test match in October 2003. He was the vice-captain of the Indian ODI team between 2007 and 2008. In a match against England at the 2007 World Twenty20, he famously hit six sixes in one over bowled by Stuart Broad — a feat performed only three times previously in any form of senior cricket, and never in an international match between two teams with Test match status. In the same match, he set the record for the fastest fifty in Twenty20 Internationals and in all T20 cricket, reaching 50 runs in 12 balls, which was a record for fastest half century in International cricket, until it was broken by Dipendra Airee during 2023 Asian Games but Yuvi's achievement is still an unbreakable fastest 50 record in the ICC Cricket World Cup and among ICC full member nations. During the 2011 World Cup, he became the first player to take a 5-wicket haul and score a 50 in the same World Cup match. During the 2011 World Cup, Yuvraj Singh played eight innings in nine matches and scored 362 runs with a remarkable average of 90.50. He also took 15 wickets in the tournament, maintaining an economy rate of 5.02.

Strange deaths in Gandhi & Vadra Family

Sanjay Gandhi died in a plane crash in 1980. Indira Gandhi was assassinated in 1984. Rajiv Gandhi died in bomb explosion in 1991.

In 2001, Robert's sister Michelle had died in a car accident on the Delhi—Jaipur highway. Two years later in 2003, Robert's estranged brother, Richard committed suicide. Later in 2009, Robert's father, Rajender hanged himself in his bedroom, where he lived alone because he was separated with his wife Maureen.

PAKISTAN

Pervez Musharraf

Pervez Musharraf (11 August 1943 – 5 February 2023) was a Pakistani army general and politician who served as the tenth president of Pakistan from 2001 to 2008. He also served as the 10th Chairman Joint Chiefs of Staff Committee from 1998 to 2001 and the 7th Chief of Army Staff from 1998 to 2007.

Constitutional changes

Shortly after Musharraf's takeover, Musharraf issued Oath of Judges Order No. 2000, which required judges to take a fresh oath of office. On 12 May 2000, the Supreme Court asked Musharraf to hold national elections by 12 October 2002. After President Rafiq Tarar's resignation, Musharraf formally appointed himself as President on 20 June 2001. In August 2002, he issued the Legal Framework Order No. 2002, which added numerous amendments to the Constitution.

2002 general elections

Musharraf called for nationwide political elections in the country after accepting the ruling of the Supreme Court of Pakistan. Musharraf was the first military president to accept the rulings of the Supreme Court and holding free and fair elections in 2002, part of his vision to return democratic rule to the country. In October 2002, Pakistan held general elections, which the pro-Musharraf PML-Q won wide margins, although it had failed to gain an absolute majority. The PML-Q formed a government with far-right religious parties coalition, the MMA and the liberals MQM; the coalition legitimised Musharraf's rule.

After the elections, the PML-Q nominated Zafarullah Khan Jamali for the office of prime minister, which Musharraf also approved. After first session at the Parliament, Musharraf voluntarily transferred the powers of chief executive to Prime Minister Zafarullah Khan Jamali. Musharraf succeeded to pass the XVII amendment, which grants powers to dissolve the parliament, with approval required from the Supreme Court. Within two years, Jamali proved to be an ineffective prime minister as he forcefully implemented his policies in the country and caused problems with the business class elites. Musharraf accepted the resignation of Jamali and asked his close colleague Chaudhry Shujaat Hussain to appoint a new prime minister in place. Hussain nominated Finance minister Shaukat Aziz, who had been impressive due to his performance as finance minister in 1999. Musharraf regarded Aziz as his right hand and preferable choice for the office of Prime minister. With Aziz appointed as Prime minister, Musharraf transferred all executive powers to Aziz as he trusted Shaukat Aziz. Aziz proved to be extremely capable in running the government; under his leadership economic growth reached to a maximum level, which further stabilised Musharraf's presidency. Aziz swiftly, quietly and quickly undermined the elements seeking to undermine Musharraf, which became a factor in Musharraf's trust in him. Between 2004 and 2007, Aziz approved many projects that did not require Musharraf's permission.

In 2010, all constitutional changes carried out by Musharraf and Aziz's policies were reverted by the 18th Amendment, which restored the powers of the Prime Minister and reduced the role of the President to levels below that of even the pre-Musharraf era.

He suspended the country's democratic process and imposed two states of emergency, leading to his conviction for treason. During his rule, he implemented both liberal reforms and authoritarian measures, while also forming alliances and impacting the situation in Balochistan. The legacy of Musharraf's era serves as a cautionary tale for future leaders in Pakistan.

Presidency (2001-2008)

The presidency of Pervez Musharraf helped bring the liberal forces to the national level and into prominence, for the first time in the history of Pakistan. He granted national amnesty to the political workers of the liberal parties like Muttahida Qaumi Movement and Pakistan Muslim League (Q), and supported MQM in becoming a central player in the government. Musharraf disbanded the cultural policies of the previous Prime Minister Nawaz Sharif, and quickly adopted Benazir Bhutto's cultural policies after disbanding Indian channels in the country.

His cultural policies liberalised Pakistan's media, and he issued many television licences to the private-sector to open television centres and media houses. The television dramas, film industry, theatre, music and literature activities, were personally encouraged by Pervez Musharraf. Under his policies, the rock music bands gained a following in the country and many concerts were held each week. His cultural policies, the film, theatre, rock and folk music, and television programs were extremely devoted to and promoted the national spirit of the country. In 2001, Musharraf got on stage with the rock music band, Junoon, and sang the national song with the band.

On political fronts, Musharraf faced fierce opposition from the ultra-conservative alliance, the MMA, led by clergyman Maulana Noorani. In Pakistan, Maulana Noorani was remembered as a mystic religious leader and had preached spiritual aspects of Islam all over the world as part of the World Islamic Mission. Although the political deadlock posed by Maulana Noorani was neutralised after Noorani's death, Musharraf yet had to face the opposition from ARD led by Benazir Bhutto of the PPP.

On 18 September 2005, Musharraf made a speech before a broad based audience of Jewish leadership, sponsored by the American Jewish Congress's Council for World Jewry, in New York City. He was widely criticised by Middle Eastern leaders, but was met with some praise among Jewish leadership.

Support for the war on terror and Afghanistan relations

Musharraf allied with the United States against the Taliban in Afghanistan after the September 11 attacks. As the closest state to the Taliban government, Musharraf was in negotiations with them in the aftermath of the attacks regarding the severity of the situation before allying with the U.S. and declaring to stamp out extremism. He was, however criticised by NATO and the Afghan government of not doing enough to prevent pro Taliban or al-Qaeda militants in the Pakistan-Afghanistan border region.

Tensions with Afghanistan increased in 2006, with Hamid Karzai, then president of Afghanistan, accusing Musharraf of failing to act against Afghan Taliban leaders in Pakistan, claiming that the Taliban leader Mullah Omar was based in Quetta, Pakistan. In response, Musharraf hit back saying "None of this is true and Karzai knows it." George W. Bush encouraged the two leaders to unite in the war on terror during a trio meeting.

Violence in the Khyber Pakhtunkhwa escalated in the late 2000s amid fighting between militants and Pakistani soldiers backed by the U.S.

Relations with India

After the 2001 Gujarat earthquake, Musharraf expressed his sympathies to Indian prime minister Atal Bihari Vajpayee and sent a plane load of relief supplies to India.

In 2004, Musharraf began a series of talks with India to resolve the Kashmir dispute. In 2004 a cease-fire was agreed upon along the Line of Control. Many troops still patrol the border.

Relations with Saudi Arabia

In 2006, King Abdullah of Saudi Arabia visited Pakistan for the first time as King. Musharraf honoured King Abdullah with the Nishan-e-Pakistan. Musharraf received the King Abdul-Aziz Medallion in 2007.

Nuclear scandals

From September 2001 until his resignation in 2007 from the military, Musharraf's presidency was affected by scandals relating to nuclear weapons, which were detrimental to his authoritative legitimacy in the country and in the international community. In October 2001, Musharraf authorised a sting operation led by FIA to arrest two physicists Sultan Bashiruddin Mahmood and Chaudhry Abdul Majeed, because of their supposed connection with the Taliban after they secretly visited Taliban-controlled Afghanistan in 2000. The local Pakistani media widely circulated the reports that "Mahmood had a meeting with Osama bin Laden where Bin Laden had shown interest in building a radiological weapon;" it was later discovered that neither scientist had any in-depth knowledge of the technology. In December 2001, Musharraf authorised security hearings and the two scientists were taken into the custody by the JAG Branch (JAG); security hearings continued until early 2002.

Another scandal arose as a consequence of disclosure by Pakistani nuclear physicist Abdul Qadeer Khan. On 27 February 2001, Musharraf spoke highly of Khan at a state dinner in Islamabad, and he personally approved Khan's appointment as Science Advisor to the Government. In 2004, Musharraf relieved Abdul Qadeer Khan from his post and initially denied knowledge of the government's involvement in nuclear proliferation, despite Khan's claim that Musharraf was the "Big Boss" of the proliferation ring. Following this, Musharraf authorised a national security hearing, which continued until his resignation from the army in 2007. According to Zahid Malik, Musharraf and the military establishment at that time acted against Abdul Qadeer Khan in an attempt to prove the loyalty of Pakistan to the United States and Western world.

The investigations backfired on Musharraf and public opinion turned against him. The populist ARD movement, which included the major political parties such as the PML and the PPP, used the issue to bring down Musharraf's presidency.

The debriefing of Abdul Qadeer Khan severely damaged Musharraf's own public image and his political prestige in the country. He faced bitter domestic criticism for attempting to vilify Khan, specifically from opposition leader Benazir Bhutto. In an interview to Daily Times, Bhutto maintained that Khan had been a "scapegoat" in the nuclear proliferation scandal and said that she didn't "believe that such a big scandal could have taken place under the nose of General Musharraf". Musharraf's long-standing ally, the MQM, published criticism of Musharraf over his handling of Abdul Qadeer Khan. The ARD movement and the political parties further tapped into the public anger and mass demonstrations against Musharraf. The credibility of the United States was also badly damaged; the US itself refrained from pressuring Musharraf to take further action against Khan. While Abdul Qadeer Khan remained popular in the country, Musharraf could not withstand the political pressure and his presidency was further weakened. Musharraf quickly pardoned Abdul Qadeer Khan in exchange for cooperation and issued confinement orders against Khan that limited Khan's movement. He handed over the case of Abdul Qadeer Khan to Prime minister Aziz who had been supportive towards Khan, personally "thanking" him: "The services of Dr. Qadeer Khan are unforgettable for the country."

On 4 July 2008, in an interview, Abdul Qadeer Khan laid the blame on President Musharraf and later on Benazir Bhutto for transferring the technology, claiming that Musharraf was aware of all the deals and he was the "Big Boss" for those deals. Khan said that "Musharraf gave centrifuges to North Korea in a 2000 shipment supervised by the armed forces. The equipment was sent in a North Korean plane loaded under the supervision of Pakistan security officials." Nuclear weapons expert David Albright of the Institute for Science and International Security agreed that Khan's activities were government-sanctioned. After Musharraf's resignation, Abdul Qadeer Khan was released from house arrest by the executive order of the Supreme Court of Pakistan. After Musharraf left the country, the new Chairman of the Joint Chiefs of Staff Committee General Tärik Majid terminated all further debriefings of Abdul Qadeer Khan. Few believed that Abdul Qadeer Khan acted alone and the affair risked gravely damaging the Armed Forces, which oversaw and controlled the nuclear weapons development and of which Musharraf was Chairman of the Joint Chiefs of Staff until his resignation from military service on 28 November 2007.

Corruption issues

When Musharraf came to power in 1999, he promised that the corruption in the government bureaucracy would be cleaned up. However, some claimed that the level of corruption did not diminish throughout Musharraf's time.

Domestic politics

Musharraf instituted prohibitions on foreign students' access to studying Islam within Pakistan, an effort that began as an outright ban but was later reduced to restrictions on obtaining visas.

In December 2003, Musharraf made a deal with MMA, a six-member coalition of hardline Islamist parties, agreeing to leave the army by 31 December 2004. With that party's support, pro-Musharraf legislators were able to muster the two-thirds supermajority required to pass the Seventeenth Amendment, which retroactively legalised Musharraf's 1999 coup and many of his decrees. Musharraf reneged on his agreement with the MMA and pro-Musharraf legislators in the Parliament passed a bill allowing Musharraf to keep both offices.

On 1 January 2004, Musharraf had won a confidence vote in the Electoral College of Pakistan, consisting of both houses of Parliament and the four provincial assemblies. Musharraf received 658 out of 1170 votes, a 56% majority, but many opposition and Islamic members of parliament walked out to protest the vote. As a result of this vote, his term was extended to 2007.

Prime Minister Zafarullah Khan Jamali resigned on 26 June 2004, after losing the support of Musharraf's party, PML(Q). His resignation was at least partially due to his public differences with the party chairman, Chaudhry Shujaat Hussain. This was rumoured to have happened at Musharraf's command. Jamali had been appointed with the support of Musharraf's and the pro-Musharraf PML(Q). Most PML(Q) parliamentarians formerly belonged to the Pakistan Muslim League party led by Sharif, and most ministers of the cabinet were formerly senior members of other parties, joining the PML(Q) after the elections upon being offered positions. Musharraf nominated Shaukat Aziz, the minister for finance and a former employee of Citibank and head of Citibank Private Banking as the new prime minister.

In 2005, the Bugti clan attacked a gas field in Balochistan, after Dr. Shazia was raped at that location. Musharraf responded by dispatching 4,500 soldiers, supported by tanks and helicopters, to guard the gas field.

Women's rights

The National Assembly voted in favour of the "Women's Protection Bill" on 15 November 2006 and the Senate approved it on 23 November 2006. President General Pervez Musharraf signed into law the "Women's Protection Bill", on 1 December 2006. The bill places rape laws under the penal code and allegedly does away with harsh conditions that previously required victims to produce four male witnesses and exposed the victims to prosecution for adultery if they were unable to prove the crime. However, the Women's Protection bill has been criticised heavily by many for paying continued lip service and failing to address the actual problem by its roots: repealing the Hudood Ordinance. In this context, Musharraf has also been criticised by women and human rights activists for not following up his words by action. The Human Rights Commission of Pakistan (HRCP) said that "The so-called Women's Protection Bill is a farcical attempt at making Hudood Ordinances palatable" outlining the issues of the bill and the continued impact on women.

His government increased reserved seats for women in assemblies, to increase women's representation and make their presence more effective. The number of reserved seats in the National Assembly was increased from 20 to 60. In provincial assemblies, 128 seats were reserved for women. This situation has brought out increased participation of women in the 1988 and 2008 elections.

In March 2005, a couple of months after the rape of a Pakistani physician, Dr. Shazia Khalid, working on a government gas plant in the remote Balochistan province, Musharraf was criticised for pronouncing Captain Hammad, a fellow military man and the accused in the case, innocent before the judicial inquiry was complete. Shazia alleged that she was forced by the government to leave the country.

In an interview given to The Washington Post in September 2005, Musharraf said that Pakistani women who had been the victims of rape treated rape as a "moneymaking concern", and were only interested in the publicity to make money and get a Canadian visa. He subsequently denied making these comments, but the Post made available an audio recording of the interview, in which Musharraf could be heard making the quoted remarks. Musharraf also denied Mukhtaran Mai, a Pakistani rape victim, the right to travel abroad, until pressured by US State Department. The remarks made by Musharraf sparked outrage and protests both internationally and in Pakistan by various groups i.e. women groups, activists. In a rally, held close to the presidential palace and Pakistan's parliament, hundreds of women demonstrated in Pakistan demanding Musharraf apologise for the controversial remarks about female rape victims.

Assassination attempts

Musharraf survived multiple assassination attempts and alleged plots. In 2000 Kamran Atif, an alleged member of Harkat-ul Mujahideen al-Alami, tried to assassinate Musharraf. Atif was sentenced to death in 2006 by an Anti Terrorism Court. On 14 December 2003, Musharraf survived an assassination attempt when a powerful bomb went off minutes after his highly guarded convoy crossed a bridge in Rawalpindi; it was the third such attempt during his four-year rule. On 25 December 2003, two suicide bombers tried to assassinate Musharraf, but their car bombs failed to kill him; 16 others died instead. Musharraf escaped with only a cracked windshield on his car. Amjad Farooqi was an alleged mastermind behind these attempts, and was killed by Pakistani forces in 2004 after an extensive manhunt.

On 6 July 2007, there was another attempted assassination, when an unknown group fired a 7.62 submachine gun at Musharraf's plane as it took off from a runway in Rawalpindi. Security also recovered two anti-aircraft guns, from which no shots had been fired. On 17 July 2007, Pakistani police detained 39 people in relation to the attempted assassination of Musharraf. The suspects were detained at an undisclosed location by a joint team of Punjab Police, the Federal Investigation Agency and other Pakistani intelligence agencies.

Fall from the presidency

By August 2007, polls showed 64 per cent of Pakistanis did not want another Musharraf term. Controversies involving the atomic issues, Lal Masjid incident, the unpopular War in North-West Pakistan, the suspension of Chief Justice Iftikhar Muhammad Chaudhry, and widely circulated criticisms from rivals Benazir Bhutto and Nawaz Sharif, had brutalised the personal image of Musharraf in public and political circles. More importantly, with Shaukat Aziz departing from the office of Prime Minister, Musharraf could not have sustained his presidency any longer and dramatically fell from the presidency within a matter of eight months, after popular and mass public movements called for his impeachment for the actions taken during his presidency.

Suspension of the Chief Justice

On 9 March 2007, Musharraf suspended Chief Justice Iftikhar Muhammad Chaudhry and pressed corruption charges against him. He replaced him with Acting Chief Justice Javed Iqbal.

Musharraf's moves sparked protests among Pakistani lawyers. On 12 March 2007, lawyers started a campaign called Judicial Activism across Pakistan and began boycotting all court procedures in protest against the suspension. In Islamabad, as well as other cities such as Lahore, Karachi, and Quetta hundreds of lawyers dressed in black suits attended rallies, condemning the suspension as unconstitutional. Slowly the expressions of support for the ousted Chief Justice gathered momentum and by May, protesters and opposition parties took out huge rallies against Musharraf, and his tenure as army chief was also challenged in the courts.

Lal Masjid siege

The Lal Masjid mosque in Islamabad had a religious school for women and the Jamia Hafsa madrassa, which was attached to the mosque. A male madrassa was only a few minutes drive away. In April 2007, the mosque administration started to encourage attacks on local video shops, alleging that they were selling porn films; and massage parlours, which were alleged to be used as brothels. These attacks were often carried out by the mosque's female students. In July 2007, a confrontation occurred when government authorities made a decision to stop the student violence and send police officers to arrest the responsible individuals and the madrassa administration.

This development led to a standoff between police forces and armed students. Mosque leaders and students refused to surrender and fired at police from inside the mosque building. Both sides suffered casualties.

Return of Benazir Bhutto and Nawaz Sharif

On 27 July, Bhutto met for the first time with Musharraf in the United Arab Emirates to discuss her return to Pakistan. On 14 September 2007, Deputy Information Minister Tariq Azim stated that Bhutto will not be deported, but must face corruption charges against her. He clarified Sharif's and Bhutto's right to return to Pakistan. On 17 September 2007, Bhutto accused Musharraf's allies of pushing Pakistan to crisis by refusal to restore democracy and share power. Bhutto returned from eight years exile on 18 October. Musharraf called for a three-day mourning period after Bhutto's assassination on 27 December 2007.

Sharif returned to Pakistan in September 2007 and was immediately arrested and taken into custody at the airport. He was sent back to Saudi Arabia. Saudi intelligence chief Muqrin bin Abdul-Aziz Al Saud and Lebanese politician Saad Hariri arrived separately in Islamabad on 8 September 2007, the former with a message from Saudi King Abdullah and the latter after a meeting with Nawaz Sharif in London. After meeting President General Pervez Musharraf for two-and-a-half hours discussing Nawaz Sharif's possible return. On arrival in Saudi Arabia, Nawaz Sharif was received by Prince Muqrin bin Abdul-Aziz, the Saudi intelligence chief, who had met Musharraf in Islamabad the previous day. That meeting had been followed by a rare press conference, at which he had warned that Sharif should not violate the terms of King Abdullah's agreement of staying out of politics for 10 years.

Resignation from the Military

On 2 October 2007, Musharraf appointed General Tariq Majid as Chairman Joint Chiefs Committee and approved General Ashfaq Kayani as vice chief of the army starting 8 October. When Musharraf resigned from military on 28 November 2007, Kayani became Chief of Army Staff.

2007 presidential elections

In a March 2007 interview, Musharraf said that he intended to stay in office for another five years.

A nine-member panel of Supreme Court judges deliberated on six petitions (including Jamaat-e-Islami's, Pakistan's largest Islamic group) for disqualification of Musharraf as a presidential candidate. Bhutto stated that her party may join other opposition groups, including Sharif's.

On 28 September 2007, in a 6–3 vote, Judge Rana Bhagwandas's court removed obstacles to Musharraf's election bid.

2007 state of emergency

On 3 November 2007, Musharraf declared emergency rule across Pakistan. He suspended the Constitution, imposed a state of emergency, and fired the Chief Justice of the Supreme Court again. In Islamabad, troops entered the Supreme Court building, arrested the judges and kept them detained in their homes. Independent and international television channels went off air. Public protests were mounted against Musharraf.

2008 general elections

General elections were held on 18 February 2008, in which the Pakistan Peoples Party (PPP) polled the highest votes and won the most seats. On 23 March 2008, President Musharraf said an "era of democracy" had begun in Pakistan and that he had put the country "on the track of development and progress". On 22 March, the PPP named former parliament speaker Yusuf Raza Gilani as its candidate for the country's next prime minister, to lead a coalition government united against him.

Impeachment movement

On 7 August 2008, the Pakistan Peoples Party and the Pakistan Muslim League (N) agreed to force Musharraf to step down and begin his impeachment. Asif Ali Zardari and Nawaz Sharif announced sending a formal request or joint charge sheet that he step down, and impeach him through parliamentary process upon refusal. Musharraf refused to step down. A charge-sheet had been drafted and was to be presented to parliament. It included Mr. Musharraf's first seizure of power in 1999—at the expense of Nawaz Sharif, the PML(N)'s leader, whom Mr. Musharraf imprisoned and exiled—and his second in November 2007, when he declared an emergency as a means to get re-elected as president. The charge-sheet also listed some of Mr. Musharraf's contributions to the "war on terror".

Musharraf delayed his departure for the Beijing Olympics, by a day. On 11 August, the government summoned the national assembly.

Exile

On 18 August 2008, Musharraf announced his resignation. On the following day, he defended his nine-year rule in an hour-long televised speech. However, public opinion was largely against him by this time. A poll conducted a day after his resignation showed that 63% of Pakistanis welcomed Musharraf's decision to step down while only 15% were unhappy with it. On 23 November 2008 he left for exile in London where he arrived the following day.

Return to Pakistan

Since the start of 2011, news had circulated that Musharraf would return to Pakistan before the 2013 general election. He himself vowed this in several interviews. On Piers Morgan Tonight, Musharraf announced his plans to return to Pakistan on 23 March 2012 to seek the Presidency in 2013. The Pakistani Taliban and Talal Bugti threatened to kill him should he return. On 24 March 2013, after a four-year self-imposed exile, he returned to Pakistan. He landed at Jinnah International Airport, Karachi, via a chartered Emirates flight with Pakistani journalists and foreign news correspondents. Hundreds of his supporters and workers of APML greeted Musharraf upon his arrival at Karachi airport, and he delivered a short public speech.

Electoral disqualification

On 16 April 2013, three weeks after he returned to Pakistan, an electoral tribunal in Chitral declared Musharraf disqualified from contesting elections, effectively quashing his political ambitions (several other constituencies had previously rejected Musharraf's nominations). A spokesperson for Musharraf's party said the ruling was "biased" and they would appeal the decision.

Jail, house arrest and bail

Two days later, on 18 April 2013, the Islamabad High Court ordered the arrest of Musharraf on charges relating to the 2007 arrests of judges. Musharraf had technically been on bail since his return to the country, and the court now declared his bail ended. Musharraf escaped from court with the aid of his security personnel, and went to his farm-house mansion. The following day, Musharraf was placed under house arrest but was later transferred to police headquarters in Islamabad. Musharraf characterised his arrest as "politically motivated" and his legal team has declared their intention to fight the charges in the Supreme Court. Further to the charges of this arrest, the Senate also passed a resolution petitioning that Musharraf be charged with high treason in relation to the events of 2007.

On Friday, 26 April 2013, a week after one court had voided his bail and caused his arrest in the "arrest of judges" case, another court ordered house arrest for Musharraf in connection with the death of Benazir Bhutto. On 20 May, a Pakistani court granted bail to Musharraf. On 12 June 2014 Sindh High Court allowed him to travel to seek medical attention abroad.

Fourth assassination attempt

On 3 April 2014, Musharraf escaped the fourth assassination attempt, resulting in an injury of a woman, according to Pakistani news.

Judicial hearings and return to exile

On 25 June 2013, Musharraf was named as prime suspect in two separate cases. The first case was subverting and suspending the constitution, and the second was a Federal Investigation Agency probe into the conspiracy to assassinate Bhutto. Musharraf was indicted on 20 August 2013 for Bhutto's assassination in 2007. On 2 September 2013, a first information report (FIR) was registered against him for his role in the Lal Masjid Operation in 2007. The FIR was lodged after the son of slain hard line cleric Abdul Rahid Ghazi (who was killed during the operation) asked authorities to bring charges against Musharraf.

On 18 March 2016, Musharraf's name was removed from the Exit Control List and he was allowed to travel abroad, citing medical treatment. He subsequently lived in Dubai in self-imposed exile. Musharraf vowed to return to Pakistan, but has not done so. It was first disclosed in October 2018 that Musharraf was suffering from amyloidosis, a rare and serious illness for which he has undergone treatment in hospitals in London and Dubai; an official with Musharraf's political party said that Musharraf would return to Pakistan after he made a full recovery.

In 2017, Musharraf appeared as a political analyst on his weekly television show Sab Se Pehle Pakistan with President Musharraf, hosted by BOL News.

On 31 August 2017, the anti-terrorism court in Rawalpindi declared him an "absconder" in Bhutto's murder case. The court also ordered that his property and bank account in Pakistan be seized.

Verdict

On 17 December 2019, a special court declared him a traitor and sentenced him in absentia to death for abrogating and suspending the constitution in November 2007. The three-member panel of the special court which issued the order was spearheaded by Chief Justice of the Peshawar High Court Waqar Ahmed Seth. He was the first Pakistani Army General to be sentenced to death. Analysts did not expect Musharraf to face the sentence given his illness and the fact that Dubai has no extradition treaty with Pakistan; the verdict was also viewed as largely symbolic given that Musharraf retained support within the current Pakistani government and military.

Musharraf challenged the verdict, and on 13 January 2020, the Lahore High Court annulled the death sentence against Musharraf, ruling that the special court that held the trial was unconstitutional. The unanimous verdict was delivered by a three-member bench of the Lahore High Court, consisting of Justice Sayyed Muhammad Mazahar Ali Akbar Naqvi, Justice Muhammad Ameer Bhatti, and Justice Chaudhry Masood Jahangir. The court ruled that the prosecution of Musharraf was politically motivated and that the crimes of high treason and subverting the Constitution were "a joint offence" that "cannot be undertaken by a single person."

Personal life

Musharraf was the second son of his parents and had two brothers—Javed and Naved. Javed retired as a high-level official in Pakistan's civil service. Naved is an anaesthetist who has lived in Chicago since completing his residency training at Loyola University Medical Center in 1979.

Musharraf married Sehba, who is from Karachi, on 28 December 1968. They had a daughter, Ayla, an architect married to film director Asim Raza, and a son, Bilal. He also had close family ties to the prominent Kheshgi family.

Death

On 5 February 2023, Musharraf died at age 79 due to amyloidosis. He had been hospitalised a year prior due to the disease. His body was returned to Karachi, Pakistan, from Dubai on 6 February. His funeral prayers were offered at a mosque in Karachi's Gulmohar Polo Ground in Malir Cantonment on 7 February. He was laid to rest with military honours in an army graveyard.

"Absolute power corrupts absolutely". We have seen this in Pakistan number of times.

Many Prime Ministers & Presidents were killed by Pakistani people themselves or exiled.

1. *Liaquat Ali Khan was killed while delivering a speech in Rawalpindi in October 1951*

2. *Zulfikar Ali Bhutto was hanged in the courtyard of Rawalpindi District Jail on 4 April 1979.*

3. *Muhammad Zia-ul-Haq died in a mysterious plane crash on 17 August 1988.*

4. *Benazir Bhutto died in a bomb explosion at an election rally on 27 December 2007, Rawalpindi's Liaquat National Bagh.*

5. *Nawaz Shariff lived in exile*

6. *Musharraf also was exiled.*

2009 attack on the Sri Lanka national cricket team

The 2009 attack on the Sri Lanka national cricket team occurred on 3 March 2009, when a bus carrying Sri Lankan cricketers, part of a larger convoy, was fired upon by 12 gunmen near Gaddafi Stadium in Lahore, Pakistan. The cricketers were on their way to play the third day of the second Test against the Pakistani cricket team. Six members of the Sri Lanka national cricket team were wounded and six Pakistani policemen and two civilians were killed.

The attack was believed to have been carried out by Lashkar-e-Jhangvi. In August 2016, three of the terrorists involved in the attack were killed during a police raid in Lahore. In October, the attack's mastermind was killed in eastern Afghanistan during a military operation, while hiding there.

In December 2019, Sri Lanka agreed to play two match test series in Pakistan and marked test cricket return to Pakistan after a decade since the terror attack.

Muhammad Mian Soomro

Muhammad Mian Soomro (born 19 August 1950) is a Pakistani politician, banker and senator who currently serves as the federal minister for Privatization. Born to a Native Sindhi family originally linked to the Soomra dynasty, he previously served as the chairman of the Senate from 2003 to 2009, the Caretaker prime minister of Pakistan from 2007 to 2008, and the acting president of Pakistan from 18 August 2008 to 9 September 2008.

President of Pakistan

As required by the constitution, Soomro (in his position as Chairman of the Senate) automatically became President on 18 August 2008, upon the resignation of Pervez Musharraf. The constitution also required that a new President be elected by Parliament within 30 days.

Asif Ali Zardari was elected President and subsequently sworn in on 9 September 2008, succeeding Soomro.

Asif Ali Zardari

Asif Ali Zardari (born 26 July 1955) is a Pakistani politician who is the president of Pakistan Peoples Party Parliamentarians and was the co-chairperson of Pakistan People's Party. He served as the 11th president of Pakistan from 2008 to 2013, the first president born after Independence. He is the widower of twice-elected Prime Minister of Pakistan Benazir Bhutto. He has been a member of the National Assembly of Pakistan since August 2018.

At the inauguration on 9 September 2008, Afghan President Hamid Karzai was a guest of honour, which was a signal for much closer cooperation between the two nations in addressing the tribal insurgency along the Afghanistan-Pakistan border. After the election, Zardari promised to approve the constitutional provision that removed the President's power to dismiss Parliament, but public scepticism remained on whether he would actually carry out his promise. His economic competence was questioned after allegations that he had raised grain procurement prices through inflationary subsidies and scrapped the capital gains tax. His first parliamentary speech was overshadowed by 20 September Islamabad Marriott Hotel bombing. A few days later, he went to the United Nations Headquarters in New York City on his first overseas trip as president.

From 23 to 26 September 2008, he met with various foreign leaders, including U.S. President George W. Bush and Chinese President Hu Jintao. He suffered political embarrassment by flirting with U.S. vice presidential candidate Sarah Palin and making tongue-in-cheek comments about her. Although, at the United Nations General Assembly, he publicly condemned U.S drone attacks in Pakistan, The Washington Post reported that he had signed a "secret deal" when he met with senior American officials that arranged for the coordination of Predator strikes and a jointly approved list of prominent targets. He and Indian Prime Minister Manmohan Singh agreed to resume peace talks by the end of 2008.

Economic crises

From 14 to 17 October 2008, he was in China to negotiate foreign aid, as Pakistan faced the possibility of defaulting on its payments. China refused to offer any aid commitments, but instead promised to provide assistance in the development of two nuclear power plants and more future business investments.

After Saudi Arabia, Britain, China, the United States, and the United Arab Emirates refused to provide any bailout, he officially asked the International Monetary Fund (IMF) for assistance in solving Pakistan's balance of payments problem on 22 October.

He went to Saudi Arabia from 4 to 6 November in hopes of obtaining financial aid and securing trade agreements. However, leaked cables revealed increasingly strained relations between Zardari and Saudi royalty, primarily because of Saudi distrust of Zardari and preference for Sharif. Weaker cooperation led to decreased oil subsidies as part of a broader Saudi policy of withholding monetary assistance.

In mid-November 2008, Zardari's government officially sent a letter of intent to the IMF regarding a bailout to help increase its foreign exchange reserves. In a $11.3 billion multi-year loan package, Pakistan received a $7.4 billion loan for 2008–10. The IMF stipulated stringent reform conditions, which included rebuilding the tax structure and privatising state enterprises. The World Bank and Asian Development Bank withheld a combined $3 billion aid in the 2010–11 fiscal year and the IMF withheld since May 2010 the last segment of its aid package.

In January 2011, the MQM withdrew from the government. Zardari's ruling coalition averted a government collapse by accepting the opposition's economic proposals, which restored gas subsidies and abandoned many of the IMF's suggested reforms.

In an effort to curb government expenditures, Zardari swore in an "austerity cabinet" in February 2011 which reduced the cabinet from 60 ministers to 22.

China Pakistan Economic Corridor

Pakistan and China on 22 May 2013 inked several Agreements and Memoranda of Understanding (MoUs) that mainly included the long-term Economic Corridor plan, maritime cooperation and satellite navigation. President Asif Ali Zardari and Chinese Premier Li Keqiang witnessed the signing ceremony as the representatives of the two countries inked the documents at a ceremony held at the Aiwan-e-Sadr. The visit of Chinese Premier Li Keqiang marked the signing of important documents aimed at long-term cooperation between the two countries in multiple areas.

Completion of presidential tenure

Zardari completed his five-year term on 8 September 2013, becoming the first democratically elected president in the 66-year-long history of Pakistan to complete his tenure. He received a guard of honour while leaving the Aiwan-e-Sadr. He was succeeded by Mamnoon Hussain as president.

7

(2011-2020)

INDIA - 2011 Cricket World Cup - 2012 Summer Olympics – 'Saffron terror' remark controversy - Sachin Tendulkar - 2014 Indian general election - 2016 Summer Olympics - 2016 Indian banknote demonetization - Pradhan Mantri Jan Dhan Yojana - 2016 Indian Line of Control strike - 2019 Indian general election - 2019 Balakot airstrike - Muslim Women (Protection of Rights on Marriage) Act, 2019 - 2019 Supreme Court verdict on Ayodhya dispute - Article 370 revoked in J&K - Drugs trafficking - Citizenship (Amendment) Act, 2019

PAKISTAN - Mamnoon Hussain - Arif Alvi - Shahid Khaqan Abbasi - Imran Khan - Shehbaz Sharif - Anwaar ul Haq Kakar - Why does China want Pakistan's donkeys? – 90% beggars arrested abroad are Pakistanis - Drugs trafficking

INDIA

2011 Cricket World Cup

The 2011 Cricket World Cup Final was the final match of the 2011 Men's Cricket World Cup, the 10th edition of ICC's championship of One Day International (ODI) cricket. The match was played between India and Sri Lanka at the Wankhede Stadium, Mumbai, India on Saturday 2 April 2011. It was the first time that two Asian teams had faced each other in an ODI World Cup final. India won the match by six wickets—its second World Cup win after the 1983 tournament—and became the third team to have won the title more than once, after Australia (1987, 1999, 2003, 2007) and the West

Indies (1975 and 1979). India became the first country to win Cricket World Cup in their own country.

India at the 2012 Summer Olympics

India competed at the 2012 Summer Olympics in London, from 27 July to 12 August 2012. A total of 83 athletes, 60 men and 23 women, competed in 13 sports. Men's field hockey was the only team-based sport in which India had its representation in these Olympic Games. India also marked its Olympic return in weightlifting, after the International Weightlifting Federation imposed a two-year suspension for the nation's athletes in Beijing because of a doping scandal.

This was India's 2nd most successful Olympics in terms of total medal tally, having won a total of 6 medals (2 silver and 4 bronze), doubling the nation's previous record (3 medals at the 2008 Beijing Olympics). Two medals each were awarded to the athletes in shooting and wrestling. India also set a historical milestone for the female athletes who won two Olympic medals for the first time. Badminton player and world junior champion Saina Nehwal became the first Indian athlete to win an Olympic bronze medal in the women's singles. Boxer Mary Kom, on the other hand, lost to Great Britain's Nicola Adams in the semi-final match, but settled for the bronze in the first ever women's flyweight event.

Medalists

Medal	Name	Sport	Event
Silver	Vijay Kumar	Shooting	Men's 25 m rapid fire pistol
Silver	Sushil Kumar	Wrestling	Men's freestyle 66 kg
Bronze	Gagan Narang	Shooting	Men's 10 m air rifle
Bronze	Saina Nehwal	Badminton	Women's singles

Medal	Name	Sport	Event
Bronze	Mary Kom	Boxing	Women's flyweight
Bronze	Yogeshwar Dutt	Wrestling	Men's freestyle 60 kg

'Saffron terror' remark controversy: Sushil Kumar Shinde to clarify, stand-off to end soon: sources

Feb 20, 2013 NDTV - India News

New Delhi: The row over Sushil Kumar Shinde's "saffron terror" remark might end shortly, sources said, adding that the Home Minister is expected to make a clarification as the UPA government, desperate to transact important legislative business, makes every effort to ensure that Parliament functions when the Budget Session convenes tomorrow.

A belligerent BJP has made it clear that its attack on Mr Shinde will dominate proceedings as the session opens. But, sources said, the main Opposition party has agreed to withdraw its protest of Mr Shinde withdraws his comments.

Feb 20, 2013 The Hindu

Shinde apologises for 'Hindu terror' remark ahead of budget session

The Home Minister had said in Jaipur last month, "We have got an investigation report that be it the RSS or BJP, their training camps are promoting Hindu terrorism." He later said he meant "saffron terrorism" not "Hindu terrorism."

Union Home Minister Sushilkumar Shinde on Wednesday expressed "regret" over his controversial "Hindu terror" remark made in the Congress' Jaipur conclave last month, a step aimed at pacifying a combative Bharatiya Janata Party ahead of the crucial Budget session.

In a statement, Mr. Shinde said his comments had created a misunderstanding. "It has been understood to mean that I was linking terrorism to a particular religion and was accusing certain political organisations of being involved in organising terror camps," he said.

Sachin Tendulkar

Sachin Ramesh Tendulkar, (born 24 April 1973) is an Indian former international cricketer who captained the Indian national team. He is widely regarded as one of the greatest batsmen in the history of cricket. He is the all-time highest run-scorer in both ODI and Test cricket with more than 18,000 runs and 15,000 runs, respectively. He also holds the record for receiving the most man-of-the-match awards in international cricket. Tendulkar was a Member of Parliament, Rajya Sabha by nomination from 2012 to 2018.

Tendulkar took up cricket at the age of eleven, made his Test match debut on 15 November 1989 against Pakistan in Karachi at the age of sixteen, and went on to represent Mumbai domestically and India internationally for over 24 years. In 2002, halfway through his career, Wisden ranked him the second-greatest Test batsman of all time, behind Don Bradman, and the second-greatest ODI batsman of all time, behind Viv Richards. The same year, Tendulkar was a part of the team that was one of the joint-winners of the 2002 ICC Champions Trophy. Later in his career, Tendulkar was part of the Indian team that won the 2011 Cricket World Cup, his first win in six World Cup appearances for India. He had previously been named "Player of the Tournament" at the 2003 World Cup.

Tendulkar is the leading run-scorer in Test matches, with 15,921 runs, as well as in ODI matches, with 18,426 runs. He is the only player to score more than 30,000 runs combined in all forms of international cricket (Test, ODI, and Twenty20). He is the 16th player and the first Indian to score 50,000 runs in all forms of domestic and international recognised cricket (First-class, List A, and Twenty20). He achieved this feat on 5 October 2013, during a Champions League Twenty20 match for his IPL team Mumbai Indians against Trinidad and Tobago.

2014 Indian general election

General elections were held in India in nine phases from 7 April to 12 May 2014 to elect the members of the 16th Lok Sabha. With 834 million registered voters, they were the largest-ever elections in the world until being surpassed by the 2019 elections. Around 23.1 million or 2.7% of the total eligible voters were aged 18–19 years. A total of 8,251 candidates contested the 543 elected Lok Sabha seats. The average election turnout over all nine phases was around 66.40%, the highest ever in the history of Indian general elections.

Since the last general election in 2009, the anti-corruption movement by Anna Hazare, and other similar moves by Baba Ramdev and Arvind Kejriwal (founder of Aam Aadmi Party), gathered momentum and political interest. Kejriwal went on to form a separate political party, Aam Aadmi Party, in November 2012. The 2012 presidential election resulted in Pranab Mukherjee of Indian National Congress becoming the president. Andhra politics was further shaken following the death of its chief minister, Y. S. Rajasekhara Reddy. His son, Y. S. Jaganmohan Reddy, then broke from the INC and founded the YSR Congress Party, taking several politicians with him.

The final session of parliament started on 6 February and ended on 21 February. Amongst the agenda in the final session was passing The Lokpal and Lokayuktas Bill, 2013 in tackling corruption and the creation of Telangana.

When it became clear that the BJP would win the election, Narendra Modi tweeted, "India has won! Bharat ki Vijay. Ache din ane wale hai (good days are ahead)." This tweet instantly became India's most retweeted Twitter post. Manmohan Singh congratulated Modi by telephone. Congress President Sonia Gandhi accepted the defeat and congratulated the new government saying, "I congratulate the next government. I take full responsibility for the loss of Congress." Rahul Gandhi also did the same saying, "The new government has been given a mandate by the people. As Congress Vice President I hold myself responsible. The Congress party has done badly."

With this election, BJP came to power with NDA (National Democratic Alliance). Narendra Modi becoming a Prime Minister proved to be a turning point in the Indian Politics.

India at the 2016 Summer Olympics

India competed at the 2016 Summer Olympics in Rio de Janeiro, Brazil, from 5 to 21 August 2016. Indian athletes have appeared in every edition of the

Summer Olympics since 1920, although they made their official debut at the 1900 Summer Olympics in Paris.

India left Rio de Janeiro with two medals. These medals were won only by female athletes for the first time in history, a silver to badminton player P. V. Sindhu in the women's singles, who became India's youngest individual Olympic medallist and the first Indian woman to win an Olympic silver, as well as a bronze to freestyle wrestler Sakshi Malik in the women's 58 kg, who became the first female wrestler from India to win an Olympic medal. Several Indian athletes came close to increasing the medal haul, finishing in fourth place, including tennis tandem Mirza and Rohan Bopanna in the mixed doubles; Bindra, who narrowly missed out the podium by a half-point in the men's 10 m air rifle before retiring from the sport; and Karmakar, who surprised the global audience with her high-risk Produnova routine in the women's vault. For the first time, the Indian shooters failed to earn a single medal since 2004, and the boxers since 2008.

Medalists

Medal	Name	Sport	Event
Silver	P. V. Sindhu	Badminton	Women's singles
Bronze	Sakshi Malik	Wrestling	Women's freestyle 58 kg

2016 Indian banknote demonetization

On 8 November 2016, the Government of India announced the demonetisation of all ₹500 and ₹1,000 banknotes of the Mahatma Gandhi Series. It also announced the issuance of new ₹500 and ₹2,000 banknotes in exchange for the demonetised banknotes. Prime Minister Narendra Modi claimed that the action would curtail the shadow economy, increase cashless transactions and reduce the use of illicit and counterfeit cash to fund illegal activity and terrorism.

The announcement of demonetisation was followed by prolonged cash shortages in the weeks that followed, which created significant disruption throughout the economy. People seeking to exchange their banknotes had to stand in lengthy queues, and several deaths were linked to the rush to exchange cash.

According to a 2018 report from the Reserve Bank of India ₹15.3 lakh crore (15.3 trillion rupees on the short scale) of the ₹15.41 lakh crore in demonetised bank notes, or approximately 99.3%, were deposited in banks, leading analysts to state that the effort had failed to remove black money from the economy. The BSE SENSEX and NIFTY 50 stock indices fell over 6 percent on the day after the announcement. The move reduced the country's industrial production and its GDP growth rate. It is estimated that 1.5 million jobs were lost. The move also saw a significant increase in digital and cashless transactions throughout the country.

Initially, the move received support from some central bankers as well as from some international commentators. The move was also criticised as poorly planned and unfair, and was met with protests, litigation, and strikes against the government in several places across India. Debates also took place concerning the move in both houses of Parliament.

This demonetization was very cleverly planned. The bank accounts opened for the poor people were without any condition of minimum balance to expand the financial base came in handy for the people to deposit black money and were caught. When demonetization was announced, there was a rush to spend Rs 500 & Rs 1000 notes. Many people purchased gold. Some others booked rail tickets, air tickets with a view to cancel the tickets subsequently and get the refund etc. Large amounts of the currency notes were found thrown as garbage on the streets. Some of the amounts were deposited in the bank accounts of the poor who opened Bank accounts under Pradhan Mantri Jan Dhan Yojana.

Pradhan Mantri Jan Dhan Yojana

Pradhan Mantri Jan Dhan Yojana (PMJDY) Under this, a person not having a savings account can open an account without the requirement of any minimum balance and, in case they self-certify that they do not have any of the officially valid documents required for opening a savings account, they may open a small account.

Pradhan Mantri Jan Dhan Yojana (transl. Prime Minister's Public Finance Scheme) is a financial inclusion program of the Government of India open to Indian citizens (minors of age 10 and older can also open an account with a guardian to manage it), that aims to expand affordable access to financial services such as bank accounts, remittances, credit, insurance and pensions. This financial inclusion campaign was launched by the Prime Minister of India Narendra Modi on 28 August 2014. He had announced this scheme on his first Independence Day speech on 15 August 2014.

Run by Department of Financial Services, Ministry of Finance, under this scheme 15 million bank accounts were opened on inauguration day. The Guinness Book of World Records recognized this achievement, stating: "The most bank accounts opened in one week as a part of the financial inclusion campaign is 18,096,130 and was achieved by the Government of India from August 23 to 29, 2014". By 27 June 2018, over 318 million bank accounts were opened and over ₹792 billion (US$12 billion) were deposited under the scheme.

This also started an era of DBT (Direct Benefit Transfer). The transaction that completely stopped black money and also ensured that money reached to the concerned person.

2016 Indian Line of Control strike

On 29 September 2016, teams of Indian Army commandos crossed the Line of Control into Pakistani-administered Kashmir to attack targets up to a kilometer within territory held by Pakistan. The raid occurred ten days after four militants had attacked an Indian army outpost at Uri on 18th September 2016 in the Indian state of Jammu and Kashmir, and killed 19 soldiers. Estimates of casualties from India's cross-border attack varied widely, with figures of 12 to 70 being reported. The Pakistani government eventually acknowledged the deaths of two soldiers and injuries to nine, while one Indian soldier was captured.

2019 Indian general election

General elections were held in India in seven phases from 11 April to 19 May 2019 to elect the members of the 17th Lok Sabha. Votes were counted and the result was declared on 23 May. The election resulted in a landslide victory for the BJP which won 303 seats and formed the government.

Around 912 million people were eligible to vote, and voter turnout was over 67 percent – the highest ever, as well as the highest ever participation by women voters.

The Bharatiya Janata Party received 37.36% of the vote, the highest vote share by a political party since the 1989 general election, and won 303 seats, further increasing its substantial majority. In addition, the BJP-led National Democratic Alliance (NDA) won 353 seats. The BJP won 37.76% of votes, while the NDA's combined vote was 45% of the 603.7 million votes that were polled. The Indian National Congress won 52 seats, failing to get 10% of the seats needed to claim the post of Leader of the Opposition. In addition, the Congress-led United Progressive Alliance (UPA) won 91 seats, while other parties won 98 seats.

2019 Balakot airstrike

The 2019 Balakot airstrike was a bombing raid conducted by Indian warplanes on 26 February 2019 in Balakot, Pakistan, against an alleged terrorist training camp.

Muslim Women (Protection of Rights on Marriage) Act, 2019

The Muslim Women (Protection of Rights on Marriage) Act, 2019 is an Act of the Parliament of India criminalising triple talaq. In August 2017, the Supreme Court of India declared triple talaq, which enables Muslim men to instantly divorce their wives, to be unconstitutional. The minority opinion suggested the Parliament to consider appropriate legislation governing triple talaq in the Muslim community.

In December 2017, citing the Supreme Court judgment and cases of triple talaq in India, the government introduced The Muslim Women (Protection of Rights on Marriage) Bill, 2017. The bill proposed to make triple talaq in any form—spoken, in writing, or by electronic means—illegal and void. Punishment for breach of the law was proposed to include up to three years imprisonment for the husband pronouncing triple talaq. The bill was passed by the Lok Sabha, the lower house of the

Parliament of India, on the same day, but was stalled by the opposition in the Rajya Sabha, the upper house.

The bill was reintroduced and passed by the Lok Sabha and by the Rajya Sabha in July 2019. Consequently, the bill received assent of the President of India. The act also entitles an aggrieved woman to demand a maintenance for her dependent children. It was subsequently notified as law in the same month. The acts stands to be retrospectively effective from 19 September 2018.

However, Muslim men are still allowed to be polygamous and can also give a divorce easily by paying paltry sums.

2019 Supreme Court verdict on Ayodhya dispute

The final judgement in the Ayodhya dispute was declared by the Supreme Court of India on 9 November 2019. The Supreme Court ordered the disputed land (2.77 acres) to be handed over to a trust (to be created by the government of India) to build the Ram Janmabhoomi (revered as the birthplace of Hindu deity, Rama) temple. The court also ordered the government to give an alternative 5 acres of land in another place to the Uttar Pradesh Sunni Central Waqf Board for the purpose of building a mosque as a replacement for the demolished Babri Masjid.

Revocation of the special status of Jammu and Kashmir

On 6 August 2019, the Government of India revoked the special status, or autonomy, granted under Article 370 of the Indian Constitution to Jammu and Kashmir—a region administered by India as a state which consists of the larger part of Kashmir which has been the subject of dispute among India, Pakistan, and China since 1947.

The President of India issued an order under the power of Article 370, overriding the prevailing 1954 Presidential Order and nullifying all the provisions of autonomy granted to the state. The Home Minister introduced a Reorganisation Bill in the Indian Parliament, seeking to divide the state into two union territories to be governed by a lieutenant governor and a unicameral legislature. The resolution seeking the revocation of the temporary special status under Article 370 and the bill for the state's reorganisation was debated and passed by the Rajya Sabha – India's upper house of parliament – on 5 August 2019. On 6 August, the Lok Sabha – India's lower house of parliament – debated and passed the reorganisation bill along with the resolution recommending the revocation.

Article 370 of the Indian constitution gave special status to Jammu and Kashmir — a state in India, located in the northern part of the Indian subcontinent. The Article conferred power on Jammu and Kashmir to have a separate constitution, a state flag and autonomy over the internal administration of the state. The Constituent Assembly of Jammu and Kashmir, after its establishment, was empowered to recommend the articles of the Indian constitution that should be applied to the state or to abrogate the Article 370 altogether. After consultation with the state's Constituent Assembly, the 1954 Presidential Order was issued, specifying the articles of the Indian constitution that applied to the state. The Constituent Assembly dissolved itself without recommending the abrogation of Article 370, the article was deemed to have become a permanent feature of the Indian Constitution. This article, along with Article 35A, defined that the Jammu and Kashmir state's residents live under a separate set of laws, including those related to citizenship, ownership of property, and fundamental rights, as compared to residents of other Indian states.

Drugs trafficking

Drugs are pushed in Punjab across the borders of Pakistan which basically come from Afghanistan.

Citizenship (Amendment) Act, 2019

The Citizenship (Amendment) Act, 2019 (CAA) was passed by the Parliament of India on 11 December 2019. It amended the Citizenship Act, 1955 by providing an accelerated pathway to Indian citizenship for persecuted religious minorities from Afghanistan, Bangladesh and Pakistan who are Hindus, Sikhs, Buddhists, Jains, Parsis or Christians, and arrived in India before the end of December 2014. The law does not grant such eligibility to Muslims from these countries. The act was the first time that religion had been overtly used as a criterion for citizenship under Indian law, and it attracted global criticism.

The Bharatiya Janata Party (BJP), which leads the Indian government, had promised in previous election manifestos to offer Indian citizenship to members of persecuted religious minorities who had migrated from neighbouring countries. Under the 2019 amendment, migrants who had entered India by 31 December 2014, and had suffered "religious persecution or fear of religious persecution" in their country of origin, were made eligible for citizenship. The amendment also relaxed the residence requirement for naturalisation of these migrants from twelve years to six. According to Intelligence Bureau records, there will be just over 30,000 immediate beneficiaries of the bill.

The amendment has been criticized as discriminating on the basis of religion, particularly for excluding Muslims. The Office of the United Nations High Commissioner for Human Rights (OHCHR) called it "fundamentally discriminatory", adding that while India's "goal of protecting persecuted groups is welcome", this should be accomplished through a non-discriminatory "robust national asylum system". Critics express concerns that the bill would be used, along with the National Register of Citizens (NRC), to render many Muslim citizens stateless, as they may be unable to meet stringent birth or identity proof requirements. Commentators also question the exclusion of persecuted religious minorities from other regions such as Tibet, Sri Lanka and Myanmar. The Indian government said that since Pakistan, Afghanistan and Bangladesh have Islam as their state religion, it is therefore "unlikely" that Muslims would "face religious persecution" there. However, certain Muslim groups, such as Hazaras (mostly Shias) and Ahmadis, have historically faced persecution in these countries.

The passage of the legislation caused large-scale protests in India. Assam and other northeastern states witnessed violent demonstrations against the bill over fears that granting Indian citizenship to refugees and immigrants will cause a loss of their "political rights, culture and land rights" and motivate further migration from Bangladesh. In other parts of India, protesters said that the bill discriminated against Muslims, and demanded that Indian citizenship be granted to Muslim refugees and immigrants as well. Major protests against the Act were held at some universities in India. Students at Aligarh Muslim University and Jamia Millia Islamia alleged brutal suppression by the police. The protests have led to the deaths of several protesters, injuries to both protesters and police officers, damage to public and private property, the detention of hundreds of people, and suspensions of local internet mobile phone connectivity in certain areas. Some states announced that they would not implement the Act. In response, the Union Home Ministry said that states lack the legal power to stop the implementation of the CAA.

PAKISTAN

In the last 75 years, Pakistan completely destroyed Pak occupied Kashmir (POK) which it calls "Azad Kashmir". Still crying and trying to get Kashmir which is a part of India. This area of Jammu & Kashmir has developed to a great extent since removal of Clause 370 and the world has seen the change during the latest G20 summit.

Mamnoon Hussain

Mamnoon Hussain (21 December 1941 – 14 July 2021) was a Pakistani politician and industrialist who served as the 12th President of Pakistan from 2013 to 2018. He was first appointed Governor of Sindh in June 1999 by President Rafiq Tarar; but was removed from the post in October 1999 due to the 1999 military coup d'état. Hussain was then nominated for the presidency by the PMLN in July 2013 and was elected through an indirect presidential election. Hussain took over the presidency after an oath administered by the Chief Justice of Pakistan on 9 September 2013. Hussain maintained a low-key profile as president and his role was rarely seen in the nation's politics, although he was involved in a Polio eradication program.

Arif Alvi

Arif-ur-Rehman Alvi (born 29 July 1949) is a Pakistani politician currently serving as the 13th President of Pakistan, in office since 9 September 2018. He was a member of the National Assembly of Pakistan from June 2013 to May 2018 and again from August to September 2018. A founding member of the

Pakistan Tehreek-e-Insaf (PTI), Alvi was elected as President of Pakistan on 4 September 2018 following the 2018 Pakistani presidential election.

Shahid Khaqan Abbasi

Shahid Khaqan Abbasi (born 27 December 1958) is a Pakistani politician and businessman who served as the 21st prime minister of Pakistan from August 2017 to May 2018. Abbasi is the senior vice President of the Pakistan Muslim League-N (PML-N), and secretary-general of Pakistan Democratic Movement (PDM), an anti-PTI coalition of political parties in Pakistan. He has been a Member of the National Assembly of Pakistan since October 2018. Previously, he served as a member of the National Assembly for 8 non— consecutive terms since 1988.

Imran Khan

Imran Ahmad Khan Niazi (born 5 October 1952) is a Pakistani politician and former cricketer who served as the 22nd prime minister of Pakistan from August 2018 until April 2022. He is the founder and chairman of the political party Pakistan Tehreek-e-Insaf (PTI).

Born to a Niazi Pashtun family in Lahore, Khan graduated from Keble College, Oxford. He began his international cricket career in a 1971 Test series against England. Khan played until 1992, served as the team's captain intermittently between 1982 and 1992, and won the 1992 Cricket World Cup, Pakistan's only victory in the competition. Considered one of cricket's greatest all-rounders, Khan was later inducted into the ICC Cricket Hall of Fame. Founding the Pakistan Tehreek-e-Insaf (PTI) in 1996, Khan won a seat in the National Assembly in the 2002 general election, serving as an opposition member from Mianwali until 2007. PTI boycotted the 2008 general election and became the second-largest party by popular vote in the 2013 general election. In the 2018 general election, running on a populist platform, PTI became the largest party in the National Assembly, and formed a coalition government with independents with Khan as prime minister.

As prime minister, Khan addressed a balance of payments crisis with bailouts from the IMF. He presided over a shrinking current account deficit, and limited defence spending to curtail the fiscal deficit, leading to some general economic growth. He enacted policies that increased tax collection and investment. His government committed to a renewable energy transition, launched the Ehsaas Programme and the Plant for Pakistan initiative, and expanded the protected areas of Pakistan. He presided over the COVID-19 pandemic, which caused economic turmoil and rising inflation in the country, threatening his political position.

Amid a constitutional crisis, Khan became the first prime minister to be removed from office through a no-confidence motion in April 2022. In August, he was charged under anti-terror laws after accusing the police and judiciary of detaining and torturing an aide. In October, Khan was disqualified by the Election Commission of Pakistan from taking office for the current term of the National Assembly of Pakistan, regarding the Toshakhana reference case. In November, he survived an assassination attempt during a political rally in Wazirabad, Punjab.

On 9 May 2023, Khan was arrested on corruption charges at the Islamabad High Court by paramilitary troops who smashed their way into the courthouse. Protests broke out throughout Pakistan resulting in the arrest of several thousands of Khan's supporters along with military installations being ransacked. After his release, he blamed the Chief of Army Staff Asim Munir for his arrest. The army responded by terming 9 May as "Black Day", with Minister of MoPD Ahsan Iqbal terming it as Pakistan's 9/11. He was sentenced to a three-year jail term on 5 August 2023 and was subsequently arrested for the second time.

Economic policy

In domestic economic policy, Khan inherited a twin balance of payments and debt crisis with a large current account deficit and fiscal deficit in 2018, Khan's government sought a bailout from the IMF. In exchange for the bailout, Khan's government slashed subsidy spending in the energy sector and unveiled an austerity budget to curb the fiscal deficit and limit government borrowing. Also, the IMF demanded that the Pakistani government depreciate the rupee, and improve tax collection. Khan's government decided to raise import tariffs to collect higher tax revenues and devalued the currency, this alongside the heavy import duty helped to curtail the current account deficit. Pakistan's overall balance of payment's position improved significantly following record-high remittances in 2020, which stabilised the central bank's foreign exchange reserves. The fiscal deficit narrowed to less than 1% of GDP by 2020 due to the government's austerity policies. Thus the rate of debt accumulation had significantly slowed, but Pakistan's debt remained high due to the high borrowing of previous governments in which the current government had to allocate $24 billion to pay off loans taken during the tenure of previous governments.

Shehbaz Sharif

Shehbaz Sharif is a Pakistani politician and businessman who served as the 23rd prime minister of Pakistan, in office from April 2022 to August 2023. He is the current president of the Pakistan Muslim League (N) (PML-N). Previously in his political career, he served as the Chief Minister of Punjab three times, making him the longest-serving Chief Minister of Punjab.

On 10 April 2022, Sharif was nominated as candidate for Prime Minister by opposition parties following a vote of no confidence in incumbent Prime Minister Imran Khan after the 2022 Pakistani constitutional crisis.

He was elected Prime Minister on 11 April 2022. He took the oath of office on the same day, administered by the Chairman of the Senate, Sadiq Sanjrani, acting for President Arif Alvi, who was on medical leave after complaining of "discomfort". Pakistan Democratic Movement's government faced with worst economic crisis in Pakistan since its independence, Sharif-led administration hoped for a relief deal with the IMF and improved relations with the United States, but received only limited response. Chinese foreign minister Qin Gang has expressed clear concerns about Pakistan's internal instability, despite China providing economic support for its longtime ally.

Daily Mail defamation case

On July 14, 2019, The Daily Mail published a news with the headline: "Did the family of Pakistani politician who has become the poster boy for British overseas aid STEAL funds meant for earthquake victims?" According to the report, Shehbaz Sharif stole aid funds from the UK's Department for

International Development (DFID) following the 2005 earthquake. It was written by Daily Mail journalist David Rose. Investigations have shown that the UK donated more than £500 to the earthquake victims in Pakistan through the DFID, a UK government organisation.

Daily Mail apology

Daily Mail publishers and Shehbaz's lawyers signed an agreement of settlement with Tomlin Order in the second week of December 2022 after which Daily Mail removed the defamatory article and apologized to the prime minister and his son-in-law. The ANL has promised it will never repeat these false allegations at any forum and has already worked with Google to remove all articles carrying Daily Mail's article.

Toshakhana Records

On 12 March, 2023, The Government of Pakistan released a record of Toshakhana Gifts Retained by Government Officials from 2003-2023, 90 gifts were retained by Mian Muhammad Shehbaz Sharif from Toshakhana.

Anwaar ul Haq Kakar

Anwaar-ul-Haq Kakar (born 1971) is a Pakistani politician who is currently serving as the Caretaker Prime Minister of Pakistan, in office since August 2023. He succeeded Shehbaz Sharif. He previously served as the spokesperson of the Government of Balochistan from 2015 to 2017.

Why does China want Pakistan's donkeys?

The newspaper reports

The demand for donkey hides in China is insatiable. While donkeys may not hold significant value in other parts of the world, they are regarded as valuable assets in China.

The Chinese recognize the worth of a donkey's hide and the products derived from it, which remain highly sought after in the country. However, Chinese donkey breeders have failed to meet the market demand, resulting in the need to import donkeys from other regions such as Africa and Pakistan.

Utilization in China

Donkey hides offer numerous purported medicinal benefits to the Chinese population, including the treatment of anemia, reproductive issues, and insomnia, although these claims lack clinical proof.

The primary product derived from donkey hides is called Eijao, a traditional medicine that has been used in China for thousands of years. Previously reserved for the Chinese royal class, the demand has now extended to the middle class.

The production of this medicine involves mixing collagen extracted from donkey hides with mineral-rich water from China's Shandong province. The collagen is obtained through a 99-step process of boiling the donkey's skin, performed at specific times of the year.

But, why Pakistan?

Pakistan ranks as the third largest producer of donkeys, while Africa has the highest production. China's estimated donkey population is 4.9 million.

Pakistan has been exporting donkeys to China in recent years, with two major donkey farms located in Dera Ismail Khan and Mansehra, involving foreign partnerships. Apart from live donkeys, there have also been instances of illegal exports of donkey hides from Pakistan to China.

Between 2014 and 2016, Pakistan exported nearly 200,000 donkey skins to China. Unfortunately, this also led to an increase in the fraudulent sale of donkey meat as beef in Pakistani markets. As Pakistan is a Muslim country, this constituted a serious crime, prompting the government to ban donkey and donkey hide exports.

'90pc of beggars' arrested abroad are of Pakistani origin, Senate body told

Nadir Guramani | Published September 27, 2023

Dawn reports

The Senate Standing Committee on Overseas Pakistanis was informed on Wednesday that a growing number of beggars from Pakistan were moving abroad, which has spurred "human trafficking".

Overseas Ministry Secretary Zulfikar Haider made this disclosure during a discussion in the Senate panel on the issue of skilled and unskilled labour leaving the country.

In a startling revelation, Haider informed the committee that a staggering "90 per cent of beggars" arrested in foreign countries were of Pakistani origin.

He explained that many beggars exploited pilgrim visas to travel to Saudi Arabia, Iran, and Iraq.

The official further revealed that a significant number of pickpockets apprehended in holy sites like Haram were also Pakistani nationals.

During the discussion, Haider also noted that Japan had emerged as a new destination for such visitors.

He emphasised Pakistan's historical role in exporting skilled labour and expressed optimism that the country's foreign remittances would increase when professionals went abroad. He added that Saudi Arabia now preferred skilled labour over untrained individuals.

Senator Rana Mehmoodul Hasan highlighted Japan's demand for skilled workers from different countries, with India, Nepal, and Pakistan sending varying numbers of individuals.

Hasan also mentioned that as many as 50,000 engineers in Pakistan were unemployed.

"India chand par pahonch gaya hai, aur hum rozana koi chaand charha dete hain (India has reached the moon, while we stumble every day)," the senator added.

"Our people are now ready to work on wages lower than those of workers of Nepal and India."

Regarding the Middle East, he mentioned that approximately three million people were in Saudi Arabia, 1.5m Pakistanis were in the UAE, while 0.2m were in Qatar.

Haider acknowledged that Bangladesh and India had surpassed Pakistan in this aspect, citing concerns about the skills and trustworthiness of Pakistani workers in the eyes of foreign employers.

On the other hand, Senator Sherry Rehman pointed out that Pakistan was witnessing an influx of skilled mountaineers from Nepal, emphasising that "Pakistan's own people generally lacked the same level of expertise in mountain climbing."

Drugs trafficking

Most of the illegal drugs in Pakistan come from neighbouring Afghanistan. The unemployment rate in Pakistan is influenced by the presence of low-skilled graduates and the overall poor quality of education.

8

(2021 ONWARDS)

Economy of India - 2022–2023 Pakistani economic crisis - India Pakistan Comparison (GDP, Currency, Population) - Religious discrimination in Pakistan - Religious Composition of India

Economy of India

The economy of India has transitioned from a mixed planned economy to a mixed middle-income developing social market economy with notable public sector in strategic sectors. It is the world's fifth-largest economy by nominal GDP and the third-largest by purchasing power parity (PPP). According to the International Monetary Fund (IMF), on a per capita income basis, India ranked 139th by GDP (nominal) and 127th by GDP (PPP). From independence in 1947 until 1991, successive governments followed Soviet model and promoted protectionist economic policies, with extensive Sovietization, state intervention, demand-side economics, natural resources, bureaucrat driven enterprises and economic regulation. This is characterised as dirigism, in the form of the Licence Raj. The end of the Cold War and an acute balance of payments crisis in 1991 led to the adoption of a broad economic liberalisation in India and indicative planning. Since the start of the 21st century, annual average GDP growth has been 6% to 7%. The economy of the Indian subcontinent was the largest in the world for most of recorded history up until the onset of colonialism in early 19th century. India accounts for 7.2% of the global economy in 2022 in PPP terms, and around 3.4% in nominal terms in 2022.

India still has informal domestic economies; COVID-19 reversed both economic growth and poverty reduction; credit access weaknesses contributed to lower private consumption and inflation; and new social and infrastructure equity efforts. Economic growth slowed down in 2017 due to the shocks of "demonetisation" in 2016 and the introduction of the Goods and Services Tax in 2017. Nearly 70% of India's GDP is driven by domestic consumption. The country remains the world's sixth-largest consumer market. Apart from private consumption, India's GDP is also fueled by government spending, investments, and exports. In 2022, India was the world's 6th-largest importer and the 9th-largest exporter. India has been a member of the World Trade Organization since 1 January 1995. It ranks 63rd on the Ease of doing business index and 40th on the Global Competitiveness Index. Due to extreme rupee/dollar rate fluctuations India's nominal GDP fluctuates significantly. With 476 million workers, the Indian labour force is the world's second-largest. India has one of the world's highest number of billionaires and extreme income inequality. The number of income tax returns filed has been increasing year on year reaching a record 6,77,00,000 income tax returns for the 2023-24 financial year filed by 31st July 2023; this was a 16.1% increase on the previous year when 5,83,00,000 tax returns were filed by 31 July 2022. Income-Tax Department said that it was a "fair indication of widening of [the] tax base" that 53,67,000 of the tax returns were by people who had never filed a tax return before.

During the 2008 global financial crisis, the economy faced a mild slowdown. India endorsed Keynesian policy and initiated stimulus measures (both fiscal and monetary) to boost growth and generate demand. In subsequent years, economic growth revived. According to the World Bank, to achieve sustainable economic development, India must focus on public sector reform, infrastructure, agricultural and rural development, removal of land and labour regulations, financial inclusion, spur private investment and exports, education, and public health. The period between 2004 and 2014 is referred to as India's lost decade as India fell behind other BRIC economies.

In 2022, India's ten largest trading partners were the United States, China, United Arab Emirates (UAE), Saudi Arabia, Russia, Germany, Hong

Kong, Indonesia, South Korea, and Malaysia. In 2021–22, the foreign direct investment (FDI) in India was $82 billion. The leading sectors for FDI inflows were the service sector, the computer industry, and the telecom industry. India has free trade agreements with several nations and blocs, including ASEAN, SAFTA, Mercosur, South Korea, Japan, Australia, UAE, and several others which are in effect or under negotiating stage.

The service sector makes up more than 50% of GDP and remains the fastest growing sector, while the industrial sector and the agricultural sector employs a majority of the labor force. The Bombay Stock Exchange and National Stock Exchange are some of the world's largest stock exchanges by market capitalisation. India is the world's sixth-largest manufacturer, representing 2.6% of global manufacturing output. Nearly 65% of India's population is rural, and contributes about 50% of India's GDP. It has the world's fifth-largest foreign-exchange reserves worth $561 billion. India has a high public debt with 83% of GDP, while its fiscal deficit stood at 6.4% of GDP. India faces high unemployment, rising income inequality, and a drop in aggregate demand. India's gross domestic savings rate stood at 29.3% of GDP in 2022. In recent years, independent economists and financial institutions have accused the government of manipulating various economic data, especially GDP growth. India's overall social spending as a share of GDP in 2021–22 will be 8.6%, which is much lower than the average for OECD nations.

2022-2023 Pakistani economic crisis

The 2022–2023 Pakistani economic crisis is an ongoing economic crisis and part of 2022–2023 political unrest in Pakistan. It has caused severe economic challenges for months due to which food, gas and oil prices have risen.

The Russian invasion of Ukraine has caused fuel prices to rise worldwide. Excessive external borrowings by the country over the years raised the spectre of default, causing the currency to fall and making imports more expensive in relative terms. By June 2022, inflation was at an all time high, along with rising food prices.

Poor governance and low productivity per capita in comparison with other low to middle-income developing countries have contributed to a balance of payment crisis, where the country is unable to earn enough foreign exchange to fund the imports that it consumes. Pakistan's economic crisis is the biggest crisis since its independence.

According to Indian strategic affairs specialist Sushant Sareen, Pakistan has doubled its debt roughly every five years over the last 25-year period. Starting from a debt of Rs. 3.06 billion at the beginning of General Musharraf regime in 1999, the debt stood at Rs. 62.5 billion at the end of the Imran Khan government in 2022. While the debt grew at around 14 percent per year on average, the GDP was growing at only 3 percent per year on average. This led to an unsustainable debt burden. In the fiscal year 2022–23, the debt servicing obligations of Rs. 5.2 trillion exceed the entire federal government revenue. In 2022, Pakistan experienced a trifecta of challenges, as political unrest, an economic crisis, and destructive floods gripped the nation. Economically, the country is grappling with severe inflation, a declining currency, and critically low foreign reserves, posing significant concerns for its financial stability.

Pakistan's economic crisis was at the centre of a political standoff between Prime Minister Shahbaz Sharif and his predecessor Imran Khan in 2022, which led to Khan's ouster in April 2022. Sharif accused Khan of economic mismanagement and mishandling of the country's foreign policy, forcing him to step down in a no-confidence vote. Amid ousting, he ignited "Haqeeqi Azaadi" in english "Real Independence" in context of from foreign superpowers after 1947 Independence from British Empire political movement which caused nationwide political unrest calling for early elections and civilian supremacy which in result worked as a catalyst for already worsening economic condition. During 2019 Imran Khan tried to make a deal with IMF and agreed with the several terms and conditions which resulted the increase in inflation but Imran Khan failed to gain IMF loan.

2022

Information Minister Maryam Aurangzeb told a news conference held on 19 May 2022, that Pakistan was committed to "controlling rising inflation, stabilizing foreign exchange reserves, strengthening the economy and reducing the country's dependence on imports". Import of unnecessary and luxury items was banned. Sharif had said at the time that the decision would "save the country's precious foreign exchange" and that Pakistan would have to "pursue austerity."

In late May 2022, the government lifted the cap on fuel prices - a condition for advancing the long-stalled bailout deal with the International Monetary Fund (IMF). IMF also insisted Islamabad to raise electricity prices, ramp up tax collection and make sizeable budget cuts.

Federal Minister for Planning and Development Ahsan Iqbal told reporters on 14 May 2022, that Pakistanis could reduce their tea consumption to "one or two cups" a day as imports were putting additional financial pressure on the government. "The tea we import is imported on credit," Iqbal said, adding that businesses should be shut down first to save electricity. According to the Observatory of Economic Complexity, the South Asian nation of 220 million is the world's largest tea importer, having bought more than $640 million worth of tea in 2020.

Inflation in Pakistan rose to 21.3% in June, the highest since December 2008 when inflation stood at 23.3%.

Finance Minister Miftah Ismail said that a loan of $2.3 billion from a Chinese consortium of banks had been credited to the Pakistani central bank's account in late June.

2022 Pakistan floods in summer cause over $30 billion dollars in economic losses in Pakistan.

At the end of March 2022, the State Bank of Pakistan's reserves stood at $11.425bn, but they gradually tanked to an almost four-year low of $6.715bn on 2nd December. Pakistan's foreign exchange reserves equal to just five weeks of merchandise imports.

The consistent depreciation of the rupee is said to be deepening the economic crisis. At the end of March, the rupee stood at 183.48 to $1. On 9th December 2022, it closed at 224.40.

2023

In January 2023, Muhammad Aurangzeb, the CEO of Pakistan's largest bank, Habib Bank commented publicly on the prevailing economic situation that it could be a "big blow to the economy" if the stakeholders didn't make the right decisions swiftly.

In late January, Pakistan lifted the artificial cap on its currency, causing the rupee to plunge 20% against the dollar in a few days. The government raised fuel prices by 16%. And the Pakistani central bank raised its interest rate by 100 basis points to battle the country's highest inflation in decades, expected to be as high as 26% in January.

In February 2023, a Moody economist predicted that inflation in Pakistan could average 33% in the first half of the year 2023. China lent Pakistan further 700 million dollars to shore up Forex reserves. Pakistan's Consumer price index (CPI) further jumped to 31.5%, the highest annual rate in 50 years. Also Fitch downgrades Pak's sovereign credit rating from CCC+ to CCC-. The New York-based ratings agency warned that a default could be a "real possibility".

In March 2023, the food inflation rate in Pakistan witnessed a significant increase, with urban areas experiencing a rate of 47.1 percent and rural areas facing a slightly higher rate of 50.2 percent. Moody's downgrades Pakistan's rating to Caa3; changes outlook to stable from negative. Finance Minister Ishaq Dar said that China approved a rollover of a $1.3 billion loan for cash-strapped Pakistan, which would help shore up its depleting foreign exchange reserves. The World Bank further recorded the Consumer price index (CPI) for food items on a year on year basis at 45.1%, the second highest in South Asia after Sri Lanka. The Consumer price index (CPI) raced to 35.4 per cent in the highest annual rise in prices on record, driven mainly by skyrocketing costs of food, electricity, beverage, and transport. The inflation number was the highest annual rate since available data - July 1965 - according to the research firm Arif Habib Ltd, and is expected to rise in the upcoming months.

In April 4, the World Bank projected about 4 million Pakistani people falling below the lower middle-income ($3.6/day) poverty line amid economic growth plummeting to just 0.4% against a target of 5pc.

In May 2023, Pakistan's inflation rate reached 38%, surpassing Sri Lanka to become the highest country in Asia.

In June 2023, the Pakistani government unveiled a "Economic Revival Plan" according to which, plans on investments in key areas of production such as on agriculture, mining, Information Technology, defence and the energy sector were discussed. PM Shehbaz Sharif also lauded China for assisting his country in the current economic crisis.

Federal budget

On 10 June 2022, the government unveiled a new 47 billion budget for 2022-23 to persuade the IMF to resume the 6 billion bailout deal, which was agreed upon by both sides in 2019. However, the IMF expressed dissatisfaction with the budget for 2023-24 submitted by Pakistani authorities two weeks before the bailout expired, which indicated that Pakistan would not receive its bailout.

Impact on industry

In October 2022, the All Pakistan Textile Mills Association (APTMA) announced that 1,600 garment mills were closed across the country due to withdrawal of power subsidies and, as a result, five million people lost their jobs. In December 2022, APTMA stated that mills across the country were running at less than 50% capacity utilization and textile exports could fall further from 2023.

A number of leading companies listed on the Pakistan Stock Exchange announced closure of plants. Car assemblers such as Pak Suzuki Motors, Toyota Indus, and Honda Atlas Cars, whose production relies completely on parts imported from other countries, shut down assembly plants after they failed to secure letters of credit due to foreign exchange curbs imposed by the government. Other notable companies to shut factories due to low demand and poor economic conditions include Millat Tractors, Ghandhara Tyre & Rubber Company, Nishat Chunian, and Fauji Fertilizer Bin Qasim.

Shortage of foreign exchange reserves and depreciation in Pakistani rupee created difficulties in importing crude oil, leading to a temporary closure of Pakistan's largest petroleum refinery–Cnergyico, in February 2023.

Delays in securing letters of credit resulted in ships and containers of pharmaceutical raw material, medicines and healthcare devices imported from other countries to be stuck at seaports for prolonged periods. Several pharmaceutical companies shut down due to "unaffordable cost of production". As a consequence, a shortage of medicines and equipment was reported across the country, forcing hospitals to postpone surgeries and treatment.

In April 2023, almost all of the country's 30 mobile phone assembly units, including three run by foreign brands, have shut down. This puts the future of 20,000 employees at stake.

In June 2023, Shell plc announced that it would exit the Pakistani market by selling its entire 77.42% stake in Shell Pakistan.

International opinion

Chinese officials blamed the West for Pakistan's economic crisis, and state media continues to talk about the strengths of the China-Pakistan Economic Corridor. "Only China has given a full plan. From this perspective, it is the Western world that 'abandoned' Pakistan, and China is the one that extended a helping hand. And if Pakistan wants complete self-help, it cannot completely rely on China, it still has to fight for itself," wrote Liu Qingbin, senior researcher at the China Digital Economy Institute.

The US has expressed serious concerns about Pakistan's debt to China. "We have been very clear about our concerns not just here in Pakistan, but elsewhere all around the world about Chinese debt, or debt owed to China," said US State Department Counselor Derek Chollet during his visit to Islamabad on 15 February 2023.

Since the Gulf Arab states that have traditionally supported Pakistan are now unwilling to continue to provide economic assistance, outside analysis indicates that Pakistan can only seek further loan support from China.

India Pakistan Comparison (GDP)

INDIA   PAKISTAN

1980 $ 186.33 B	1980 $ 34.8 B
2021 $ 3,176.30 B	2021 $ 348.2 B

India Pakistan Comparison (Currency)

1 $ = 4.78 Indian Rupees in 1949

1 $ = 3.31 Pakistani Rupee in 1949

1 $ = 83.27 Indian Rupees on 7th Nov 2023

1 $ = 286.47 Pakistani Rupee 7th Nov 2023

India Pakistan Comparison (Population)

India 357,021,100 (1950)

Pakistan 37,696,264 (1950)

India 1,407,563,842 (2021)

Pakistan 231,402,117 (2021)

Religious discrimination in Pakistan

Religious discrimination in Pakistan is a serious issue for the human rights situation in modern-day Pakistan. Hindus, Christians, Sikhs, Shias, and Ahmadis among other religious minorities often face discrimination and at times are even subjected to violence. In some cases Christian churches and the worshippers themselves have been attacked. Khawaja Nazimuddin, the 2nd Prime Minister of Pakistan, stated: "I do not agree that religion is a private affair of the individual nor do I agree that in an Islamic state every citizen has identical rights, no matter what his caste, creed or faith be".

Overview

One of the significant issues being faced by minority communities is the abuse of the blasphemy law. People belonging to minority religions are often falsely accused of using derogatory remarks against the Islamic prophet Muhammad, resulting in fines, lengthy prison sentences, and sometimes the death penalty. Often these accusations are made to settle personal vendettas and, due to the bias against minorities, victims are often immediately presumed guilty without any substantive evidence.

According to 1951 census, Non-Muslims constituted 14.20% of total Pakistan's (West Pakistan and East Pakistan) population. In West Pakistan (now Pakistan), the Non-Muslims constituted 3.44% of the total population while East Pakistan (now Bangladesh) had a significant share comprising 23.20 per cent of the population therein. One reason for low Non-Muslim percentage is because of higher birth rates among the Muslims. Another reason was due to constant migration of India and Pakistan's respective minorities after the partition of India in 1947. However, the main reason as to why the population of minorities declined was due to the separation of East Pakistan (present day Bangladesh) which constituted almost 18% of Pakistan's Hindu population according to the 1961 Pakistani census. After the independence of Bangladesh, all minorities (mostly Hindus) that lived in the former East Pakistan were no longer counted in the census as they were officially Bangladeshis, and not Pakistanis. Due to the fact that Hindus made up the large bulk of the minority population, the percentage of Pakistan's minorities plummeted. Religious minority groups in Pakistan feel the effects of this legal and political marginalization and disenfranchisement in their daily lives.

In the 1951 census, West Pakistan had 1.6% Hindu population, while East Pakistan (modern Bangladesh) had 22.05%. By 1997, the percentage of Hindus remained stable at 1.6% in Pakistan, while in Bangladesh, it had dropped to 9.2% by 2011, with non-Muslims accounting for 10.2% of the population.

In 1999 the United Nations Human Rights Council approved the first resolution against defamation of religions. However these resolutions have been severely criticized by the United States, various European nations and freedom of religion groups as these resolutions contained language which could be used to discriminate against minority religions, and in March 2010 the UN refused to enact the most recent resolution.

In 2011 religious intolerance was reported to be at its height, hundreds of minorities, women, journalists and liberals were being killed by Islamist fundamentalist extremists, while the Government remained mostly a silent spectator, often only making statements which condemned the ruthless acts of violence by the extremists but taking no real concrete action against them.

Progress on religious freedom is being made gradually as Pakistan transitions to democracy from Zia's legacy, in 2016 Sindh with Pakistan's largest Hindu minority passed a bill that outlawed forced conversions. However, the bill was never ratified by the Governor. The bill was tabled by a faction of the Pakistan Muslim League which in Sindh is led by Sufi leader Pir Pagara, called PML-F, Pakistan Muslim League functional. In 2014, NGOs estimated that around 1000 girls from minority groups every year are being forcibly converted to Islam. In November 2019, a parliamentary committee was formed to prevent act of forced conversion in Pakistan.

During the COVID-19 pandemic in Pakistan, reports emerged that rations were being denied to minority Hindus and Christians in the coastal areas of Karachi. The Saylani Welfare Trust, carrying out the relief work, said that the aid was reserved for Muslims alone. On 14 April, the US Commission on International Religious Freedom expressed concern with the discrimination. Other organisations, including Edhi Foundation, JDC Welfare Organization and Jamaat-e-Islami are reported to have stepped forward to provide relief to the minorities.

Freedom of religion in Pakistan

In 2022, Freedom House rated Pakistan's religious freedom as 1 out of 4, noting that the blasphemy laws are often exploited by religious vigilantes and also curtail the freedom of expression by Christians and Muslims, especially Ahmadis. Hindus have spoken of vulnerability to kidnapping and forced conversions.

Religious minorities in Pakistan, including Hindu and Christian communities, have been subjected to forced conversions and persecution, while facing the oppressive impact of blasphemy laws. Unfortunately, these communities have been unable to exercise their constitutionally granted freedom of religion, enduring significant challenges and restrictions.

Unlike Pakistan, India saw rise in percentage of religious minorities as observed by Pew Research Center.

Religious Composition of India

1. Population growth and religious composition

By Stephanie Kramer

India's population has more than tripled in the six decades following Partition, from 361 million (36.1 crore) people in the 1951 census to more than 1.2 billion (120 crore) in 2011. As of 2020, India gains roughly 1 million (10 lakh) inhabitants each month, putting it on course to surpass China as the world's most populous country by 2030, according to the United Nations Population Division.

Though religious groups grew at uneven rates between 1951 and 2011, every major religion in India saw its numbers rise. For example, Hindus increased from 304 million (30.4 crore) to 966 million (96.6 crore), Muslims grew from 35 million (3.5 crore) to 172 million (17.2 crore), and the number of Indians who say they are Christian rose from 8 million (0.8 crore) to 28 million (2.8 crore).

Indian Muslim Population

It is observed that there are many areas all over India where Muslim population is found to be concentrated. Even Police do not dare to enter those areas. Mewat is one such area located on the border of Haryana and Rajasthan. Whenever any Hindu procession passes thru these areas, there is stone pelting, bombing and even firing on such processions.

Fortunately there have been no terrorist attacks in any state of India since last 8-9 years. In J&K, stone pelting on soldiers is totally stopped after removal of Clause 370 but stray instances of target killing by the terrorists are still being reported.

If Pakistan is dreaming of 'Ghazwa-e-Hind', they should first try to make their house in order.